AROUND THE GLOBE
IN TWENTY YEARS

AROUND THE GLOBE
IN TWENTY YEARS

Irena Wiley

**Illustrated with drawings
by the author**

DAVID McKAY COMPANY, INC.
New York

To
JOHN

I

"... $\bigwedge_{ND}$ I AM MARRYING YOU UNDER THE LAW FOR the gypsies," pronounced the mayor. With this phrase I was catapulted into marriage and diplomatic life.

It was a warm Mediterranean day in April. We were solemnly seated, John and I, on huge gilded and most uncomfortable armchairs in the Renaissance room of the town hall of Toulon. Facing us, unshaven, in a mildewed frock coat, with a faded tricolor draped around his middle, Mayor Escatafigue was rushing through the marriage service.

This unimpressive and jet-propelled ceremony was the culmination of months of red tape, paper work, endless preparation. If you must be married abroad, choose any place on the map, even a lamasery in Tibet, but *don't* get married in France. A church marriage is not valid without a civil ceremony, and banns are required for both. Publishing the banns nearly prevented our marriage. I was born in Poland, residing in Paris, and contracting matrimony in Toulon, in the South of France. John was born in the American Consulate in Bordeaux, where his father was consul. He was now stationed in the American Embassy in Moscow. Where to publish the banns was the question that the functionary of the town hall could not resolve. He refused to do anything about it.

Luckily at that time I was staying with Admiral and Mrs. Raymond Cellier who for the previous year had been for me *in loco parentis*. In the glorious tradition of the French, the Celliers had been sailors since Louis XIV. Raymond, the last

1

of the line, with his golden eyes, his deep culture, his generous heart but stern discipline, was an example of what heredity and environment can produce. The continuous presence of the sea with its dangers, the comradeship as known among men in ships, had cleaned this naval aristocracy of the pride and decadence that so often characterize other aristocracies.

At that time, in 1934, Raymond was also a very senior naval personage in Toulon, which was the chief naval base of France. When prospects for the banns looked completely hopeless, he stormed into the mayor's office, pounded the table and demanded action. The mayor scratched his head, thought and thought and at last came up with a solution—to marry us under a provision of the law covering the nomadic gypsies, who, having no fixed domicile, eluded the requirement of banns.

During the ceremony I had my first encounter with protocol. The mayor was mumbling endlessly and I was overwhelmed by a desire for a cigarette. I started saying "Mr. Mayor, may I sm . . ." when John kicked me on the shin, stopping my sentence in mid-vowel. Apparently one does not smoke during a civil marriage ceremony.

Also, in France one apparently does not use newfangled inventions such as fountain pens.

Walter Duranty, the Moscow correspondent of the *New York Times,* accompanied John from Moscow to Toulon to act as best man. His chief function was to sign the act of marriage as John's witness. When the moment came, like a good reporter, he whipped out his fountain pen and started to affix his signature. There was consternation. Monsieur le Maire raised a protesting hand. With vehement sibilants, he interrupted the proceedings, saying "No, no, not with that pen!"

Walter, astounded, anxiously inquired the reason. "With a fountain pen," said the mayor firmly, "you might use invisible ink." Walter was handed the official inkwell and the pen of the

2

town hall. It was similar to the pens one used to find in American post offices. But it sufficed, and with a little scratching and splattering of ink from the ancient nib, John and I were duly bound in wedlock.

Then the mayor hurriedly closed the ledger, handed me a little red book and dashed out for his noonday game of "boules." The little red book was my marriage certificate, which in France has entries for twenty-one children and a cryptic inscription printed in red: "If your child is born with red and streaming eyes, consult a doctor. It is not the result of a draft."

I would like to mention that on our wedding night, which we spent on the estate of a friend, a bolt of lightning came in through one window of our bedroom, went over our bed, and out through another window, crashing into a telegraph pole. I was sure that it was an omen that I would give birth to at least a Tamerlane. Alas, I did not. And the red book remains empty.

The next few days resembled the very early movies, in which everybody was always in a desperate hurry, running with jerky movements.

John was then counselor of embassy in Moscow, a post now called deputy chief of mission; he had been given only one week's leave of absence to marry, honeymoon, and bring back the bride; so the day after our marriage we took the train to Moscow via Vienna.

Mayor Escatafigue never knew how appropriate the gypsy wedding was for us and how the sign of the gypsies shaped our life. In the next twenty years we were to be stationed in Russia, Belgium, Austria, Estonia, Latvia, Colombia, Portugal, Iran, Panama, and Washington, not counting trips to Turkey, Lebanon, China, Japan, and Greece, and to almost all the countries of South America.

What gypsy could roam more?

After a week of honeymoon spent mostly on trains except for three hilarious days in Vienna, we arrived at the Russian frontier.

The Moscow express left the last Polish station behind and slowly moved eastward. After ten minutes it stopped before a weather-beaten wooden arch astride the track which displayed the commanding and disquieting slogan: "Workers of the world, unite!" On both sides stretched many lines of barbed wire, reminding us of familiar photos of wartime trenches. At some distance, beyond swampy fields, there stood a high watchtower of the type used by foresters. In this melancholy and remote spot of Byelorussia, the tower was designed for another purpose. The forest that had stood here from time immemorial had been cut down in the process of frontier delimitation after the Treaty of Riga. A belt some hundreds of yards wide was cleared along the full length of Soviet boundary from the Baltic to the Black Sea, to make a no man's land patrolled day and night by frontier guards. Stalin's Russia officially welcomed the foreign proletariat but, more efficiently than ever in history, persisted in isolating her multilingual subjects from the "polluting" contact of the West.

The passengers of our car kept an absolute silence, a behavior instinctively observed by all foreigners about to cross into the Soviet Union. We looked at a stone frontier marker with the letters R.P., meaning Republic of Poland, at another with the letters C.C.C.P., the Cyrillic equivalent of U.S.S.R. Beyond the latter lay the flat plain stretching all the way to China and the Pacific. The Polish crew left the train and a Soviet crew took over. The train crossed the boundary under the arch; in another few minutes we stopped at the Soviet customhouse. In the darkness I could barely distinguish the ramshackle buildings and the nondescript barracks occupied by the passport and customs officials. We had to change trains as the standard European gauge ended at the frontier station

4

of Negoreloye. Here was another feature of the Russian will to isolate themselves from the West: when the first Russian railroads were about to be built in the eighteen-forties, the Imperial General Staff insisted that their gauge should be broader than in the neighboring Germany and Austria, in order to slow down any military invasion.

We boarded the Moscow-bound train, with its old locomotive decorated with a big red star pinned to its breast, and leaking steam and water at every pore.

In fact, the whole train was a prewar antique. Slowly it got us to Moscow next morning, puffing all the way. From the station we were whisked off to the National Hotel.

Ambassador Bullitt, my first chief, had filled our sitting room with white flowers. It was a heart-warming gesture, but the result was far from festive. In Moscow the only flowers to be found in April were chrysanthemums which are so hardy they survive even revolutions and long winters. But a lot of them, especially white ones, tend to create a funeral parlor atmosphere.

John deposited me under the flowering bushes and departed for the Chancery, leaving me to unpack and organize our first home. Instead of plunging into wifely duties, I dashed out to get my first glimpse of Moscow. I had learned enough Russian from my White Russian friends in London not to worry about finding my way back.

For hours I roamed the squares and streets of the downtown city surrounding the hotel. There was little traffic but on the sidewalk a featureless, gray crowd flowed sluggishly like a muddy river. It was not the shabbiness, the poverty of their clothes, but it was the stillness of their unsmiling faces that made me wonder with anguish about a regime that created such an atmosphere of anonymous hopelessness.

An Asiatic gloom and decrepitude seemed to grip the city. Every wall that was not cracked was peeling; every house

5

and every church needed repair, every building had the un-cared-for look of things unloved. Between the crumbling Orthodox churches closed for years, with their tarnished golden onion-shaped cupolas, and the disintegrating Empire façades of czarist public buildings there would suddenly appear the prison-like, battleship gray of the Soviet buildings. Grim and bare, those new buildings had an air of austere disdain of their surroundings. This strange mixture of architecture clearly showed that Moscow was in but not of Europe, in fact apart from both Europe and Asia.

At first I lingered to look at shop windows until I found that the display consisted only of large, official portraits of Stalin and Lenin, displayed with pots of my previous acquaintances, the bedraggled white chrysanthemum.

Many times when I would stop in front of a shop, one of the women, wrapped in a shawl, would timidly approach me, asking *"Inostranka?"* (foreigner) I was hatless, gloveless, in a gray knitted suit but they knew at once that I was from the "outside" world. When I would answer "Yes" to her question, she would ask to touch the fabric of my suit, then whisper "How soft it is." There was no jealousy or resentment, only a pathetic joy in seeing something feminine and nice. When approached by one of those women I wanted to take off my dress and give it to her, then and there, or at least, like St. Martin, cut it in half. Having long hair but not so long as Lady Godiva I had to resist the impulse.

After long hours, when I was trailing back to the hotel, a workman noticing my red lacquered nails stopped and exclaimed, "Did you murder someone that your fingers are dipped in blood?"

When in the evening John came back from the office, he found me sitting in the dark, in the middle of the chrysanthemums, with the red nail polish gone from my nails, disconsolately but stubbornly reading the last verse of Tiutchev's poem:

> With your mind you can't understand Russia,
> You cannot measure her by the usual yardstick.
>   She has a special nature.
> In Russia you can only believe.

The next morning my diplomatic life started with a bang and . . . a whimper. It was May first, the great annual Soviet celebration with its massive parade through Red Square, a spectacle at which the presence of the entire diplomatic corps was required.

When John and I got to the diplomatic stand, I saw to my dismay that no seats were provided, although the parade was supposed to last some seven hours. That is when I realized with foreboding what a role feet play in diplomatic life. The hymn of the Foreign Service should be a paraphrase of Kipling's verse "Feet, feet, feet, feet, feet; we can stick out hunger, thirst and weariness but not the chronic standing on our feet."

From our standing-room-only podium, I had my first view of Stalin. On the muted red granite mausoleum where Lenin's embalmed body was kept on exhibit, there stood a group of squat middle-aged men, clad in dark overcoats, mufflers and workingmen's caps, most of them with little beards and pince-nez. These were the Soviet elite including the members of the sinister Politburo. In the mathematical center of the mausoleum was Stalin. He appeared taller than his minions, but only because he alone stood on a little stool, or at least so I was told. The parading crowds had no doubt that he was the ruler. He remained invisible throughout the year, hidden behind the walls of the Kremlin, and May Day was one of the very rare occasions when the Soviet people could have a glimpse of his piercing eyes and graying mustache.

The parade was an imposing spectacle, a masterpiece of organization. It was very difficult to synchronize the movement of all these multitudes through the narrow medieval streets leading to and from Red Square, to let them pass ceremoniously in front of the reviewing dignitaries. There were many thousands of soldiers in long brown overcoats and peaked caps, all brotherly alike and advancing like a moving human wall. Then flashing and gleaming came the guns, tanks, planes with waving crimson flags. This military display was followed by countless civilian organizations—workers, athletes and school children. Strangely, this part of the parade resembled a church procession—the same gravely marching crowds, the fervent singing, the flowing banners. Only instead of icons, huge transparencies of Stalin and Lenin, the saints of the Communist hagiology, were carried reverently.

Watching the marching people with their dedicated, proud faces so different from the defeated and anxious crowds I had seen on the previous day in the streets, I realized how full of riddles Russia is. And that "yes" and "no" can be the answer to any question.

After five hours we were permitted to go home. And thus ended my first diplomatic venture, leaving me hungry, weary, puzzled and interested.

II

THE NEW APARTMENT BUILDING IN MOSCOW WHICH WAS to house the embassy staff was not yet completed. Actually it never was really finished. An American correspondent once remarked apropos of the building that it took him a year to find out that *ne rabotayet,* the word is Russian for "out of order," did not mean elevator. We lived temporarily in two rooms of the National Hotel, a relic from czarist days. Nothing had been changed since the time when rich boyars visited Moscow. Our suite was a Victorian paradise of raspberry plush, gold tassels, potted palms, heavy contorted furniture with swirling, flowery carvings, and that badge of luxury, an untuned grand piano. A tea cozy, in the form of a Russian doll with crinoline skirts, was on the piano. One day, looking for cigarettes, John discovered that she concealed a litter of new-born mice, six pink hairless babies. So long as we stayed at the National, I fed and took care of them. One mouse, a very friendly one that we named Otto Otto, even followed us when we moved to our own embassy quarters. He had stowed away in a packing case.

The food of the National Hotel was very appetizing but highly lethal. When served at our dining-room table, meat and fish were covered with a thick layer of jelly or hard mayonnaise, molded in curlicues and other strange shapes. These signs of artistic creativity aided to disguise the essential un-freshness of the animal matter (at that time refrigeration was unknown in Moscow). The urge for self-preservation made me

9

get a Sterno stove, pots and pans, and cookbooks. Armed with good will and abysmal ignorance, I started cooking in our bedroom. I can still see myself seated on the red velvet gilded chair in front of the Sterno stove trying to understand the cabalistic language of a recipe.

I was completely unprepared to face any household problems, not only because I am entirely innocent of any culinary talent but because domesticity had never entered into my upbringing.

I had had only one previous cooking experience, a terrifying one if not novel. Friends with whom I was staying in London asked me to boil the rice for supper. Full of enthusiasm, I filled a huge pot with rice, adding some water. An hour or so later I was playing the part of the sorcerer's apprentice who learned how to create water but not to shut it off. When my friends returned they found me disheveled and frantic. Every single receptacle in the house—kitchen utensils, flower vases, teacups, and finally even the bathtub—was full of rice that still kept flowing from the pot like white lava out of an erupting volcano. For the next two weeks we had rice for breakfast, lunch and dinner, puddings, risottos, pilafs, rice cakes, and just plain rice—indeed, anything the determination and imagination of my two hostesses could devise.

In Moscow, as in many foreign cities, my problem was not only the problem of cooking but that of food itself. When the American housewife envies the Foreign Service wife her cook, she does not realize that abroad food sometimes comes into your kitchen alive and we have to be not only cook but executioner as well. The screaming chicken, the gobbling turkey, the jumping fish that we have to face before any meal is prepared are a far cry from the friers all cleaned, cellophane wrapped, and from the turkey without feathers, without its head, looking like a wax sculpture that could easily tempt even a vegetarian since they become so completely anonymous. But

10

when one sees one's dinner running around the kitchen full of zest for life, it is another story.

In Moscow in 1935 there was one open market where one could get, if lucky, a few potatoes, wrinkled heads of cabbage, and some old carrots.

There was a shop for foreigners where one could get many things if one paid hard currency. And it was really like eating gold every time we bought food at the *torgsin,* as it was called. At a dollar an egg, $10 a chicken, I knew how Midas felt.

One day when shopping there I saw crawfish, which is one of my favorite foods. In Eastern Europe it is a staple food in the summer months, as many streams are filled with them.

They were plentiful and cheap, so I bought a dozen of them for our dinner. To keep them alive I put them in our bathtub full of water to await the moment that they would be our *plat de résistance.* But we had to go out to dinner that night and I left them in the tub, much to John's disgust as he was cheated out of a bath. By the next day, having cherished them for nearly twenty-four hours, I began to be attached to my crawfish. I already knew the characteristics of every one of them, the one that was lazy, the one that was a bully, the one that had initiative. So, of course, not being a cannibal, I could not eat my new friends. I was faced with a dilemma, what to do with them. They could not stay in the bathtub indefinitely. If I returned them to the shop, somebody else would eat them, an idea I could not face. Suddenly I got the answer, to put them back where they came from, the Moskva River.

I collected them into an old straw hat and drove to the river. I climbed down the bank. While I was putting them one by one in the water, a policeman tapped me on the shoulder and asked, "What are you doing?" "Can't you see, I am putting crawfish in the river," I answered. I also added "American Embassy," a magic formula at that time since we had just recognized Russia and the political honeymoon was still on.

He then stood guard over me until I parted with the last of the crawfish. He watched me with an unforgettable expression of bewilderment.

After that experience and until we moved into the embassy and had a cook, we lived on canned sardines and macaroni.

Within a short time Moscow taught me Oriental resignation to all housekeeping tragedies—a useful attitude for all wives who start housekeeping in difficult posts. We should try to do our best. But if the main course is stolen from the kitchen by a black panther just before dinner—as once happened in Panama—or you find asparagus you gave to your cook for lunch, beautifully arranged as a centerpiece on the table, you take it as a matter of course.

The apartment that was finally assigned to us in the building known as the Mokhovaya House, after the street it was on, was a bride's delight—a bride of course with a tendency for the macabre, as from the enormous windows of our two communicating studio rooms, the view was on an annex of the Medical School, where one could see students dissecting cadavers in a Rembrandtesque chiaroscuro. The view from our bedroom was luckily less obviously sinister as it overlooked the Kremlin, with its towers crowned with the imperial, double-headed eagles borrowed by the Russians centuries ago from the splendors of moribund Byzantium. We could also see, a perpetual delight, the Church of St. Basil, which with its many-colored shining domes looked like a flowering bush of fuchsia in the rain.

When at last we were settled, I had to give my first official dinner, a large one. As Bill Bullitt was absent, the dinner was at the embassy residence. For formal occasions we had to engage extra waiters. I held a rehearsal the day before the dinner, since these waiters were completely untrained. Having a workable knowledge of Russian, I spent hours in showing them how to serve on the left, to remove plates on the right,

12

which glasses for which wines, and all the rest of the dinner party ritual. I overheard one of the waiters saying "Madame Wiley must be very superstitious, she wants us to do everything the same way all the time."

I had forgotten, though, to tell them that waiters like children should be seen but not heard. During dinner I noticed that they whispered remarks to our Russian guests. I eavesdropped and heard "You can eat the fish, it is fresh" and "Take a lot of the dessert, it is not passed around the second time."

The fish and the dessert were all right, but not the meat. At that time meat was very scarce in Russia. The courier who used to bring our supply from Poland forgot it at the frontier station. There I was faced with a formal dinner for some thirty people, all high-ranking Soviet officials, ambassadors and important personages, and I had no main dish to give them. I telephoned wildly to all the embassies and legations, but all were in the same boat, completely meatless. In desperation I stormed into a Russian butchershop demanding meat, any meat, or I would complain to the Kremlin. This was a gratuitous threat, but it sounded impressive, and I think it did impress. An hour later the butcher telephoned that I could have a roast if I would buy the whole cow. So I did. An underfed Soviet cow, eaten the very day it was butchered, is not eatable. At dinner that night when my guests were trying unsuccessfully to cut the meat, they only managed to play a sort of weird tiddly-winks. John said loudly across the table, "You had better show our guests the horns, so that they'll know it isn't a horse."

It was perhaps the only time I did not properly appreciate John's Irish sense of humor.

In housekeeping in the United States only ignorance produces surprises. But abroad no skill, no knowledge can shield one from the strange, the grotesque, the unexpected. Sometimes it is language that creates curious results, as in the case of the Mexican Minister's wife in Warsaw. One day, expecting visitors for lunch, she asked her cook Maria to prepare stewed pears for dessert. She told her to peel them and boil them in syrup, adding vanilla, lemon, and cinnamon. There was a look of amazed rebellion on Maria's face when she heard the orders and, to the astonishment of the Minister's wife, she complained bitterly that it was too much work. But her complaint was overruled.

When the dessert appeared on the table, the hostess to her horror saw that a green "goo" was being served. It had been made of peas, not pears. With quick presence of mind, she announced to her surprised guests that they were being served the great national dish of Mexico, her favorite dessert. Heroically, and with a smile, she swallowed a big helping of the revolting mess. What had happened was that in Polish pears and peas are very similar in sound, *grushka* and *groshek,* and she had mistakenly ordered stewed peas. The poor cook had spent hours peeling each and every pea.

The wife of the Minister at least learned how to mind her peas and pears in Polish.

I believe in the necessity and beauty of legends, but one myth has to be shattered. The myth that the diet of diplomats consists chiefly of foie gras, caviar, partridge, and champagne. Caviar appears in our life occasionally but only when stationed in Russia or Persia—not counting, of course, those pathetic international cocktail canapés, over which a caviar bird has flown. Our steady diet quite often is based on milk full of Malta fever, fruits with amebas, ham with trichinosis, water that has to be carefully boiled, and salads optimistically soaked in permanganate. In many, many posts abroad eating is a dangerous adventure.

In Moscow a Soviet official, who was a friend of John's, urged him when attending Soviet banquets "Don't eat it if you can't peel it." This is a little drastic; it limits one to a very few fruits and nuts—if one can assume that cracking is like peeling.

One of my many duties was to learn the protocol of wine—when and where and how to serve it. I found out that champagne plays mostly a symbolic role in diplomatic life, chiefly at official receptions and dinners, especially when toasts are drunk.

I did not have many opportunities to learn about wine in Moscow, except that there was a red Soviet concoction which bore an amazing label "Burgundy Bordeaux type, Great Wine of the Caucasus." This should puzzle any student of grape geography. Nearly as puzzling as one we were later to see in Manchuria on a bottle of "Scotch." It had been christened "Queen George." The bottling was beautiful and for those who could not read English it looked completely authentic. The strong yellow liquor bore little resemblance to whisky.

The lack of opportunity to learn about wines in Moscow was compensated for by John's knowledge of the subject. Born in Bordeaux, where his father had been not only the American consul but a true wine connoisseur, John probably learned about wine and mother's milk at the same time.

Perhaps even before, to judge by the story of his birth. When John came into existence, his father was out to lunch. When he eventually returned, he was greeted with the happy news. The doctor explained, though, that there had been a very critical moment, sort of touch and go. When born, the child was not breathing. But due, the doctor explained, to his own genius and ready presence of mind, the situation had been saved. He had called for a bottle of cognac and with it had massaged the infant. The baby let out a scream, breathed, and all was well.

John's father was alarmed. He summoned the butler. "Which bottle of cognac did you open for this?" he demanded. The butler replied, "One of the bottles in the sideboard." Mr.

Wiley replied indignantly, "A bottle of cooking brandy from the kitchen would have done equally well." The butler had chosen one of three authentic bottles of Napoleon Fine cognac. To this day John is convinced that his father was absolutely right.

Vodka, the great national drink of Russia, was at that time fit to be put in a lamp, not in a human stomach. Prior to 1917 vodka was rectified many times to acquire tastelessness and smoothness. Otherwise, it was as raw as our moonshine. The postrevolutionary Russian did not bother about this, perhaps rightly, since vodka is not a drink for people with a discerning taste. It is drunk for its effect, and is never sipped. In Eastern Europe vodka is literally tossed down, bottoms up. Our Russian friends did not seem to mind gulping many glasses of it. But then their stomach juices are remarkable and possibly different from ours.

The most striking example of Russian stomach fortitude came one night after a dinner party at our house. We were always running short of food in Moscow, so we kept a supply of canned goods on hand. For this dinner I had planned to serve a fish course, using canned fish we had imported from abroad. In the afternoon I found to my stupefaction that the large oval cans had swollen into the shape of footballs. When I applied the can opener to one of them, it was like sticking a pin into a balloon inflated with poison gas. I fled from the stench. The cook improvised another dish and the sad story of the fish was forgotten until much later that night.

After all the guests had left, I went again into the kitchen. I screamed.

Our two Russian housemaids were sitting around the table, wolfing the horrible fish. In response to my shrieks of alarm, both young women amiably repeated, *nichevo, nichevo;* the fish was very good; indeed, delicious. I wanted at once to call a doctor, an ambulance and a stomach pump, but the girls roared with laughter and repeated *nichevo, nichevo*. The next morning the two girls appeared as usual, fresh, rosy and bright-eyed. They had not even needed bicarbonate of soda. There was not a hiccup or burp between them.

An important task ahead of me when we moved into our apartment was to find servants.

One of the first gestures of the Russian Revolution in its infancy was to abolish the servant class. It was Lenin himself who brought it back as he learned very quickly that he could not clean his room, cook his food, and at the same time do all the work expected of him. We, the Foreign Service wives, are often envied since when stationed abroad we have servants to do many of our household chores. However, in our case, as in Lenin's, it is not a luxury but a necessity. A Foreign Service wife cannot, even if like the goddess Siva she had two hundred hands, add much housework to all her other duties.

Outside of the United States, the kitchen is not mechanized. In many countries of the world, the electricity makes only sporadic and feeble appearances. No timesaving devices are possible as the current is so weak, indifferent or sporadic that there are no electric ranges—no mixers, washing machines, electric irons or vacuum cleaners. Frequently stoves are heated by wood or charcoal. Carpets are swept with brooms. Floors are cleaned with a rag on all fours. Even the water for one's bath is often heated in the kitchen.

At the time of our marriage, the Celliers had with them the most perfectly trained and charming maître d'hôtel, a Savoyard named Rémy. He could do everything, even to darning stockings or giving permanents. The Celliers did not think too highly of my housekeeping talents and realized what difficulties were ahead of me as the wife of the counselor of a large embassy. After consulting Rémy, they decided to let him go with us to Moscow to manage our household. I was delighted with the prospect, not only because Rémy would take the load off my inexperienced shoulders but because of my sincere friendship for him.

All was arranged for his departure. John got him a visa, and deposited the money for his trip so he could join us in Moscow. A few days after our arrival to Russia, I received a letter from Rémy, a letter I have always kept. He began: "Dear madame, between God and you I have chosen God." He went on to explain that for a long time he had felt the call to become a priest and that he had again consulted his conscience and definitely decided to take the vows of priesthood instead of coming to Russia. Today he is a priest in Savoy.

When we moved into an embassy apartment we acquired the services of a Viennese cook, Walter, a Volga-German girl, Anna, and a Russian kitchen maid. Anna was very young, untrained, but intelligent and gay. She had an odd but harmless idiosyncrasy. Whenever we were absent from Moscow for a few days, she surrounded the sofa in our living room with all the potted and flowering plants she could find, dressed herself in my very best evening dress, and reclined in a Madame de Récamier pose. Then our cook Walter would sing Austrian *lieder* to her. We heard about it from friends who had dropped in at our apartment unannounced, to be greeted by this enchanting *tableau vivant*.

My struggle with that erratic, untrained staff ended in a few months. The greatest gift of the penates, an excellent Chinese servant, appeared to assume control of our domestic life. It was Fu who started the dynasty of Chinese servants which luckily still continues in our household. Fu was not only a superb cook, an excellently trained butler and valet, but also a human being of superior intelligence. His wife Yui-chen, tiny, lovely looking, had the same qualities of heart and mind. With the advent of Fu and Yui-chen all household problems vanished for me.

The Chinese servant idea of paradise on earth is to own a

restaurant. They deny themselves much in order to save for this goal. But before leaving their employer, they always train someone else to take their places. That is their code. When Fu asked us to facilitate the arrival of his brother-in-law Han from Harbin we knew that a restaurant was in prospect, somewhere.

When Han had been trained to perfection, Fu left us to open a restaurant in New York. Happily, Han proved to have the same fine qualities as his family.

Years later, in Portugal, we met in a restaurant where he was a waiter a six-foot, smiling Chinese, Wong. He used to visit Han. One day he appeared at the embassy with all his possessions. He liked us and decided to join our household. He has been with us ever since. He is so strong he can lift a piano, yet, for all his strength, he is a most gentle soul. There is no household chore that he cannot do, and does do with a zest.

Han of course by now has a restaurant in New York.

To the hard core of our Chinese servants we added many local ones. I have been happy with all of them in our many posts—thanks to my mother. In my parents' household, a maid or a cook never left except to get married when young or to go to the cemetery when old. It was Mother who taught me that servants were not a timesaving device, a machine with hands and feet, or a zombie. The minute they came to us they were a part of the family. To establish this personal relationship with the people who work for you takes a lot of your time, especially in large embassies, but it is very rewarding.

Another thing I learned was that you cannot expect the same quality of domestic service in every country. In many backward and poor countries of the world where children are shockingly undernourished and illiterate, when grown they have little physical resistance and slow reactions. Efficiency is the slogan of the American housewife. Patience should be that of the Foreign Service wife. I believe we should have that word engraved in gold letters on our hearts when we go abroad.

Cleanliness also is one unending fight. It does not take an American Foreign Service wife long to realize that there are many countries in the world where Pasteur is still unknown and where cleanliness is considered a foreign superstition. A typical answer was made by my Persian cook who, after being repeatedly asked to cover the food so as to keep off the cloud of flies, said, quite shocked, "But, madam, why do you mind? They eat so little."

III

While I was laboriously trying to find my way through the mysteries of housekeeping, I was faced by what at that time seemed to me a terrifying monster—protocol.

For me protocol was something like the Old Man of the Sea, perched on one's neck, paralyzing every movement, something completely unnecessary and terribly outmoded. I know better now!

My many governesses had taught me "les manières." In my memory still echoes a sentence of a white-haired Irish governess who called me Eileen, instead of my own name, Irena. She would brush my hair for hours, repeating solemnly, "When in doubt use a fork." Thin and scanty tutelage I was bringing to my first post.

In Moscow, John was counselor, William C. Bullitt was the Ambassador and unmarried, so I became automatically the number one woman of the embassy. I was saved from becoming a nervous wreck by my abysmal, blissful ignorance of the responsibilities and demands of diplomatic life. Coming as I had from art school and an artist's environment, I imagined that the same informality reigned in every stratum of society.

I always thought that in life one only needed St. Augustine's advice, "Love and do what you want." It is not so in diplomacy. No love of your neighbor will teach you which fork to use when eating an artichoke or where to seat the Archbishop of Canterbury when he dines with you.

For that, I discovered, we have protocol, which constitutes

21

a rigid pattern of precedence and procedure which fits international relations like a beautifully tailored strait jacket.

Diplomatic life, like any game, has its set of inflexible rules. They are very few, but one has difficulty playing the game without knowledge of them. The rest, of course, is one's own personality. Experience, kindness, tact, patience and a few other such odds and ends also are most useful. These, however, are learned in another book. Strangely enough, protocol, like law, is here to help rather than to hinder. It is much easier to know than to guess at, invent or improvise behavior for each occasion.

Not only did I not know the rules of this game, but I thought that I could do very well without them. Of course, John, having been in the Foreign Service for many years, was my patient mentor and prevented me from committing unforgivable diplomatic mistakes. I had a tendency toward seating congenial people next to each other at dinners, oblivious of rank. I did not always know when to take my leave at official events, where one arrives by the clock and leaves by the same tyrannical instrument.

Apart from John, my diplomatic guardian angel in Moscow was the doyenne of the Diplomatic Corps, the wife of the Italian Ambassador, Countess Attolico. She was beautiful, charming, and a well-trained ambassadress. She took me under her wing and kept an eagle eye on my protocol behavior. She would call me up and say, "Irena, I know that the Danes have left cards. Have you returned them?" I would humbly confess that I had not, and then I learned that cards have to be returned within a week. On another occasion she scolded me for going on an official visit without a hat, and I learned that when calling, regardless of climate or mood, one must wear a hat, stockings and gloves.

This stern necessity of being, as an ambassadress, always well-groomed, was one of my losing battles. By inclination I am sloppy, and during daylight hours have the sartorial instincts of an Indian squaw. I am given to slacks, Chinese coolie coats, and bare feet. Through my profession—I am a sculptress—I am also disorderly, with cement dust on my hair, wood shavings in my pockets, and color-stained fingernails. And I detest hats! Having very long hair, a hat always has a tendency to slide askew, giving me an unmerited inebriated look. I compromised by always wearing tiny beanies on the top of my head except for one spectacular hat which I would replace only every few years. I called it my "Te Deum" hat, as one simply has to be visibly hatted when a Te Deum is sung in church on official occasions.

But too often, alas, I did not live up to the sartorial image of an ambassadress.

If I felt rebellious against the constant tyranny of formal clothes, I always enjoyed the colorful and exciting paraphernalia that goes with state functions, the resplendent evening gowns, tiaras, feathers, decorations.

During my apprenticeship I learned that the usefulness of protocol is its impersonality. There is no resentment attached to being seated at the end of the table, below the salt, knowing that one is relegated there not by the dislike or caprice of one's hosts but in conformity with a written rule. But this rule is sometimes hard on the young, as I soon found out. As the Counselor's wife I sat quite low at the table, with the younger generation. But the minute Ambassador Bullitt went off on one of his many important trips, John would become chargé d'affaires and I would go zooming up, sitting among ambassadors and other high officials. My bad luck was that at the time, whenever I was so promoted, protocol usually seated me between the Japanese Ambassador, who spoke only Japanese, and the British Ambassador, who refused to speak at all. Oh, those long, long Russian dinners from ten until two o'clock! I tried and tried to get a few words out of the British Ambassador, but to all my primitive and standard questions, "Do you like the theatre?" and "Do you like Pushkin?" the answer was always "No." End of conversation. One evening, after a hundred curt "Noes," I got mad and said, "What on earth do you like, Mr. Ambassador?" He looked at me sideways with his light-blue eyes veined with red and said: "I like only three things: whisky, Shakespeare and sleep." I gave up my efforts but, curiously enough, I liked him.

I also learned that when a chief of state is present at a party, you can never leave ahead of him, you are stuck—short of a ruptured appendix. I learned never to use the crystal-gazing method of seating official guests but always to be guided by the protocol section at the various Foreign Offices. I found out that protocol is not the invention of idiots to befuddle fools nor was it devised by stuffed shirts for their own weird amusement; on the contrary, it is as essential in official life as traffic regulations are to circulation of motor cars in a large city.

And then there are times when an Act of God precludes the use of protocol.

When John was stationed in Holland long before our marriage, it was customary for the legation staff, which numbered about ninety, garbed in frock coats, to present formal New Year greetings at the palace. Queen Wilhelmina was, curiously enough, an extremely shy and nervous woman with no repertoire of small talk. The Minister went first, then John headed the staff Indian file into the royal presence. John, to give the proper example to those who followed, bowed very low. He was alone in the middle of the great salon with its parquet floor. While he bowed a rear suspender button fell to the floor with a shattering clatter. It rolled interminably in large concentric circles.

The Queen, the Court, the Minister, and the diplomatic staff watched the button in hypnotic fascination. Only when the button collapsed did the Queen address John. "How long have you been in Holland?" Queen Wilhelmina asked anxiously, fingering her pearl necklace. "Nine months, your Majesty," John replied. There the conversation ended.

I learned painfully that protocol is not like a human skeleton, on the inside supporting the whole structure of the body and giving it its shape, but more like the shell of a lobster, the hard shell that gives protective covering to what is essential. And the essential is politeness, friendliness, and broad understanding.

Another side of diplomatic life which revolted me at first was what looked like unforgivable artificiality in human relations.

I remember how horrified I was by an ambassadress who greeted everybody with inattentive eyes, but a charming, glued-on, artificial smile. I remember saying to John: "The first time you see me smile that way, shoot me." I was wrong. Now I am not, of course, preaching or condoning hypocrisy. But what is our aim when we go to a strange unknown country? Isn't it to understand and to like the people who suddenly surround us? And there is only one international key that opens every door of friendship, and that is a smile. What is more understood and more understanding?

A smiling face is absolutely essential for a woman in diplomatic life. Not Pope's "Eternal smiles his emptiness betray," but a smile which comes from a desire for friendship.

People talk so much about our armor of banal politeness. But even if it is an armor, it is not banal. It requires so much discipline, so much courage, to be able to face people always—and I mean always—with amiability. Our Lord teaches us to love our neighbor, which I never found too hard to do. But liking him is another matter. How easy to love but how impossible to like the mean, the vain, the cruel, the petty, those who talk all the time and say nothing, those who talk to harm, those who are rude and patronizing. That is when the smile is one's life preserver. St. Thérèse of Lisieux once wrote: "When someone irritates you, when you dislike that person, give her your most beautiful smile." So when officials greet you with a ready-made smile, don't condemn them. They may not be hypocrites. They may be just trying to be better human beings.

IV

IN OUR MANY POSTS THERE WERE ONLY A FEW OCCASIONS when I felt that I was living in the Hanging Gardens of Semiramis, suspended high above everyday reality. Strangely enough, the first occasion was at a dinner at the Kremlin.

This aggressively proletarian capital, with its eternal inveighing and invectives against the decadent West, preserved sumptuous luxury for the elite. Paradoxically, of all our many posts, it was in Moscow that John had to wear his white tie and tails the most. The Russians at that time did not use them much, but expected them from the diplomats on formal occasions, which were very frequent.

This magnificent party at the Kremlin was the first and to my knowledge the last of its kind. It stands out in my memory because it was so unexpected in that drab, dreary, sad, uneasy city, suddenly to be transported for one night into glamour. One felt as a tragedian might feel if suddenly cast in a light operetta staged in a gay, mythical kingdom of waltzes and romance.

It was held in the great reception rooms of the Kremlin. In every corner were long tables covered by white damask cloth. Pyramids of fruit, great platters of salmon, hollowed blocks of ice filled with caviar, partridges, pheasants, cakes, were displayed as in some wild dream of Gargantua.

This delirious abundance of food, which characterized all Russian official parties, was such a contrast to the empty food stores, the barren markets, such a departure from the diet of the people, which consisted largely of cabbage, potatoes, and coarse bread, that it revealed the Asiatic love of ostentatious luxury and complete disregard of human decency. The philosophy of the ruling hierarchy of that time—undamaged since the beginning of time—was plenty for the few and little for the masses. Let them eat cabbage, but for us the salmon of the Volga, the sturgeon from the Caspian, the wild game from Siberia.

I did not know Russia before the Revolution, but I am sure that this party, to which we were invited by the invisible Stalin, could not have been outdone by any czar. All the pomp of empire was there, in the blazing crystal chandeliers, illuminating the great white and gold rooms, in the food, in the flowing champagne, in the multitude of servants.

As we entered the fortress-like beauty of the Kremlin, we passed several great halls. To the right, as we went in, there was a special room reserved for Litvinov, high Soviet dignitaries, and the chiefs of diplomatic missions.

Since John was chargé d'affaires, during a prolonged absence of the Ambassador, we were at once escorted toward the huge "table d'honneur." But in the enormous center hall there were a great number of tables. John spotted a very small one near a wall. He grabbed me by the wrist. "Let's beat it and have dinner together," he whispered.

I was enchanted, since during our first year of marriage I doubt if we had eaten more than two meals alone. In a flash we escaped and were blissfully ensconced at our table for two.

It is wonderful to be young, newlywed, all dressed up, and sitting in the flattering light of the fabulous chandeliers. A multitude of servants brought food and Russian champagne. John declined the champagne. The Soviet product at that time was abominable. But a waiter leaned over, put his mouth to John's ear. "You can drink this; just try it," he insisted. John did and it was superb; obviously from the old imperial cellars.

28

John loves food and drink, and everywhere he seems to have waiters as bosom friends.

Alas, I soon found out that if there is no peace for the wicked, there is also no solitude for diplomats. We were just beginning to enjoy our crowded isolation when we were joined by Troyanovsky, then the Soviet Ambassador to Washington. The son of a czarist officer, he was a man of good breeding and charm. With him was Kalinin, titular chief of state of the U.S.S.R. With his cheerful peasant face, his little blond beard, gay eyes, his simplicity and directness (a quality seldom found in Soviet officials) Kalinin looked like the perfect prototype of a proletarian president. Without ado they sat down at our table and a strange conversation ensued.

Kalinin, who knew that I was a sculptress, started with a tirade about the uselessness, the stupidity of diplomacy compared to other forms of work. He said to me, "You and I can talk together and understand each other since we are both craftsmen, not silly diplomats," and added with nostalgia: "Before the Revolution, I was a locksmith, a very good one. I made ninety gold rubles a month, and now look at me, just a president." He asked, "You are an artist, why aren't you a Bolshevik?"

I answered, "I do not like Bolsheviks." Kalinin looked shocked. "But you don't know any, so how can you judge?" I looked around the ballroom, filled with high officials of the party, all of them present except Stalin. Kalinin, with the back of his hand, disdainfully waved them away. "Those are not Bolsheviks. A real Bolshevik is as rare as a white fox. I and one other are perhaps the only ones in this entire building tonight."

True, Kalinin was in a gay mood. The champagne had been flowing in torrents, but his frankness was revealing. The old veterans of the Russian Revolution did not like the new generation of Communists that was already beginning to emerge.

Happily, because of his great popularity with the people, he escaped the purges and was permitted to die a natural death.

Strange things always happened at parties in Moscow. John and I gave a large reception for a visiting magnate of the American press. The embassy was crowded with all the top level of Soviet life. I was talking to Radek, famous *Izvestia* editorial writer, when a Russian came up and whispered something in his ear. Radek was leaning against the wall and I saw that his face turned as white as the wall itself, which is not a fanciful expression. He looked as if he were ready to faint, excused himself, and left. For the next fifteen minutes, being the hostess, I was busy with some purely housekeeping problems. Suddenly looking around, I saw that there was not a single Russian left. They had all evaporated silently without a word of good-by. John was terribly interested and very puzzled.

The Americans then slowly departed and John and I returned to our own apartment. The doorbell rang. In came Boris Sergeivich Steiger, looking anxiously over his shoulder. His visit was obviously surreptitious.

Steiger, ostensibly a high official of the Commissariat of Education, was the GPU agent whose job it was to watch the Diplomatic Corps. He had become a great friend of ours and had been one of the Russian guests who had melted so suddenly into the Moscow night. I knew that he had come with news. I was almost jumping out of my skin with curiosity.

"Take it very seriously," he announced solemnly. He repeated: "Take it very seriously." "Take what seriously?" John asked. "Kirov has been assassinated in Leningrad," Steiger explained, and then he was gone. All the Russians at the embassy had at once appreciated the dire consequences of Kirov's death. Kirov had been one of the very top Communists in Leningrad. He had been killed by another Communist. Why, no one has ever really found out. That very night the purges began. Steiger subsequently told John that an average of seven thousand people a day were exiled to the Arctic Circle or to Central Asia. Later, of course, many were tried publicly and executed, while many others were killed without trial, including Yenykidze, a Georgian and the Secretary of the powerful Central Committee; the suave and elegant Karakhan, probably the most able of Soviet diplomats, and Steiger himself.

Up to that time we had seen the Russians constantly and quite freely. That same night Stalin pulled down the iron curtain. From that time until we left Moscow, Russian contact with the Diplomatic Corps, or any foreigner for that matter, was rigidly controlled and restricted.

During the sinister time of the purges I had the unique experience of having a bridge partner arrested and deported while playing three no trump. My partner, Florinski, then chief of protocol, had just made the bid when he was called to the telephone. He came back smiling and explained that he had to leave for half an hour, but would be back and would we please wait for him. He has not been seen since. There were no charges. There was no trial. He just vanished.

Outside of the spectacular affair at the Kremlin, there has been one, and only one, great party in the Moscow of the U.S.S.R. It was a ball given by our Ambassador William C. Bullitt, staged by me and Charlie Thayer. It was one of the rarest occasions, more rare and precious than the whooping crane, when ideological differences and Communist hates were dissolved into an atmosphere of fun and friendship.

One day Bill Bullitt—knowing me he should have known better—sent me a telegram from Washington, where he was on consultation. "Returning next month. Arrange a party. The sky is the limit."

I have always wanted to design and stage a ballet, but this was far more exciting. In Europe or America, a "sky is the limit" party presents no challenge. But in Moscow in the spring of 1935, there was nothing in the shops, nothing in the market, not a flower, not a scrap of material. Everything had to be invented, created. The training I had had in art schools, where all our parties had to be arranged on a shoestring, came in handy. But the most important factor for the success of the Bullitt ball was Charlie Thayer. Charlie at that time was a young secretary of the embassy, endowed not only with an unfettered imagination but also with Napoleon's scorn for the word "impossible." We immediately held a conference.

As the party was to be at the end of April, we decided to make it a green, white and gold Spring Festival. Green trees, green grass, white tulips, white lambs with gilded horns and hoofs, and white roosters in gold and glass cages.

The only thing that did not present any problem were the tulips. A courier going to Holland produced on his return thousands of blooming bulbs. But where to get the green trees with Moscow still covered with snow and the trees still stark naked. And of course pines and firs were too sad and wintry. Undaunted, Charlie telegraphed to Yalta, in the Caucasus, but back came the answer "Spring late here too." The sun lamp of Bill Bullitt saved the day. We had a dozen young birch trees uprooted, stuck them in the Ambassador's bathtub, and put the lamp on them. And on the day of the party, obligingly, the trees burst forth with lovely green leaves.

Our greatest headache was the lambs, as the collective farm sent us sheep instead. Their smell was overpowering and persisted even after hours of careful shampooing and perfuming. Shampooing six large sheep in a small bathroom is an experience I hope never to repeat. But as all the perfumes of Araby were of no avail, we compromised for half a dozen baby goats. With their gilded horns and hoofs, leaping and playing on a small scenically arranged and fenced-in platform, they were most decorative.

The white roosters were plentiful and we solved the problem

of glass cages by collecting all the glass towel racks from the bathrooms of the unwilling embassy staff. They made spectacular cages.

In the dining room we had a 60-foot table built with alternate segments scalloped out. They were thickly planted with tulips and tiny concealed electric fans made the flowers sway as in a breeze. Beyond the tulips, in the space reserved for a sumptuous buffet, we wanted grass, so as to make the table look like a garden. The grass nearly defeated us until suddenly I remembered that in some parts of Poland one used to sow oats on wet cheesecloth to have green squares for decorating the Easter table. Immediately we covered the Embassy's attic floor with yards and yards of wet cheesecloth, scattered chicory seeds, and waited. The Buddhists are right: "No seed will die, every seed will grow." The seeds sprouted superbly and we had an emerald-green grass for our table.

To achieve a real effect of spring, I thought we should have at least one wild newborn animal. The director of the Moscow Zoo produced a most charming baby bear, plus a trained nurse to keep an eye on him. We also prepared a baby bottle for him and a tree complete with limbs, where he could clamber or rest.

The director of the Zoo was so intrigued by our party that every time there was a birth at the Zoo he would ring me up. "Madame Wiley, I have something for your party. A giraffe has just been born." Another day he would offer a wolf cub or a baby llama or some other strange creature. To my regret I had to refuse them all as John had taken an unreasonable but firm stand against any more wildlife for this party.

As it turned out, the baby bear nearly created a diplomatic incident. During the ball General Yegorov, then chief of staff, took it tenderly in his arms, whereupon the bear immediately proceeded to unhousebreak all over the general's gala uniform.

Yegorov, furious and cursing, rushed out of the Embassy, leaving Charlie and me upset and uneasy.

We started to breathe freely again only when an hour later the general reappeared at the party, gay as a lark, in a new uniform and, with the rest of the guests, stayed until dawn.

Apropos of larks, birds were the only dismal fiasco of that memorable evening.

The dining room looked radiant with the tables of grass and swaying tulips, the white roosters in glass cages around the room, goats dancing in one corner, a baby bear sleeping at the other end, and white birches tracing lacy patterns on the white walls.

But the ball room, which at the Spasoo House, the Ambassador's residence, is formal, dull and stark, marble walled, was very difficult to bring to life. My first plan of glassing over the floor, pumping water under the glass and putting a lot of tropical fish and marine life so as to make an aquarium to dance on, was rejected even by Charlie. He definitely disapproved of gallons of water and fish on the embassy floor. Perhaps he was right. We had already one decorative scheme, as the stage director of the Kamerney Theater had flowers painted on slides to be projected on the walls, but the room still needed some life and gaiety.

I don't know what evil spirit inspired me to arrange an aviary. We got some great fish nets, soaked them in gold powder and glue, and stretched them around four huge marble pillars at the end of the room.

It did look lovely when filled with hundreds of little finches, produced, of course, by our friend the Zoo director. The finches were singing and flying merrily behind the gold mesh. I was delighted with my idea until the dance began. I had not realized that the noise of the band and the strong lights would terrify the birds. I still feel sad and remorseful when I remember how the poor things flew around wildly for hours, hitting

34

the net in a heartbreaking panic. Luckily many escaped through the net, and for days the Embassy was filled with finches flying about. The brocade furniture was covered with their droppings, to the understandable annoyance of the Ambassador.

It was perhaps the gayest party ever given in Moscow. Everybody from the Red hierarchy was there except Stalin. The mustached General Budenny, a Cossack, and the last great cavalry leader of history, with his center of gravity almost touching the floor, his arms folded on his chest and his legs working like locomotive pistons, danced the trepak around and around the huge floor. Mrs. Litvinov, the wife of the Foreign Minister, all night long hugged one of the baby goats passionately to her ample bosom, while the ill-fated Radek tried to pour champagne into the bear's milk bottle.

When morning came all the roosters started to crow, but still the guests did not leave. It was nine o'clock when the last ones reluctantly straggled out.

Certainly never before and probably never again will the Soviet Union have had such a gloriously good time.

V

WHEN A DIPLOMAT IS IN THE FIELD HE FREQUENTLY becomes a passionate collector. By nature I am more a sentimental hamster than a collector of antiques or objects of art. I keep cracked, faded presents from people I like, pieces of colored glass, broken shells with curious shapes, odd bits of stone, and old Christmas cards. I do not quite reach the sublime heights of the grandfather of a French friend of mine. After his death my friend went through the attic of his mansion. She found a large trunk labeled *Petits bouts de ficelle ne pouvant plus servir a rien*. On examining the contents she discovered that the label was entirely correct. She found only bits and pieces of useless string which he had amassed over the long years and which truly could serve no useful purpose.

Normally when shopping I have a tendency to emulate Socrates. On viewing a display of goods for sale, he remarked "How many things I do not want!" Nevertheless, on arrival at a new post I invariably catch the antique-buying fever, spurred on by the competition of other diplomats and by my great conceit that, as an artist, I can do better than others.

It all started in Moscow, where hunting for antiques was practically the only diversion, replacing as entertainment the corner drugstore, clubs, and movies.

In the late afternoon the members of the Moscow Diplomatic Corps would saunter nonchalantly in and out of antique shops, called *kommissionny* in the Soviet jargon, with mysterious expressions and secretive smiles. There were strict rules

36

in that hunt, never to divulge one's sources, never knowingly to overbid somebody else's haggle, and never to reveal the price one paid. That game had to do only with the ruble stores, not with the ones called *torgsins*, "selling to foreigners," where one could buy only with foreign currency fabulous treasures at fabulous prices. *Torgsins* were, of course, only patronized by the very rich.

Once, when on a freezing winter day I was looking at the pathetic bric-a-brac in a *kommissionny*, I noticed an old man. He was wearing a threadbare jacket; his feet were wrapped in newspapers tied with string. He had a sweet, distinguished face, and his bedraggled poverty did not conceal an air of breeding. He was trying to sell a dirt-encrusted silver goblet and was having an argument with the salesgirl. She was offering only the trifling value of the cup's actual weight in silver. He was asking more, since it was old and had long been in the family. The girl was adamant, so he sadly withdrew saying that he would think it over.

I was so moved that I rushed after him. In the street I told him that I thought his cup was beautiful, and asked him if he would sell it to me for whatever price he thought was right. His face lit up with a lovely smile. He was perhaps more pleased that I appreciated his heirloom than that I was offering a fair sum for it.

I happily paid him what he asked and, all aglow, feeling like Lady Bountiful, I returned home. After cleaning the silver, I discovered to my horrified amazement that it was a rare eighteenth-century embossed cup with the Moscow hallmark, worth a hundredfold what I had paid. I felt so ashamed that for many weeks I remained on the lookout for the old man in the threadbare jacket in order to make restitution. But I never saw him again.

This episode made me realize that every antique offered for sale in the countries behind the iron curtain represents sorrow and suffering, that every object tells a story of want and pain. After that all the fun of antique hunting vanished, and I gave it up. The antique shop had become for me a graveyard of human hopes.

I turned instead to modern art. As the Soviet officials knew that I was a sculptress, the GPU was not suspicious when I wanted to meet artists. American diplomats were still permitted to see a lot of Russians anyhow. John and I met writers, stage directors, dancers, musicians.

Russia has not had any plastic art since the splendid era of the old icons. Only once across the dark and empty horizon of Russian art was there a flash, like that of lightning, which started a blazing trail throughout the artistic world. At the turn of the century there appeared in Russia a group of painters—Kandinski, Malevich, Chagall, Taltin—all men of talent and vision.

If one can ever pinpoint the beginning of a new school of art, one can say that Western abstract art started there. One of the possible explanations as to why abstraction in art began in Russia is its proximity to China. While the Chinese communicate visually, using characters which actually are abstract images, the Western world communicates phonetically, using letters to create words.

Curiously enough, these painters emigrated to France and Germany and left no followers behind. Only Malevich remained in Russia. But finally he abandoned painting when the Soviet regime took over art as an instrument of propaganda.

Once I was asked by the head of the Moscow Art Department to help him choose a hundred paintings out of five hundred to be sent to an exhibition in Chicago. I walked endlessly through rooms where, like reflections in mirrors, countless faces of Stalin glared at me, where conventional pictures of workers with bulging muscles were achieving the Second Five-Year Plan, where a few Victorian, sentimental photographic landscapes failed to reflect the melancoly beauty of the Russian scenery. I told the director, "Send everything." The artists were so uniformly bad that there was no reason for hurting the feelings of any particular painter.

Something that has always puzzled me is that the Russians who are so devoid of talent in pictorial art have genius in decorative art. Their painted stage settings, for example, are inspired. While there is not even a half-decent picture in the entire gallery of Russian art, pictures painted merely as part of the scenery of a play are magnificent.

Russian village art also shows great imagination and talent. John and I were interested and delighted by the black-lacquered boxes in the shops in Moscow. These boxes of every shape and form had perfectly charming miniatures painted on the lids. Though no longer representing religious subjects, these miniatures were under a strong Byzantine influence, but of a Byzantium gone lighthearted and gay, unorthodox and "liberated."

On those boxes a Red Army soldier looked like St. George, the workers and peasants like saints and prophets. And every picture of a mother and child needed only the switch from the red star behind her head to a halo to become an icon of the Virgin Mary. We were very curious about the artists who, while following the party line in their subjects, could produce works with so much religious feeling.

The mystery was solved when we found out that the *artel* (the traditional form of Russian artisan association) not as yet interfered with by the authorities—from which those miniatures came was in the village of Palekh. This village had been for three centuries the center of icon painters.

I wanted very much to go to Palekh. After months of haggling with the Foreign Office, we received the necessary permission. Our little party started by car. It took sixteen hours to cover the 150 miles of flat, dull landscape from Moscow to

Palekh since the bumpy dirt road was more appropriate for tanks than other vehicles.

We were met at the outskirts of the village by an excited and delighted delegation of the *artel* workers, as we were the first foreigners to visit Palekh since the Bolshevik Revolution.

The men who surrounded us had gay faces and the clear eyes of artisans. In their *façon d'être* there was none of that undefined uneasiness, none of that atmosphere of anxiety so characteristic of the Russians we had previously seen.

They led us triumphantly through muddy, crooked streets bordered by crooked, thatched cottages to the one-story three-room house that had been assigned to us. One large white-washed room was a combination kitchen, dining room and studio. It had a long table in the middle, a kitchen range in one corner and in another Russia's greatest blessing, a *pyechka,* a square brick stove which heats the house in winter and in which the bread is baked. In every cottage we saw the same squat stove, with an ancient grandfather quietly dozing on its top. I cannot imagine a happier way of spending one's old age than lying on top of a warm stove and from that vantage point watching the activities of the family. We got very attached to our *pyechka* grandfather who never left the top of the stove, never spoke to us but with a toothless and friendly grin gulped down each glass of vodka brought to him.

We found ourselves immediately in a completely different atmosphere from any I had seen in Russia. Here Communist ideology was only skin deep. The Palekh *artel,* like a painter's guild in the Middle Ages, has only one ideology, that of art. The villagers began their apprenticeship in infancy. Every workroom was filled with children whose favorite games were grinding colors, tracing drawings, and watching the ovens where the lacquer was fired.

The *artel* artists accepted us foreigners not as people one had to indoctrinate or be shy of but as welcome guests. Unafraid, unpolitical, they lived to paint. They talked with simplicity about their daily problems, about their desire to travel and see works of art. They told us the story of the shattering blow that nearly destroyed them when, after the Revolution, the order came: "No more icons." Unprepared for any other trade, they were desperate and lost until one of the artists had the idea of learning the art of lacquered papier-mâché. In that medium they again found a way to express themselves. They did not talk to us about religion, but I noticed how often they chose to illustrate fairy tales in which angels appeared.

They brought to my mind a poem by a revolutionary poet, Yessenin, which reflects their feelings:

> I accept all; just as it is, I take it all.
> I am ready to travel the newly broken road.
> I give my whole soul to October and May.
> Only my lyre I will not give away.

The government left them pretty much alone, to paint, to illustrate, to bake their multicolored boxes, so long as they stuck to proletarian subjects or to old Russian sagas.

We spent two marvelous days with those hospitable, inspiring people, sharing their primitive accommodations and lethal diet. They shared everything with us, but their everything consisted of black bread, tea, pickled herrings, pickled cucumbers and . . . vodka. Black bread and black tea for breakfast, herring, cucumbers and vodka for lunch, herring, cucumbers, potatoes, bread and vodka for dinner, and herring and vodka during the nightlong dancing and singing. Those usually sober, frugal and destitute artists doubtless ruined themselves producing this flow of vodka as a gesture of friendship and hospitality. So, of course, I had to drink with them, so as not to hurt their feelings or shatter their high opinion of American stamina. For a nondrinker, I did pretty well during some forty-eight hours of alcoholic binge. I never once fell flat on my face nor passed out. I was, it is true, in a complete state of euphoria, probably slightly reeling but ambulant and able to discuss art problems and learn the Palekh technique of lacquer.

When we left with tender farewells and promises of return we had as many friends as there were inhabitants in the village.

In the alcoholic haze we were in, it is lucky that on the road back to Moscow there were no trees, telegraph poles nor traffic. Our car was the only one on the road.

Just before reaching Moscow, on the outskirts of a village, we saw a charming church with the Orthodox cross still shining on its onion-shaped domes. A church that had not been converted into a warehouse, a club or an antireligious museum was already such a rarity that we stopped the car to visit it.

The church was falling in ruins but like the face of an old woman with a beautiful bone structure, where under the sagging flesh, beauty remains, so this little church with its façade cracked and disintegrated, its peeling, golden domes, still retained a touching loveliness. As we approached an elderly priest came to meet us. Gaunt, with a gray, pinched face, long gray hair, in a long gray robe all soiled and patched, he had the same undefeated air as his church. He invited us to the rectory, where he worked, slept, washed and cooked. Cooking is a euphemism as he was so poor that his only cooking consisted of boiling water for tea. Black tea and black bread made up his main diet. His few parishioners were as poor as he, for those with jobs did not dare come to church for fear of being dismissed.

At that time the fight of the Communists for the Russian soul was at its height. They drowned the people with waves of propaganda deriding religion. They attacked their ears with blaring loud-speakers, their eyes with huge posters and pamphlets. But what was more effective than any verbal or visual

42

propaganda was the starving of the priests. This liquidated most of the existing clergy and the closing of seminaries prevented drastically the ordaining of new ones.

We talked for hours with Father Vladimir in his little room where poverty was not oppressive, cheered as it was by the icons shining in one corner and a violet and red fuchsia plant on the window sill. Fuchsias are loved by Russian people and are to be found even in the most destitute peasant hut. I have a theory that the shape and color of the blossoms of the fuchsia are the inspiration for Russian church architecture.

Father Vladimir told us how he was denied a bread card as his work was considered unnecessary, how the sacrifices of his parishioners kept him alive, and how in the middle of the night, so as not to be seen by the authorities, the people would come to him for confession, baptism and marriage. He said, "I don't mind hunger and cold so long as they leave me my parish, but I know that the net is closing on me and that soon I will be deported and my people will be left without a pastor."

We asked him if we could help him in any way with food or money but he explained that any help from foreigners could be a pretext for liquidating him sooner. We parted sadly. "How can we know what is going to happen to you? May I come back?" I asked. "Yes," he replied, "do come but don't come in, just drive by. If all is well, the fuchsia plant will be on the window sill, if it is not there it means I have been arrested."

VI

THE TRIP TO PALEKH WAS ONE OF THE VERY FEW WE took, since foreigners were not permitted to circulate freely in Russia. But we did make one strange voyage.

Many months after our arrival we had our first real vacation. We were overjoyed at the opportunity to be together. During the first year as newlyweds John and I were seldom alone, since something like 15,000 American tourists visited Moscow. Most of those among the 15,000 that we did not know visited us with letters of introduction. Our apartment functioned as a restaurant but, alas, without a cash register.

We made our plans very carefully. We decided to go by train to Odessa on the Black Sea, then by an Italian ship to Istanbul, and thence to Greece. The first part of the vacation went very well. We had a relatively comfortable compartment on the train. On each side the compartments were occupied by our faithful GPU companions who stuck like leeches to higher-ranking diplomats. We arrived in drab, crumbling Odessa and went to a drab and crumbling hotel, where our escorts relaxed in the lobby. We then discovered to our consternation that there was no Italian ship. Mussolini had decided to embark on the conquest of Abyssinia and had mobilized all available Italian shipping for the purpose. There was no other ship, so we were stuck in Odessa.

John came up with an idea. It looked like a forlorn hope. He put in a call to Moscow to Ambassador Bullitt. It was extremely rare in those days for a long-distance call to get *t*hrough to anyone anywhere, particularly in the case of a foreign diplomat. By some miracle John succeeded in talking to Bullitt. He asked the Ambassador to obtain permission from the Soviet government for us to go by motorcar overland to Rumania through the Ukraine. Our GPU escorts overheard the conversation. I could hear them loudly voicing the hope that permission would not be granted. To their chagrin it came and we decided to set forth at 2:00 A.M.

We embarked in an automobile of ancient vintage. There was, of course, a second car following—it contained our inevitable escorts smothered in dust. Daylight came early but, as we traveled through this extremely rich farm country—the country of the black earth—we saw people only occasionally. They looked haunted and haggard in the distance. They were the survivors of Stalin's remorseless purge of the *kulaks* in which millions were made to perish. Lovely villages loomed on the horizon like the illustrations of a fairy story—but as we entered them the fairy tale turned into a nightmare. There was not a pane of glass in the windows, not a soul in the streets, not a cat, dog or chicken. They were ghost towns.

After hours of traveling we reached the Dniester River, where we were greeted with frigid politeness by thin-lipped, severely uniformed GPU officers. The skeletonlike remains of what had once been a bridge was silhouetted against the sky, a memorial to a forgotten battle of World War I. The bridge was not rebuilt, for the Russians did not recognize the Rumanian rights to Bessarabia, and the big river was closed to all traffic. The GPU escorted us to a small boat, we were rowed across the river and landed at Bender-Tighina. As we stepped ashore on the Rumanian side the GPU in the rowboat departed, still glacial and thin-lipped.

Waiting for us on the bank was a committee of welcome that had the dash and color of the chorus of an operetta. A slim-waisted officer with heavily powdered cheeks handed me a big bouquet of lilacs with a bright yellow-gloved hand. The mayor in his best Sunday black suit greeted us in fluent French with charming affability, and another armful of lilacs. Instead of the frigid courtesy on the Soviet side, an atmosphere of warm friendliness was immediately created. How they knew we were coming is a mystery we could never fathom. As we were admiring the ancient Turkish fortress that frowned upon the river, the mayor told us that we had arrived in the nick of time. The one and only daily train out of Bender-Tighina was leaving in a few minutes. We were taken to the station. Covered with dust and very, very hungry, we departed for Kishinev.

Again, what a contrast as we traveled through Bessarabia! Here we were in the poorest Rumanian province, and yet each cottage was freshly painted in gay colors. The same gay colors were repeated in the women's clothes and in the masses of flowers surrounding the houses. When our train arrived at Kishinev we were met at the station by the prefect of the city, also bearing a large offering of flowers. It was the third bouquet of lilacs that had been deposited in my arms. With my long hair, uncombed since Odessa, covered with fine gray dust and encumbered with flowers, I looked like a mad Ophelia, but an Ophelia dragged out from under a sand pile, not out of a clear stream.

The prefect informed us that it would be some four hours before the express left for Bucharest. He offered to act as our guide and companion until traintime. And thus began a brief but strange odyssey.

We started out in the prefect's car, an early American model. As we drove through the squalid streets of Kishinev we found at every street corner a beautifully uniformed policeman directing nonexistent traffic. The prefect sat in front with the chauffeur, and at each street corner he would slow down to receive a sweeping salute worthy of the Grenadier Guards at their best. There was, however, one exception. At one intersection the policeman was not at his post. The day had become quite warm and he had sought the shade of the doorway of a church, where he was sound asleep. The prefect stopped the car. The chauffeur sounded the horn violently and loudly. The policeman finally awakened. He leapt to his feet and gave the usual sweeping salute. As we went on our way the prefect turned to John, held up his forefinger and said, "You see? Iron discipline." He was very proud.

The prefect, a most affable extravert, told us a great deal about himself. He had played a heroic role as a Rumanian officer in World War I. He had been "fatally wounded" three times.

The prefect devoted himself diligently to showing us the points of interest in Kishinev. They were few in number. We began by visiting the Prefecture, that is, police headquarters. We were greeted at the door by a police officer in uniform, a lively, rugged type who, had it not been for his uniform, could easily have been mistaken for a first-class thug. He had enough powder on his face to look like a walking advertisement for a cake mix.

We entered the prefect's magnificent office. He walked with businesslike step to his huge desk, which was covered with telephones. He picked up a phone and began talking in crisp Rumanian. He shouted and raged. At the end of the conversation he turned to us, raised his forefinger and said, "You see, iron discipline." He had staged quite an act, but we had a strange feeling that there had been no one at the other end of the line.

We then drove to the Municipal park. The prefect explained that in the park there was a monument to the great poet Pushkin. He pointed out that, although Pushkin was a Russian, the Rumanians were so broad-minded that they had left the monument undisturbed. I do not know if the prefect realized just how broad-minded they were. As a very young man, Pushkin was exiled to Kishinev by order of the Czar. He stayed there several months, and was bored to death. His "Ode to Kishinev" starts: "Accursed town of Kishinev, I will not stop cursing you till the day when heavenly lightning will strike your sinful roofs."

We were invited to walk through the park. By that time I was so exhausted that I could not even have taken a step to see Pushkin, Shakespeare or Dante in the flesh. I politely refused to leave the car. The park had nice little narrow walks bordered by hedges and flowers. The prefect, undaunted, ordered the driver to proceed through the park. To our shocked horror the car charged the hedge rows, assaulted the rosebushes and trampled flora of all kind. This was probably another example of iron discipline.

There was still some time before the departure of the train. *Faute de mieux* the prefect took us to the Kishinev cemetery. The car stopped before two graves. With a gesture of polite introduction, the prefect pointed from the car window first to one and then to the other. "Papa, Mamma." John reverently removed his hat and put on his Sunday-go-to-meeting face. We sat in respectful silence. The prefect sensed that something somewhere might somehow be wrong. He looked nervously around, and saw John's uncovered head. Then he snatched his own hat from his head. The car started on, but we continued to sit in silent vigil until we reached the station.

The prefect and his aides saw us off with great aplomb. The train was the most delightful contrast to the squalor of the Soviet Union. It was beautifully appointed.

We were starved, and the dining car was superb.

Bucharest was called the Paris of the Balkans and was indeed a city of some elegance. One outstanding event while we were there was the Consolidated National Holiday on May 10. We were invited to attend the review in the diplomatic box.

Cecil B. De Mille never achieved such heights. Seated on a

white horse, King Carol reviewed the army. He had designed their uniforms himself. They were spectacular. In one regiment each helmet was decorated with the wing of a swan. Another regiment was dressed entirely in snow white. Once upon a time this regiment had fought a battle in midsummer. Because of the heat the men removed their tunics and fought in their white shirt sleeves. They won the battle, and to commemorate the event King Carol decided that they should forever after wear white uniforms. The cavalry was impressive. The horses were good and the Rumanian officers were excellent horsemen. The masculine beauty of the officers was enough to make any girl's heart flutter.

Finally we reached Greece, where we spent what was left of our vacation.

In Athens we acquired a dilapidated taxi cab complete with meter and the most enchanting Greek chauffeur. He spoke only a few words of English but he knew and loved every inch of his country and was a perfect guide.

On the first day of our trip we arrived at Nauplia, an ancient port of Greece and in a rowboat we went to the island of Bourtzi for lunch. It is a tiny island protected by a submarine wall, entirely covered by an old Venetian fortress, with a white owl in one of its towers and ducks swimming on the amethyst sea.

We discovered that the old powder room of the fortress with its cool, enormously thick walls contained two clean metal cots. We parked. For two weeks we made Bourtzi our base of operation with the taxi ticking on the shore ready to drive us up and down the violet hills of the Peloponnese.

One very hot day, on our way to Agamemnon's tomb, after hours of traveling on desert and dusty roads, we became desperately thirsty. There were no cafés, no inns, not even a stream where we could quench our thirst. John, like a child in the night, kept repeating "I wanna drink, I wanna drink."

49

Suddenly at the top of a hill we saw an old shepherd, god-like, with the hyacinth locks and the beautifully remote face of an archaic sculpture. A figure out of mythology, he stood erect under a silver olive tree silhouetted against an opal sky. At his feet was a jug of wine. There was ageless beauty in the scene.

We stopped the car. John took out our lexicon of conversational Greek and clambered up the steep incline. "Sir," he translated painfully, "may I have a cup of your wine?" John was very pleased with himself, having been able to find the right phrase in the book. He awaited the reply. "Fine and dandy," said the shepherd with a marked midwestern accent.

The scene was as shattered as if a motorcar had flashed through the chariot race in *Ben Hur*.

We thirstily gulped down some wine. It turned out to be Resina, which tastes of rosin and nonvintage varnish. But it was liquid and cool. After thanking the shepherd for his hospitality, John inquired "Restaurant in Chicago, I suppose?" The shepherd drew himself up proudly. Indignantly he shouted, "Restaurant in Chicago, no, never! Saloon with cooking in Milwaukee." We returned to our car very puzzled and wondering what he had in mind. I think I know.

Our return from that trip was not without complications.

Lincoln's Gettysburg Address is considered the shortest of great speeches, but I know of one that was shorter, very effective, and made in a strange language. It happened on our way back to Moscow. We had heard that there was a Soviet ship making the trip from Istanbul to Odessa. We still wanted to adhere to our plan of crossing the Black Sea, so we booked passage on it.

Our arrival at the docks created quite a stir, since we looked more like a safari than mere tourists. First came John with his briefcase, then I trailed behind laden with innumerable packages of last-minute purchases, for which there was no room in the bags. We also carried all the breakable, irresistible purchases such as black earthenware jars from Corinth and glazed Turkish plates. And behind us one by one came fifteen porters with large valises on their heads.

This staggering amount of luggage is explained by the fact that in 1935 there was little one could buy in Russia. One could get icons, old jewelry, grandfather clocks, carpets, but not medicine, little or no food, and no clothing. So anyone who left on a trip outside would be loaded down with long lists from friends and colleagues of the Diplomatic Corps, lists which would waste the hours of our vacation in forced shopping. But this chore was imposed by unwritten law and we were all subject to it. That is why on the dirty headgear of our porters reposed bags full of medicines, condensed milk, spare parts for refrigerators, radios, baby food, silk stockings, deodorants, all those odds and ends that seem so essential to our Western civilization.

We arrived at the boat and there on deck stood the captain in an impeccable white uniform. He greeted us in Russian and efficiently gave orders to have our luggage distributed. Then he took us below deck to show us our cabin. We knew that the boat was not the *Normandie,* that she was old, small and uncomfortable, but we were not prepared for what we saw and, especially, for what we smelled. The dirt, the filth, was indescribable. Next to the dining room, which reeked with the odor of stale cabbage and rancid grease, was the only w.c. on the ship, which probably had been cleaned for the last time when Lenin was in knee pants. And in our cabin on the bed cover were black, fat bedbugs all ready to pounce on us.

John took one look and said, "Irena, you speak Russian. Tell the captain that he should be ashamed to permit such filth, that we are not going to spend a minute longer on this miserable boat. And make it strong!"

I hate scenes and almost never become angry enough to

be really rude. So I replied, "You tell him," knowing that John's Russian was so very limited that he would be unable to make a scene. But I underestimated his imagination. He approached the captain and snatched our passports out of his hands. Then, with a sweeping gesture of repugnance and a voice of thunder, he roared in Russian, *"Kultura, da? Kultury, nyet!"* which means "Culture, yes? Culture, no!"

The captain was abashed, for John's words struck deep. It is quite curious that the Russians are profoundly sensitive to any reflection on their culture. It seems to be the exposed nerve of their inferiority complex. The Turkish porters were overjoyed over more pay, and even more at the captain's discomfiture. They gaily transported our luggage to the railway station whence the Orient Express started us off comfortably back to Moscow.

VII

THE GREAT ITALIAN POET PETRARCH WROTE IN ONE OF his sonnets of a strange people in the north to whom the thought of death conveys no suffering. Also the Russian nervous system is remarkable in its immunity to pain.

This was made specific in a graphic description of the battle of Borodino by de Caulaincourt, ambassador, general, and equerry to Napoleon. The battle of Borodino was a most costly victory for Napoleon in which his army suffered grievous losses. De Caulaincourt wrote that on the French side the night was made hideous by the groaning and screaming of the wounded and the dying. But on the Russian side, where the losses were perhaps even greater, there was utter silence.

Years later there was another vivid illustration of Russian immunity to pain.

Margaret Sanger visited Moscow while we were there. One morning she toured the monstrous abortion clinics which were still a part of the Bolshevik credo. Mrs. Sanger came to lunch with us immediately afterwards. She was pale and shaken.

In their surgical techniques no anesthetics whatever were employed. When a woman's turn came, she stretched herself out on a table and pulled up her skirts. That was her surgical preparation. After the operation she was permitted to rest briefly on a wooden bench and then sent on her way. Mrs. Sanger, certainly a very keen observer, carefully watched the faces of the women during the operation. She did not see a single woman wince from pain or show any sign of physical suffering.

Not only is the Russian's nervous system less developed than ours, but they undoubtedly also have great stoicism. It was in Moscow that for the first time I realized the heartbreaking patience of the poor, their unmurmuring acceptance of want and drabness, their unending waiting, waiting, waiting, waiting. So many precious hours of their lives melted away in the interminable waiting, in queues before food and clothing stores, in hospitals, in stations, in the market. In Spanish there is but a single word, *esperar,* for both waiting and hoping, and in many privileged countries this linguistic optimism is often true. But not in Russia where the end result of this patient waiting was usually black bread, a head of cabbage, some old cloth—but more often nothing at all.

The Soviet regime always had money for scientific research, for laboratories, for cracking the atom, but none for decent medical care or medicine for the masses. Even we, the supposedly pampered diplomats, had trouble finding medicine. Once during some unremembered ailment I had to have a prescription filled in a pharmacy. I paid ten rubles for it. Next time the prescription was refilled it cost five rubles, and the third time one ruble. Intrigued by this fluctuating price in one week, I asked for an explanation. The pharmacist gaily told me "You see, madame, the first time we had all the ingredients necessary for the prescription, the next time only half of them, and today we have only distilled water. So I am charging you accordingly." On another occasion John had a mild eye infection. A Soviet specialist wrote out a prescription. It called for an infinitesimal amount of novocain. No pharmacy in Moscow was able to fill the prescription. Novocain was unobtainable. Happily, John got well anyhow.

This Soviet disregard for everybody's well-being, except for party members, was sadly reflected in their dentistry.

That diplomats have any teeth left is a tribute to the wonders of nature and not to the ministrations of the dentists one encounters in foreign posts. They range in their technique from the primeval to the medieval.

In Moscow the Diplomatic Corps had a special dentist, designated by the Soviet authorities. He was a nice, elderly man, a leftover from the old regime, still quite skillful in the archaic techniques of his craft, but with dental equipment that would have been more suitable for work in a stone quarry than in one's mouth. Huge antiquated foot-powered drills, chunks of sandstone for grinding coarse cement for fillings, could still be accepted gaily, but what defeated all of us were his repeated disappearances. He would be periodically arrested, vanish for a few weeks, reappear, pale and subdued, only to disappear and reappear again. As there was no one else to take his place during his absences, the Diplomatic Corps would run around disconsolately with their toothaches and swollen cheeks.

One morning, during one of his vanishing acts, I woke with a raging toothache and no hope for treatment. John got mad as only an Irishman can and telephoned the GPU demanding a dentist immediately.

We knew, of course, that there was a first-rate dental clinic in the Kremlin that took care of Russian high officials, but we had never had access to it. After John had stormed and threatened, two unsmiling, grim secret police officers appeared at our apartment. They conducted me to a waiting car, without a word. It was like a grade B suspense movie. We drove to the Kremlin hospital, where they escorted me into a most decently equipped dental office. There, pale and shaky, a young dentist was waiting. The GPU deposited me in the dentist's chair and seated themselves on each side, like Egyptian statues, never moving throughout the whole ordeal. And what an ordeal! Never have I seen a more terrified human being

55

than that dentist. Sweat was pouring down his forehead and his hands trembled like butterfly wings.

For once the roles were reversed, since usually I am the one who is cringing and panicky at a dentist's, but this time my concern over his anguish was so great that it took my mind off the painful extraction. Under the cold stare of the secret police, it took the dentist one hour to pull out my tooth. I promised myself never again to ask the GPU for a favor and in case of another abscessed tooth to pull or chisel it out myself —happily, an unfulfilled promise.

We did, though, ask for a favor, not from the GPU but from the Burobin, a frustrating institution set up by the Soviet government to take care of the material needs of the Diplomatic Corps.

When the embassy staff moved into the ten-story apartment house that had been allotted to us, there was no hot water for weeks. We begged, insisted and pestered the Burobin, but only got the standard answer *zavtza budet,* which is the Russian version of *mañana.* But finally the Burobin wheeled into action, and with a vengeance. Suddenly there was hot water everywhere. It was not only hot, it was boiling. And it boiled not only in the bathtubs and washbasins, but also in the w.c.'s. Every time one pulled the chain a geyser of steaming water would come up from the toilet bowl, bringing screams of anguish from the uninitiated. It took days to stop that new version of the hot seat.

When writing about Moscow I find myself enmeshed in things of the flesh. Perhaps because it was my first venture in housekeeping, perhaps because everyday needs cost so much effort. In Russia in everyday life man had not yet triumphed over nature. The push-button civilization had only reached the party members and the diplomatic level. But even there, if the button was present and pushed usually nothing hap-

56

pened, since the buttons were either unconnected or out of order.

While we were there it was a pathetic world of production and no distribution. Even to get a needle or thread would imply visiting countless shops and ending by importing it from a neighboring country.

Or perhaps my insistence on the material side of life comes from a subconscious desire to obliterate from memory our Russian friends, since nearly all of them have been shot or deported, to forget the unsmiling crowds in the streets, and to forget the look of panic in the eyes of the people you met when they would find out that you were a foreigner.

There are, though, in Russia oases of real happiness and it would be unfair not to mention them. One of them was the Ballet School where I spent many hours drawing and painting the students. Those Degasian interludes were not only an aesthetic joy but a real relaxation. Only people who have lived in Russia know how wound up, how nervous one gets breathing the fear-laden air.

In the Ballet School I found an atmosphere completely without fear, an atmosphere of happiness. Contrary to other artists, the ballet dancers do not have to worry much about the party line. There can be no subversive implication in an entrechat or a pirouette.

The pupils were all fervent Communists, understandably so as the government took care not only of them but also of their families. The government looked after every one of their needs and left them completely free to train. And train they did, repeating hour after hour the same exercises, all day, every day with the inspired patience of dedicated people. When I see the ballerinas floating effortlessly, violating all laws of gravity in their birdlike flights across the stage, I see them as a gardener sees a beautiful flower, knowing the toil, the care, the effort that have been necessary to permit the flower to bloom. Since my visits to the Ballet School, my artistic pleasure in watching a ballet is mixed with respect and gratitude.

The same passionate enthusiasm and devotion are found in the Russian theater.

I am not a theatergoer, as I am so talkative that it is a torture for me to listen to people talk for hours and not be able to join in the conversation. But in Moscow I went all the time, not only for the beauty of the décor, for the perfection of the acting, but also for the audience. The theater for the Russians is the only magic formula capable of throwing a bridge from their sad, drab lives into fairyland, into a world of beauty and fantasy, a world where even the grayness of their lives is seen through a multicolored prism. The audience consisted mostly of the working class, in shirt sleeves, tieless, barefoot in summer, with felt boots and sheepskins in winter. Their coarse, heavy Muscovite faces illuminated with happiness, they would sit silent and motionless until the curtain came down.

The only trace of democracy in Russia, to my knowledge, is to be found in the theater. Perhaps when Lenin, who represents the personification of the dogma and dictates of materialistic theology, carefully studied the structure of the Catholic Church he also read, remembered, and put into practice St. Thomas' saying that "amusement is necessary to sustain human life."

Perhaps that is why theater tickets are cheap, and are often given away by the Soviet government to peasants and factory workers.

That "democracy" in public amusements was strangely lacking in social life.

Before the purges we made friends with a master electrician, Ivan Vasilich, who used to repair and arrange all our electrical installations. He was a Ukrainian with some education and spoke German fluently. John and I became very fond of him, and quite often in the evening after work John would invite

58

him up for a drink. On one occasion Troyanovsky, the Soviet Ambassador to Washington, while on a visit to Moscow, came in unannounced. John cheerfully introduced Ivan Vasilich. It was an interesting demonstration of the classless stratification of the Soviet Union. To find himself in the presence of a Soviet ambassador and member of the Central Committee provoked in Ivan something akin to and perhaps even worse than stage fright. To John's amazement, the amiable Troyanovsky, whom John had known pleasantly for several years, congealed into hauteur. Ivan hurriedly backed into the outer darkness, leaving his drink untasted.

We kept on seeing Ivan till the purges started. After that he never came to our apartment but sent some of his workers in his place.

But we saw him once more, on the day we left Russia to go to our new post in Belgium.

After two years in Moscow, with an abruptness I always found bewildering, we were ordered to Belgium. When transferring its personnel from one post to another the State Department has the same mysterious technique of urgency that one finds in the angels of the Bible. "Get up and go," says the angel to Gideon or Joseph. "Pack and proceed," says the State Department.

My gypsy childhood, going from school to school, from Warsaw to Switzerland, then to London, and then finally to study in France and Italy, had conditioned me to a nomadic life. I have never had time to take root anywhere and, like some of the orchidaceous plants, I get my spiritual nourishment from the air.

Still, one never gets quite accustomed to the sadness of interrupted friendship, to the shedding of all that is familiar. But God is everywhere and so are nice people. That conviction, plus a herculean amount of packing, discarding, farewell parties, got me safely through my first transfer.

Greeting and seeing people off at stations and airports is one of the never-ending chores of diplomats. In Eastern Europe it reaches the dimensions of a gala performance, something like opening night at the Met. Everybody goes to the station, dressed in his very best, bringing flowers, books, candies and gifts. It is really *le dernier salon ou l'on cause.* One arrives long before the train is to leave and stays till the last minute. Even when one departs for a vacation, all one's friends are there to say good-by. But when it is a final, definite leave-taking, then it snowballs into spectacular magnitude. There was literally a mob at the station to say good-by when we left for Belgium. Alas, very few Russian friends were present, only a few officials from the Foreign Office. The terror of the purge had started, and being seen with a foreigner was highly dangerous. All our friends from the ballet and the stage, the writers, the artists that we liked so much were conspicuously absent.

We stood at the window of our compartment, shaking hands and blowing kisses, and receiving masses of flowers. Very soon our compartment was completely filled by the avalanche of bouquets, and I did one of the silliest things imaginable, a manifestation that is, alas, so typical of me whenever I get emotional. My brain automatically stops working.

When there was no more room in the compartment for the flowers, I opened the window on the other side of the tracks, and started a one-woman bucket brigade. As the flowers came in the front window, I heaved them unseen out the back window, not realizing at the moment that as the train pulled out it would unveil before the dismayed eyes of our friends on the platform a massive pyramid of the flowers they had offered us, lying forlornly on the tracks. I would have gladly committed hara-kiri when my stupidity suddenly dawned on me.

On the same train with us quite by chance was a woman friend of ours, an American who was quite a keen bridge player. An American correspondent whom we liked very much was close to the window of our compartment just as the train tooted and started off. He heard me complain that we lacked a fourth for bridge. He swung aboard the moving train, deaf to the anguished screams of his protesting wife, joined us in the compartment, and when the excitement of departure abated, he asked, "Well, where are the cards?" Without ticket or toothbrush, he accompanied us to the frontier, a long overnight trip, where he had to wait in the bleak Soviet station until the next evening for a train back. True, we had many hours of amusing bridge. Never have I seen an example of chivalry beyond the call of courtesy to equal this. Since then he has made a brilliant career on one of the greatest newspapers in the United States.

But something else happened as the train was slowly picking up speed. We were hanging out the window to acknowledge the last bursts of farewell and to have a last glimpse of our friends as the train left the station confines when suddenly we saw hidden behind the last pillar, all alone, our friend Ivan Vasilich. When he saw us he ran alongside the train and tossed into our still open window a bulky package. Then he stopped and waved sadly as long as we were in sight. In the package was a lovely, heavily embroidered, multicolored Ukrainian tablecloth and a little note: "It is the only thing I have left from my family. I want you to have it. Think about me sometimes. Your friend, Ivan." We have.

VIII

THE FIRST MONTH OF OUR STAY IN ANTWERP I SPENT IN A bathtub.

From Moscow, John had been transferred to Belgium as consul general in Antwerp. In 1924 the Diplomatic and Consular Services were merged and eleven years later it was still the policy of the State Department that diplomatic officers, like John, should have at least one consular post.

Before we found a house we lived in a hotel. We had a bedroom, a sitting room, and an antique bathroom with a large tin tub on gilded lions' paws in the middle of it.

On arrival in Antwerp John had the task of stopping alcohol smuggling to the U.S.A., and he had to see a lot of strange characters. John would have smugglers and informers stacked in the bedroom while seeing others in the sitting room. Since in the lobby of the hotel an unattached female was immediately pestered by persistent Don Juans who made their headquarters there, my only refuge was the bathroom. I would stuff the tub with pillows, and with a thermos of tea, cigarettes and books, sit in it for hours, threatened by a curvature of the spine but at least in serene privacy.

In 1936 Antwerp had become the headquarters for a gigantic alcohol smuggling ring. In the United States prohibition had come to an end, but the bootleggers still wanted to stay in business. Vast quantities of alcohol were shipped from Antwerp in vessels bound ostensibly for Montevideo or other innocent destinations, and the alcohol was transshipped off our coast to the bootleggers. There was quite a period after the end of prohibition when one's favorite brand of Scotch or bourbon could be the product of smuggled alcohol. This traffic had reached vertiginous dimensions.

The government of Belgium in those days was Big Business minded in a big pecuniary way. John's efforts to get the government to curb the smuggling out of Antwerp came to nothing. First of all, the Belgian government insisted that the American government buy and then dump into the ocean the enormous production of Belgian alcohol, an idea that did not particularly appeal to Washington. The final position of the Belgian government was that it was the business of the United States to protect its own coast and not the business of the Belgian Government to exercise any control whatever over illicit exports. John was faced with a thorny problem. He worked it out successfully.

Part of the time I joined the fun of chasing smugglers. John and I would go on all-night expeditions along the coast. We would stop in small ports, drinking beer and playing billiards in forlorn cafés, waiting sometimes all night for the signaled boats to appear. The dark little cafés, the deserted quays, the mysterious telephone calls, and the shadowy people who would sometimes materialize to talk to John created the atmosphere of an old-fashioned gangster film.

Our expeditions into the underworld were not only rewarding for the success of John's work, but it also brought into our lives strange human types rarely encountered in private or diplomatic life.

One of them was Captain Williamse. The local authorities were inclined to help John but, because of the attitude of the government of Belgium, there was little they could do. One day, the captain of the port told John, "There is one man here who can really help you in this problem. He is Captain Williamse. I will have him call on you tomorrow morning at eleven o'clock." Captain Williamse, clean-cut and dynamic, appeared on the dot of eleven. John explained to him that a certain ship in the harbor was loading a huge cargo of alcohol, ostensibly for Montevideo, but actually for transshipment off the American coast. What could Captain Williamse do to prevent the departure of the vessel in question? Captain Williamse calmly replied, "The solution is simple. All you have to do is to tell me whether you want the ship sunk dockside or in the channel." In horrified amusement John terminated the conversation and ushered Captain Williamse out. To my disappointment, John did not sink the bootleggers' boat, but somehow or other he did prevent it from reaching the U.S.A.

Though he was unconnected with smuggling, another strange character we met at that time was Jeff. Antwerp has a marvelous golf course where John played a lot of weekend golf. At the club was Jeff, the caddy master, who had presided over the caddy house for more than thirty years with magisterial dignity.

The club engaged a new secretary whom Jeff did not like. One Saturday night there was a gala dinner. Suddenly a strange illumination was noticed. Everyone rushed out to find the caddy house in flames. Jeff was seated tranquilly on the lawn. "Why don't you do something?" people shouted at him. "I did," he quietly replied. "I set it on fire."

Poor Jeff went to prison and everybody had to buy new golf clubs.

The golf was good and one can play most of the year in Belgium if one does not mind mist and drizzle too much. As John played one course after another, he kept running into an English colonel. He was middle-aged and had an appearance of well-bred, amiable imbecility. The colonel was a grotesque figure on the golf course. On the tee his stance and form were those of a scarecrow flapping in the breeze.

One day John had to go to Luxembourg on official business.

His visit coincided with the opening of a new golf course. Without great surprise, we saw the British colonel. We found him on the first tee.

He was with his golf companion, or rather opponent. We overheard the colonel casually remark: "We'll play for a hundred pounds, what, what?" The offer was accepted with alacrity and the match was on.

John was intrigued. He watched the colonel drive off. It was an extremely awkward and rather futile effort. The ball merely dribbled down the course, but it went right down the middle. Still intrigued, we followed the match at a discreet distance.

The drive was invariably a dribble; so was the second shot —but always down the middle. Then the colonel would go into action. His short game had an unbelievable and deadly accuracy. On the 18th green he was several holes up, an easy winner against a very competent golfer. We saw him pocket his loot with a disarming look of surprise on his innocent face.

In the clubhouse John, filled with curiosity, invited the colonel to have a drink. After chatting pleasantly, John asked the colonel: "Tell me, just for fun, what is your racket?" The colonel replied, "But, of course, I'll be delighted to."

The colonel explained that he had been retired from the Indian Army on a pension that could not keep body and soul together, that he had no qualifications that would justify anyone's employing him, but he simply had to make a living somehow. So he dedicated nine months to pitching and putting until he achieved complete mastery of this essential part of the game.

He needed to tell no more. With his disarming personality he was able to prosper by appealing to the cupidity of others. They all thought they were taking candy from a child. It is curious that the British are the only people who ever had the genius to develop a secret weapon simply by disguising intelligence with a mask of stupidity.

When we finally found a house with a large garden, we built a kennel, as we had acquired three dogs of Flemish breed called *bouvier de Flandres*—big, shaggy, black with orange-colored eyes, tougher than police dogs and overvigilant as watch dogs.

Every time a cat or indeed anything at all stirred in the neighborhood, the three dogs sounded off in stentorian tones and the night was rendered hideous. Then came a fateful day. An anonymous letter arrived. In substance the letter said, "unless the dogs renounce their nightly clamor forthwith, the dogs will come to a sticky end by poison." I was terribly upset and rushed to John for help and advice. He said, "I don't know what to do, except to read the letter to the dogs." He took me gently by the elbow and called the dogs into the house. The three dogs sat as an attentive audience while John slowly, solemnly, read the letter aloud. Not ever again did one of those dogs bark in the night.

This story may have an explanation, but if it has we don't know what it is.

It was in Antwerp that for the first time I met that overpowering force "the American Women's Club." To me the American Women's Club is controversial since, after many years and many such clubs in many lands, I cannot quite make up my mind if they should be supported or disbanded. The danger of the American Women's Club abroad is that the club is in reality a perpetual nursery where the wife of the American abroad is taken under a sheltering wing. Kind beyond words, the worthy ladies of the club feed her with baked hams, Bartlett pears, share their canned goods, their magazines, cigarettes, and give her Kleenex, soft toilet paper, and prickly heat lotion. This continuation of home life abroad is very pleasant and would be perfect if it served to prepare the housewife gradually to face successfully the brand-new world in which she has to live.

Alas, the result is that many of these people never wean themselves from this American incubator, never learn a foreign language, meet very few foreigners, shrink from native food, and ignore local customs.

Where the American Women's Club goes wrong is in magnifying household problems, developing a climate propitious for the growth of an obsession for one's own country, and induces the most dangerous pastime when abroad—comparison. Once you start to compare you are lost, as the reality of the present seldom compares favorably with the unreality of the past, veiled as it is by a haze of romanticism.

Americans who flock together abroad tend to develop nationalism rather than patriotism. One should not, like a snail, carry one's country on one's back. Its place should be in the heart, invisible but present.

In posts where there were no American Women's Clubs to shield the newcomer, the American housewife when left on her own was resourceful and competent. I found even in the youngest and least traveled a hard core of courage and the pioneer spirit. I have seen them under the most ghastly sanitary conditions, in places devoid of any amenities of civilization, organize with fantasy and gaiety a livable life for themselves and their families. I have seen them learning the language, the customs, the religion of the people, and learning that when you miss those clues a post abroad becomes a boring, exhausting, and sterile experience.

When I first met the women of the American club I was as bewildered by them as they were by me. I had been married less than two years and I had not yet been in the U.S.A. In fact I had met few American women. The ladies of the club had an easy way of explaining my puzzling behavior: "She is a foreigner" or "She is an artist," but I did not have a single clue to their mentality. Luckily the president of the club, a charming Quaker, who immediately became my great friend, served as interpreter, since at first I really needed one to understand American women.

My first encounter with the American Women's Club had to do with a Thanksgiving party.

Two delegates came to see John in his office, asking if I would be willing to do the decorations for Thanksgiving. "We heard that Mrs. Wiley is an artist and this is a very special occasion as all the American residents in Belgium come to the dinner." John answered that he was sure I would be happy to do it. But as they were leaving, John added, "I feel I should tell you that the last time Irena arranged a large party, the expense was staggering." They departed in stunned silence as the budget for the decorations was eleven dollars. But, of course, it was too late to withdraw their request.

What a mess I made of the first meeting with the decorating committee! When the ladies with shining eyes enthusiastically presented me with a collection of pumpkin-adorned paper tablecloths and paper turkeys, I rejected them in a peremptory way. I did not realize how much tradition, how much home-sickness was concentrated in those ugly paper objects.

I also could not understand the uneasy silence that greeted every one of my suggestions. It seemed to me that to place in a corner of the banquet hall a cow with horns and udders painted in gay colors, and enameled stacks of corn would be a most appropriate symbol of nature's bounty. Even the idea of sewing together autumn leaves with a gold thread to make tablecloths was not accepted. The only one of my ideas reluctantly accepted was to gild straw market baskets, fill them with carrots, eggplant, red and white cabbage, and suspend them on thick gilded cords around the room. Luckily the results pleased everybody. It was very cheap and effective and I was forgiven for my inconsiderate disdain.

Belgium also stands out in my memory for my initiation into the art and joy of food. Up to then my attitude toward food was one of scorn due to my school years in London, spent on a diet of overdone meat, underdone vegetables, sausage and mashed, Brussels sprouts, and trifles.

After meeting John, who not only is a great connoisseur but also a *cordon bleu* chef, I began to have an inkling that food was not just a boring necessity but could also be a pleasure.

But Moscow was not a post where there was any scope for the art of cooking, since the effort of getting edible food was so great that there was no incentive left for any subtlety in its preparation.

Belgium, on the contrary, is the paradise of a gourmet, and when we arrived in Antwerp after the lean, lean years of Moscow, we were staggered not only by the quality but by the profusion and variety of comestibles. We used to stand, John and I, lost in admiration, in front of show windows of butcher and pastry shops as if gazing on a beautiful picture, on the patterns made by hams, sausages, cheeses, breads and cakes. We admired, not quite believing that they were real and not painted cardboard and that we only had to walk into the shop and buy what we wanted and take it home.

Not only the *matière première* is excellent but Belgian cooking is a great art. We acquired a little book called *The Guide of the Gourmets,* where every little town had not only the names of the best restaurants, but advice on what to eat there. It was a most honest little book that could exist only in Belgium. Anywhere else there would have been a hurricane of libel suits as the book would frankly state "This restaurant has good food but bad wines"; "Too expensive but good" about another; "Watch the bill"; "Poor service, dirty but a fine 'waterzoï'." When on our many weekend trips to the beautiful old towns with which Belgium is studded, Liége, Bruges or Malines, towns full of artistic treasures, the guidebook we consulted would not be the one that told about the museums or churches, but our *Guide of Gourmets.* We would politely glance at a Renaissance town hall or a painting by van Eyck and hurriedly make a beeline for the restaurant marked with three stars in our guidebook. Those excursions, where both the spirit was willing and the flesh was weak, I still see in a haze of succulent thick soups, of plovers eggs, of *hochepot,* which is a stew into which, plus a lot of vegetables, goes every part of the anatomy of a steer with spectacular results, and, finally, incredibly exquisite apple pancakes.

This culinary orgy was not only most agreeable but taught me how much one can learn about a country from its food. A menu in a roadside inn can be the Rosetta stone which helps to decipher the character of a nation. How rich and Rabelaisian the food of Flanders, how intellectual and refined that of France and China, how heavy, unimaginative the food of the Prussian, and how wholesome, simple and plentiful is our own basic fare.

If one did not mind a touch of sophistry, one could say that plastic arts are a reflection of culinary arts, and that Brueghel and Rubens are the products of the sumptuous and abundant Flemish fare. This idea would be much more convincing if the ascetic, mystical Memling, van Eyck and van der Goes did not contradict the pattern.

Another factor that permitted us really to enjoy our Lucullan banquets was the fact that in Belgium there is no real misery. On the way to a restaurant or to a friend's house, where we knew that lavish food would be served, we never saw undernourished people. In many other countries the specter of hunger sits down with one at every meal, weighing on one's conscience. But in Belgium there was no unemployment, no serious want. There was also love of good food and genius for cooking in the poorest housewife. The greatest dishes in Belgium and France have a plebeian origin. An onion, a wilted cabbage, an old carrot, and some giblets are turned as by magic into a delicious stew by a Belgian peasant woman. A piece of low-grade meat and a bottle of cheap beer when consumed separately do not make an appetizing meal, but the imaginative Flemish woman cooks it together, adding a bay leaf, a sprig of fresh herb, and produces a most succulent dish, the *carbonnade flamande*.

This painstaking care in preparing a meal is not just a glorification of gormandizing. The simple woman in her wisdom knows the importance of having a varied and appetizing meal ready for her husband when he comes home after a hard day's work. No TV dinners for him, no quickly unfrozen food. The good dinner is there not only to please his palate but to show thoughtfulness and the desire to pamper him, to give him the pleasure of looking forward to a warm smile and a good meal when work is done.

One more thing did I learn in our gastronomic expeditions is to respect good cooking, since it is a suitable homage to pay to all those who work so hard to produce the food. Careless, bad cooking is immoral when you think of the hard work of those who grow the grains, who produce the wines, those who go to the ends of the world for spices, those who raise the cattle. This was easy for me as originally I come from a land about which a poet once said "a country where even a crumb of bread is picked up from the ground out of respect for the gifts of heaven."

I have spent so much time on the subject of food, since there is such a tendency to underestimate and even despise the role it plays in diplomatic life. Many people do not know how much understanding and good will has been created over a good meal, and that even the monstrous, torturing form of entertainment, the cocktail party, gives one not only the opportunity of meeting and seeing a lot of people of the country one is in but, curiously enough, frequently affords privacy for conversation. At a large reception one can get conveniently lost in the crowd.

IX

BEFORE GOING TO AUSTRIA, WHERE WE WERE TO BE stationed after a year in Antwerp, we took home leave. At long last I saw America. It was love at first sight. And it was a first sight in every way. Like the majority of Europeans of my generation, I had not been given even a glimpse of American history while in school. All I knew was garnered from the few books I had read. My vision of America was, to say the least, confused. For instance, it was little Eva (and no one else) who floated down the river on a cake of ice; James Fenimore Cooper's red Indians were always galloping through the woodsy background; and, of course, George Washington remained a small boy inventing truth by chopping down innumerable cherry trees.

My concept of the people of America was a composite of literary ideas, such as of Babbittry, Sinclair's Jungle, and Poe's Raven, "forever sitting," along with impressions made on me by American tourists. Amid all this welter there was one dominating reality, the generosity of America and the American people. Generosity in America is innate, and so different from that characteristic of Europe, which is often diluted by such an element as patronage or self-interest.

I also found politeness to be real in America. Being an American now by choice, rather than by the accident of birth, I can speak without conceit on this subject. One difference is this: Europeans, in general, have manners. Americans, in general, have morals. European manners, being inherited as a code of behavior, tend to become stilted and even ossified. American manners flow from a politeness springing from the heart, a spontaneous impulse changing with circumstance. I, for one, have never met a really rude American, except perhaps in the so-called International Set which seeks to emulate and assimilate things European, even the stale and outworn.

Whether they have manners or not, I am persuaded that Americans are the most instinctively polite people of the earth. One unforgettable experience may serve to support this view. During the war, while stationed in Washington, I was privileged to do art therapy in Forest Glen (an adjunct of Walter Reed Hospital). The patients were enlisted men who were considered on the borderline of insanity because of shock, amputation, wounds, or other disabilities of war. Although art therapy was then rather new in healing, we did get certain gratifying results. I had a class of fifteen to twenty boys in painting and sculpture. They were coal miners, farm hands, factory workers, mostly illiterate, and without a single college boy among them. All were very young, and all were very sick. I worked with them all day, three times a week, for a whole year. During that year I never heard a rude word from them. I was never exposed to questionable attentions or gestures. From those boys with shattered nerves, although uneducated in the formal sense, I received the utmost consideration and kindness. For me that year was to experience a miracle—it was my real school of Americanization. And so I remember it.

Our home leave was of necessity cut short because the State Department was anxious that John assume his duties in his new post as soon as possible. We both had known Vienna well in other years and were happy with the assignment to Austria.

As a young girl I had spent a year in the School of Arts and Crafts in Vienna, learning wood carving with the great sculptor Professor Hanak. Small in stature, with long, disorderly red hair and beard, he looked like a pocket version of Michelangelo's Moses. His favorite saying was that all artists fall from heaven but, alas, land on their heads. I made the mistake of repeating to John Hanak's description of an artist and he has used it against me ever since.

The Vienna I knew then was one of artists, students, museums, art talks and hard work; very different from the Vienna of diplomats, politicians, aristocracy, gala receptions that I encountered in my new role of an "excellency." The Austrians love titles and give you one on the slightest provocation—it always startled me when I was addressed as Your Excellency. At that time I probably merited more the title of Your Incompetence, which is one that would fit so many other "excellencies" I know.

One of the many things I had to learn was the protocol of the sofa. In Vienna a sofa is not just a piece of furniture made for comfort; it is a symbol of rank. The first time I sat on one, during a reception, I was politely but sternly extracted from it by a duchess to make room for an archduchess. In veiled hints it was conveyed to me that only duchesses, ambassadresses, and women over sixty had the right to sit on a sofa. Being young and the wife of a chargé d'affaires, I rated only an armchair.

Vienna society resembled a broken, precious vase that had been well glued together. Only at close range could one see its cracks and missing pieces.

The collapse of the Austro-Hungarian Empire had carried with it the disintegration of the Austrian aristocracy. When we arrived in Vienna, many were poor and landless, but desperately trying to keep their place in society. They reminded me of the houses hit by bombs, where by a strange freak the façade remained standing while the rest of the house lay in ruins and rubble.

In my student days I had encountered poverty, but nothing more pathetic than the hidden poverty of some of the great families. But enough of the aristocracy had retained their fortunes, estates and palaces to give Viennese society a gilded coating of courtly glamour. This aristocracy—to me so useless, so full of false pride and prejudices, whose ancestors lined their fur coats with Titian paintings and permitted Mozart to starve, these dukes and duchesses whom I considered more fit for a museum than for "our brave new world"—vindicated itself when Hitler came. In stress and calamity these people showed courage, deep human decency, and proved that "nobility" is not an empty word. And it was the little people, the charming "golden-hearted" Viennese, as they used to be called, that showed hearts of stone and abject cowardliness. But all this unmasking came much later. In the meantime "Congress danced" —and I danced with it.

When I look back at our stay in Austria, I see it as if cut in two with a sharp knife. The first part, up to the Nazi seizure of Austria, known as the "Anschluss," was made up of gaiety, glamour, music and dancing. The second was a nightmare of cruelty, sadism, tragedy, and brutality.

My lack of experience, my youthful callousness, prevented me from realizing what was happening under the surface of the gay life. And I had yet to believe in John's gift of prophecy. In this carefree atmosphere John, like a self-appointed Cassandra, tried to warn of Austria's coming doom. He also nagged his French and English colleagues to wake up their respective governments to the imminence of danger and make them formulate a policy that might impede Hitler's plans.

No one paid much attention to his warnings, calling him a pessimist, a killjoy. I also thought John was exaggerating, so I lightheartedly enjoyed all the fun that came my way.

The continual round of parties was saved from monotony by music. Music was in the very air you breathed. It took every form, appeared in every guise. Not only in concert halls and operas, but in every little café, where one consumed quantities of coffee with cream and a delicious chocolate cake called Sachertorte, created by the chef of Prince Metternich, Herr Sacher, for the Congress of Vienna in 1814. There was gay accordion music and singing in the *Heurigen,* that unique institution for drinking new wine on summer nights. And no official dinner was ever completely hopeless since one knew that marvelous chamber music would be served with dessert.

During the gay winter of 1938, with its balls in technicolor, its grandiose operas, there was complete unconcern for unpleasant realities.

The last great party—but one with *mene tekel upharsin* already written all over the walls of the ballrooms—was given by Chancellor Schuschnigg. It was held in the magnificent apartments of the Empress Maria Theresa in the Burg Palace. The footmen in powdered wigs, silk-embroidered uniforms and lace jabots, the gold dinner service with the coat of arms of the Hapsburgs, and a profusion of yellow and white flowers everywhere—never have I seen a more glittering sight. The ladies of the Austrian nobility wore their tiaras. Their husbands wore all their decorations. The members of the Hapsburg family had the order of the Golden Fleece around their necks. The high-ranking Austrian officers wore pale-blue tunics and dark trousers with brilliant stripes. The diplomats wore their colorful gold-embroidered uniforms, John was in white tie and tails, without a single decoration (according to American Foreign Service protocol). He looked like a king penguin in a covey of parrots.

There was certainly plenty of glamour in the Burg Palace that night. But there was also a crushing feeling of uneasiness, premonition and fear. All of us gathered around the sparkling dinner table knew that Austria's days were numbered. The Austrian officers knew that they were wearing their dress uniforms probably for the last time. And many other guests knew that their very lives would be in jeopardy with the advent of Hitler.

The undertone of anguish was due to the news of Chancellor Schuschnigg's visit to Berchtesgaden during which Hitler had vociferously demanded the unconditional union of Austria with Germany. Schuschnigg had courageously refused. On his return to Vienna he announced a plebiscite, knowing very well its outcome. Hitler knew it, too, and that is why two days before the plebiscite on March 11 the German Army marched into Austria. The dark shadow of the Nazi swastika fell over the country. Then the terror started.

With eyes of an archangel in a face of gray clay, standing in an open car, Hitler rode into Vienna on April 13, 1938. And behind him, in brown shirts with the tortured cross on their armbands, followed the horsemen of the Apocalypse. But there was an additional one, one whom St. John did not see at Patmos; the most terrifying one of all. Worse than war, worse than famine, worse than death, rode the horseman of degradation, the rider that kills the image of God in man.

It is not the physical or even the moral suffering that I remember most vividly of this nightmarish period. It is what the degradation did to some people. Circe transformed men into swine. Hitler in one day transformed them into cringing brutes. To be sure, there were many exceptions to this rule. From under flat stones, from the cracks of walls, emerged the underground Nazis, the card-bearing Austrians. Their day had come, they seized the keys of the city. They assumed the right of life and death over all who were not their kind. And how they used their power! To see primeval cruelty emerge in civilized man terrifies the soul.

John understood so well the importance of human dignity that the first thing he did after Hitler had seized Austria was to assemble the entire staff of the legation, from counselor to office boy. He told them: "Thousands of people are coming to ask for help. For most of them there is little or nothing that we can do. You will be tired, overworked and irritable, but I still ask you always to treat each of them with sympathy, courtesy, and when you can't do anything for them, when nothing else is available, give them your time and sympathy so that here at least they will be respected human beings and not hunted animals." And all rose to the occasion. Uninformed critics of the Foreign Service should have seen the compassionate behavior of our entire staff. They had only two alternatives, to be hard-boiled or heartbroken, and all of them chose the latter.

By the Anschluss Hitler opened a Pandora's box which he must have found in the deepest depths of hell. And out of this box later came the death march of Bataan and the horrors of Buchenwald, Lidice and Katyn. The annihilation of the Austrian Jews was the beginning of large-scale organized atrocities. To get help from the American Legation, a silent and tragic crowd began to queue up in the middle of the night. Like a black snake it coiled around a city block. The great artists depicting the Last Judgment on the walls of Romanesque cathedrals never quite captured a likeness equivalent to that heartbreaking look of anguish and desperate hope on the faces of the people silently waiting in the morning daylight of those spring dawns.

John cabled the State Department for twenty-four assorted New York, and Chicago telephone directories. This was an inspired move. Even today, after twenty years, I cannot look at a Manhattan telephone book without tender gratitude. It helped to save so many lives.

During the first few weeks I helped out, stamping visa applications, thus releasing the office boys for more important work. My desk was in the room where the telephone directories were kept. All day long an unending stream of desperate people would come in and pore over them for hours as if over a

Bible. Sometimes I would hear a scream of joy when someone found the name of a relative or even a person bearing the same family name, since it meant the hope of an affidavit of support, a visa to America, and thus a reprieve from a death sentence. But too often they would close the telephone book with a gesture of utter hopelessness and leave slowly, without a word.

I was at first so lost in a red haze of fury against Hitler and all he stood for that I seemed to be a one-cell organism of concentrated hatred, a useless amoeba. I was rescued by John's serenity and his Confucius-like philosophy that "It is better to light a candle than to curse the darkness." I still cursed the darkness but put my mind to lighting candles. The hard work under the strain of desperate urgency probably prevented me from indulging in hysteria or a nervous breakdown.

The problem was to get visas for refugees so that they could leave Austria. It was impossible to help everyone. Being a sculptress, I decided in so far as possible to concentrate on artists. If a hopeless visa applicant was a painter, a sculptor, a musician he would be sent directly to me. Then with the help of the Quakers, the Jewish Joint Relief or other diplomatic missions, and of many private citizens, I would try to get the required visas, visas for any place of refuge in the outside world.

The daily procession of human tragedy that passed through the legation was almost an unbearable weight, night and day, awake and asleep, on the minds of all of us. I recall a small incident that illustrates the extent to which it had become an obsession. Freddy Rheinhardt, a young secretary, now our ambassador in Rome, was operated on suddenly for appendicitis.

I was sitting beside his bed when he came out of the anesthesia. When Freddy opened his eyes he spoke in German, in a voice of deep sadness, "I am so terribly sorry, but it is impossible for me to give you a visa to the United States."

There are many spectacular, tabloid, deforming sins, but

79

the one that to me is the only unforgivable one is the sin of indifference, the negation of humanity. In that gloom and hate in which we suddenly found ourselves it was a consolation and a source of happiness to realize that no American, whether Christian, Jew or atheist, ever showed even a trace of that corroding sin. My plea for affidavits of support, those keys that opened the gate to America, never went unanswered, even when it was addressed to complete strangers.

The fateful drama of the Austrian Jews was their intense love of their country. As Schiller phrased it: "On the banks of the Danube even the Moor becomes Viennese." In Austria the Jews had not been set apart as chosen or persecuted people; they had been assimilated. The shock of suddenly becoming untouchables, of being forced to flee, seemed almost worse to them than facing annihilation. I remember a man repeating "I don't want to leave, I love Austria." Seeing my astonishment at his lack of bitterness toward the country that was treating him so brutally, he explained: "If one's brothers are murderers one does not stop loving one's mother." And how murderous the brothers were! It was not only the Germans who committed atrocities. To my enormous sadness many Austrians themselves, supposedly kind people, whose motto was *Ma Ruh will i hab*—"Peace is all I want"—suddenly turned into unfeeling brutes. I will not dwell on their surprising and terrible behavior, as one never knows "what is the cause in nature that makes these hard hearts."

Not only were the Viennese transformed but Vienna itself went through a strange metamorphosis. Before our eyes, overnight, this civilized, sophisticated capital died and was reborn a dull, provincial German city. It proved that Huan P'in, the Taoist philosopher, was right, that there is in nature "the spirit of each spot," a spirit that is not static.

In the days, weeks and months that followed the Anschluss there were many dramatic incidents. I remember particularly

80

one day, shortly after Hitler had taken over Vienna, that John telephoned me, saying: "The SS are at Professor Freud's house. I am worried about him. Take the car with the flag flying and go there at once. I'll see what can be done to protect him, but hold the fort in the meantime."

At that time of emergency the legation was terribly under-staffed; everyone was working eighteen hours a day and no one could be spared. Off I went. When I got to Freud's house, I had to push past two armed SS men who guarded the door to his apartment. There in the front room I was faced by a scene of vandalism and destruction which later, alas, became an everyday sight. Six SS men were pulling books off shelves, tearing out the pages, and throwing them on the floor. The rest were breaking the furniture. John had explained to me the psychology of brutality, and advised me that the only way to deal with bullies was to bully even more. So with a rude and commanding voice, I told them to stop immediately and asked to see the officer in charge. He was not there. I commanded them to get out immediately and, strangely enough, they did. Of course, I had no business there. Freud was not an American citizen, and the SS could have thrown me out. John was right, a show of authority left them flustered and uncertain.

I then looked for Freud and found him in his library, which being at the far end of the apartment had not yet been reached by the SS. He was sitting calm and undisturbed behind a huge desk which was entirely covered by his collection of Egyptian statuettes. He smiled when he saw me come in, and handing me a small sculpture of an Egyptian bird, asked me: "Whom does this bird resemble?" I looked at it carefully and said, "Of course, Queen Victoria." He was overjoyed that I saw the resemblance and started to talk about Egyptian myths and their influence on our civilization. There was not one word of what was going to happen to him. It was a most staggering show of philosophical detachment.

From time to time I tried to talk to him about his future. I told him that John wanted to help him get out of Vienna and asked where he wanted to go. He brushed these questions aside and resumed his talk about Egyptian religions. Only once did he flare up. It was when I asked him if he would like to go to America. "To America, never. The country where psychoanalysts have taken my thoughts and my theories and then prostituted them. Never! Never!" I stayed with him for a few hours until John had somehow or other arranged with the Nazi authorities to leave him in peace. Freud later left for England. Wealthy friends paid a substantial bribe to the Gestapo.

One morning John left very early for his office. I looked out the window and saw two Nazi brown shirts stationed in front of the house, each with a misfit, improvised uniform but each with an army rifle. I could see that they had given John a curt command. He was told to reenter the house. He explained who he was. The order was repeated more violently, whereupon John went through them like a bowling ball. John thinks this was probably the most stupid thing he ever did. The two ragtag and bobtail Nazis were undoubtedly the untrained and undisciplined dregs of the slums of Vienna. They might quite easily have been trigger-happy.

A few weeks later John, who had been working day and night, felt the absolute need of fresh air and exercise. So on a Sunday morning he set out for the golf course with a member of the legation. As they drove through the Prater, that beautiful park where the Sunday life of the Viennese concentrates, they noticed great numbers of brown shirts marching in military formation. The officers were beautifully uniformed but the rank and file looked like candidates for a mob scene in *The Beggar's Opera*. John did not give it a second thought at the time. He believed the brown shirts were merely going out to drill in the great expanses of the Prater.

On the fourth green, just as they were putting out, John and his companion found themselves suddenly surrounded by a hundred or so of these characters. They kept chanting at John: *"Sind Sie Jude?"*—"Are you a Jew?" John replied calmly in German that he was the American Chargé d'Affaires. The chant swelled into a crescendo. They started crouching, faces distorted with fury, their fists clenched, as they slowly, steadily advanced. John says that he was terrified but quite decided that he was not going to explain that he was not a Jew. He happens to be Scotch-Irish.

Just as the situation was reaching a sinister climax, the secretary of the golf club, a Viennese acquaintance of John's, providentially appeared from the clubhouse. To John's great surprise the secretary, whom John had always thought was a decent fellow, was wearing on his lapel the red badge with swastika, the emblem of a high-ranking Nazi. He laconically announced *"Der Herr ist kein Jude"*—"The gentleman is not a Jew"—and ordered the mob to withdraw. Later it was learned that on the particular Sunday there was one of the very worst Nazi pogroms, an orgy of bestial cruelty. Many Jews were killed or tortured in the immediate vicinity of the golf course.

John certainly had a close call, but one thing gave him enormous satisfaction. During the sullen withdrawal of the brown shirts, John teed off and drove to within three feet of the next pin. He made the hole in two. Around a thick clump of trees was the next tee, where John was no longer under the glare of Nazi eyes. He immediately had a sinking feeling. He says that no phrase was ever so graphic or precise. Everything within him suddenly sank and on that hole he took eighteen strokes. He did not bother to replace the divots.

As in Shakespearean dramas, there was some comic relief. An old American lady who lived in a small boardinghouse, who never read a paper or listened to the radio, on the day of Hitler's entry into Vienna tore off a swastika which was pinned on the uniform of one of the maids, saying "Don't you know that Hitler is nothing but a gangster?" She was promptly denounced, arrested, and her passport confiscated. Our consul had the greatest trouble in extracting her from jail and sending her on her way. When asked by the Gestapo: "So you don't like Hitler? Whom do you like?" "Mr. Roosevelt" was the prompt reply.

There was a Sunday, when John slipped out to the golf club and found himself to his dismay in the midst of a Nazi golf tournament. It was being conducted by the Reichsgolf-fuehrer, a brother-in-law of von Ribbentrop, the notorious Nazi foreign minister.

John tried to leave but could not. He was obliged to remain and found himself paired off with the Reichsgolffuehrer himself.

John won the tournament. There were no cheers. Obviously, it was not a popular victory. John received as first prize a large aluminum plaque with the swastika in high relief.

However grim and despicable the Nazis were, I managed once to find a faint glimmer of humor in an SS man. The news came that the house of a young friend of mine (the daughter of an archduke) was being searched by the SS. I went there to see if there was anything I could do to help and also to give her news of her brother, who was hiding. The house was guarded by black-uniformed SS men, and they would not let me in. One of the officers consented to inform my friend that I was there and permitted her to come out and sit in the car with me. When she was in the car, he said with an amiable smile (the only human one I ever saw on an SS face), "But please don't start the car. If you move I will have to shoot, and I should dislike very much to have to shoot at the wife of the American representative."

One of the oddest moments in John's career occurred during this period. He found that in order to accomplish anything he had to deal directly with the Gestapo. An American lady representing one of the great families and fortunes of the U.S.A. had married an Austrian. She bought a great estate in the Tyrol. When the Nazis assumed power they immediately seized her property. John made the usual conventional representations to have the property released. Nothing happened. John has a deep voice of considerable resonance. He finally picked up the telephone and got through to the head of the Gestapo. In a voice of condensed rage, John gave him an ultimatum: "If the property is not returned to its rightful owner by twelve noon on Thursday, I shall take *no further action* in the matter." The time limit worked; the property was returned. This may have been the strangest ultimatum in diplomatic history.

There was also the episode of additional personnel. The Anschluss with its terrors had opened floodgates of work for the legation staff. Though working fantastically long hours, they could not meet the situation.

To avert chaos, John felt obliged to engage more personnel, known in the jargon of the State Department as "local employees." They turned out to be indispensable. John at once notified the department, requesting approval and the necessary, relatively small additional funds for the payroll. No reply. As the weeks and months passed, John paid these extra employees out of his own pocket. He cabled again and still no reply. Months later, just as he was being transferred, John finally received a message from the department. It stated in substance that the department has been put to such great and unexpected expenses in entertaining the King and Queen of England during their official visit to the United States that the department deeply regretted it had no funds available for the salaries of the personnel John had employed.

When John announced this to me, he explained, "You don't know it, but we have been co-hosts *in absentia* to their Majesties." It may have been a privilege, but it was hard, indeed, on our budget.

For months "a frightful a nightfall folded a rueful a day." The telegram appointing John minister to Latvia and Estonia came as a rescue. Little did we know that a duplication of the Nazi nightmare was awaiting us in our new post. The ancient aphorism that the difference between nazism and communism is merely that it is colder in Russia proved in our case to be, alas, only too true.

X

O N A GRAY NOVEMBER DAY JOHN, I, THREE CHINESE servants, a few suitcases, and a rubber plant I had become attached to in Vienna, and from which I stubbornly refused to part, arrived in Riga, the capital of Latvia.

The bleakness, the sadness were not only in the leaden northern sky, in the flat landscape, but also in what I could see of the unimaginative, stodgily modern city itself. My boundless relief to get away from the endless, heartless, Nazi terrorism turned into a claustrophobic depression. I refrained from complaining to John but fervently hoped that he would feel the same way as J. Donald C. Rogers had, and then emulate him.

Years ago Rogers was assigned as first secretary of the legation in Albania. The day of his arrival in Tirana he sent off the most concise telegram in the history of the State Department: "I have arrived. I have resigned and I have left." But as usual John was too busy with his work to notice the dreariness of his surroundings. Now I am glad of it, as I came to like the monotonous landscape, and even the modern ugliness of Riga, which like a mask hides its medieval face. Riga was in reality two distinct cities. From broad avenues, movie houses, and neon signs only a few steps but hundreds of years separated one from narrow cobblestone streets, Gothic warehouses, Renaissance town halls, and gabled dwellings. This traveling in time was fascinating and it was uncanny to find oneself suddenly in old Riga, the city founded by Livonian knights more than seven centuries ago, the unchanged city of the medieval Hanseatic League, those great German merchants who traded with all foreign lands.

The Latvians and their neighbors, the Estonians, to whom John was also accredited as minister, had lived upon the Baltic coast since time immemorial but, until 1919, had never known independence. Their pagan ancestors had been forcibly converted into Christianity by the roving Knights of the Sword, who reduced them to serfdom. In the eighteenth century they came under the rule of the czars. Patiently, they developed their national movements and waited for the opportunity to become free. It came with the Bolshevik Revolution, and after a bitter struggle they achieved independence. Russian officials and most of the German nobles fled. Their estates were distributed among the peasants.

Except for a few impoverished German Balts who chose to remain, there was hardly any vestige of the old social order. The feudal past had been bloodlessly liquidated.

I came to respect and gradually also to like the dour, hard-working, matter-of-fact, and literate Latvians with their confidence in themselves. In 1939 they lived between the two volcanoes of nazism and communism, but they achieved a high level of prosperity, peace and progress, with bread, schools and hospitals for all. Latvia and Estonia at that time were what the U.S.S.R. advertised but did not achieve.

The President of Latvia, Karlis Ulmanis, had the genius of building a leftish, well-balanced Scandinavian type of economic life where contentment and well-being were distributed very evenly among all the people.

It was through the President that John and I were given a very lively, if fleeting and synthetic, interest in agriculture. When John presented his credentials to President Ulmanis in the old palace that had belonged to the Dukes of Courland, he was taken very much by surprise when the first question the

President asked him was, "Have you read the last number of *Wallace's Farmer*?" John had to confess that he had not. When he got back to the legation he immediately subscribed to it by cable. From that time on, John and I read it religiously. I learned much about hogs, bumper crops, how to raise potatoes, and the plaints and problems of the farmers' wives who wrote long letters to the editor.

The President had fled, years before, from the czarist oppression to the United States where he ended up as an instructor at the University of Nebraska. When he returned to contribute to the independence of his small country he could have passed as a good, solid farmer from the Middle West.

John, as minister to Estonia, had to go to Tallinn, the capital, to present his credentials and make another round of official calls. We were also obliged to find and rent a suitable legation residence and become acclimated to a new and entirely different atmosphere. All in all, it was quite a lot of work, but it was worth the effort as Estonia was a smiling country, full of *joie de vivre* and generous gestures. It had 1,500 lakes, 72 night clubs, the oldest pharmacy in the world, men who looked like Vikings, and golden-skinned, bronze-haired women with violet eyes. It is understandable that Tallinn was a favorite post of the Foreign Service bachelors. But, regardless of one's marital status, life in Tallinn was easy, gay and carefree.

We used to shuttle back and forth between the two capitals with our car filled with flat silver, pots and pans, bed linen, pillows, as the government did not furnish our legations and our household equipment did not suffice for two establishments. Those moves were not only fun but they were interesting politically, since when John wanted information on Latvia he went to Estonia, and vice versa, since each country was well informed regarding its neighbor but very reticent about its own affairs.

In Estonia John found a new solution for the language problem. To his consternation, he learned from the Chief of Protocol that he was expected to address the Estonian Army after presenting his credentials to the President. But John rose to the occasion. He composed a nice little speech, had it translated into perfect Estonian, and then practiced the phonetics with our Seventh-Day Adventist cook.

The great moment came: John, in white tie and tails, emerged from the ceremony, descended the front steps of the presidential palace, stopped, and removed his top hat in a gracious salute to the troops massed in the square. He delivered his speech in flawless Estonian with his head uncovered. He had pasted his speech inside his top hat and was able to read it without difficulty. The Estonians were delighted that John had taken the trouble to master Estonian so rapidly and marveled at his talent for languages. As if one could master Estonian!

I was annoyed no end at my inability to learn Estonian, which is vaguely related to Finnish and Hungarian, but not to Latvian, which, to make things easy, has Sanskrit roots. Born in the prebaby-sitter era, in the era of English nannies and French governesses, I learned many languages as a child. I kept collecting them as I went on, stimulated by my eavesdropping curiosity. I cannot bear not to be able to understand a conversation I might overhear in a bus or restaurant, so I would learn the language in our every post, but the languages of the Baltic States defeated me. Luckily everybody spoke both German and Russian and many spoke English, so I was not reduced to the broad smile that apologetically accompanies the sign language.

It seems, though, that learning languages is not always essential. The six-year-old daughter of a Polish diplomat who had just arrived in Tallinn was sent to a public school. Her mother was awaiting her anxiously after her first day, terribly

John Wiley

Our houseboy, Wong

Our Chinese maid, Yui-chen

Father Vladimir, a Russian
Orthodox priest, in Narva,
Estonia

Boris Sergeivich Steiger,
Moscow

A wood sculpture panel by the author in an altar of St. Thérèse de Lisieux.
President Kennedy, when a young boy, posed for the angel.

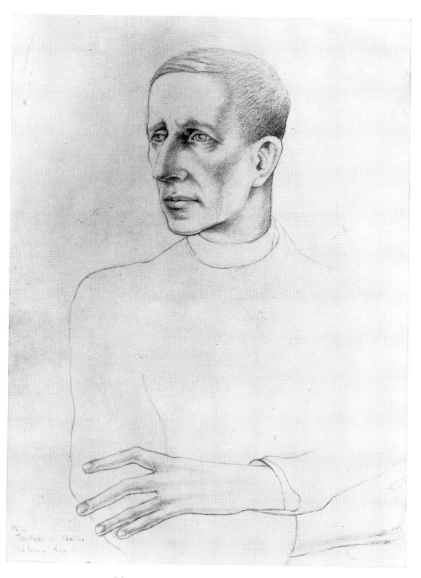

Père Teilhard de Chardin, Peking

Otto of Hapsburg, Pretender to
the throne, Vienna

A rumrunner in
Antwerp

A visa applicant waiting,
Vienna

A Jewish girl awaiting admission to the consular section, Vienna

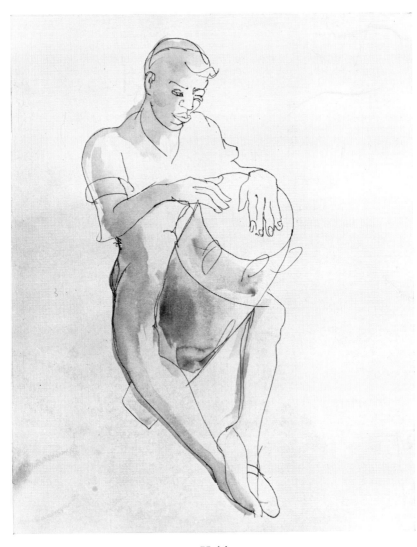

Haiti

Portrait of Franklin D. Roosevelt, presented to him by the artist-author

Arusa, Mexican bullfighter, Portugal

Indian woman and child, Colombia

Study in gray

Bibihanum, mother of a
Ghashghais tribal chief

Malek Mansur, Ghashghais
tribal chief

Majeeb Bahktiari, tribal chief,
Iran

Princess Ashraf, twin sister
of the Shah

A Druse woman, Lebanon

Panamanian child

Persian workman

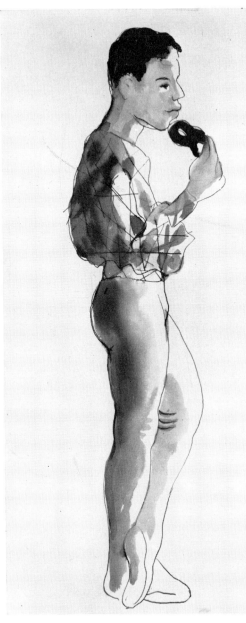

Carnival, Panama

worried about the strangeness and loneliness of a child speaking no Estonian. When the little girl came home, smiling and happy, the mother hurriedly asked "How was it?" "Very nice," said the child, "we played games and had a lot of fun." "But you don't know Estonian; how could you talk to them?" "It did not matter," explained the little girl, "they all laugh in Polish."

Another story that would be an argument against the necessity of languages was told me by the wife of a Marine Corps major, our naval attaché in Moscow. On a boat going home from the Far East, the major's wife befriended a young honeymooning couple. He was a Marine, spoke only English; she a White Russian girl, with Russian as her only language. They had married just before taking the ship and seemed blissfully happy in their wordless world.

One day the girl came to my friend who spoke Russian and said, "I am so very happy but I do need to know two sentences in English to make everything perfect." My friend asked what they were. She answered, "I would like to learn how to say, 'The bells of love are ringing in my heart' and 'Please turn over.'" In her wisdom the girl found the two best sentences to build a marriage on, first one for the soul and then one for the body. I hope they lived happily ever after.

It was in Tallinn that I learned a secret formula for preventing baldness. In Tallinn we made some very close friends and among the closest were General and Mrs. Johan Laidoner, commander-in-chief of the Estonian Army. A former czarist officer, he led the movement for national independence and thus, for the Estonians, became a sort of George Washington. He had a commanding presence; Mrs. Laidoner was a short woman with calm gray eyes and magnificent long gray hair. It was Mrs. Laidoner who gave me their secret recipe for the care of hair, a recipe that had been in her family for generations. I have used it ever since and can vouch for the magic of this formula. Here it is: heat two onions in the oven, squeeze the juice, mix with a cup of hot castor oil, rub into the scalp and leave overnight. You may lose your husband, but you will retain your hair.

Amusements were scarce in Latvia during the long winters and, just as in Moscow, diplomatic treasure hunting was the rage in Riga. The antique shops, among their pathetic assortment of ancient bric-a-brac, had an unusual collection of icons. Some were probably stolen from churches and monasteries, some abandoned or sold by families after the Russian Revolution, others smuggled across the frontier from Russia.

Icons, of course, are religious pictures painted on wood that originally came to Russia from Byzantium. Icons are not religious objects of art in our sense. In the rest of the Christian world religious pictures are a symbol, a work of the imagination, that does not represent the Absolute. To us, only in rare cases, through the will of God, are they believed to acquire divine attributes, as with some miraculous statues and pictures. A Russian icon on the contrary is a reality, a mirror of Divinity. For that reason it is stylized, remaining unchanged through centuries, as if God had thrown down photographs from Heaven, thus creating prototypes that can never be altered.

The Latvians and Estonians seldom bought them. Having little money, they were not collectors. Being Lutherans they did not accept religious art as representing the spiritual. Only diplomats and the few tourists bought icons. We acquired a few, some for their two-dimensional beauty, some just to rescue them from their undignified fate.

The story of one of these icons is particularly interesting: One day, while I was ill in bed, John went alone on a tour of the antique shops. He returned from his safari with a huge, simply enormous, new icon painted in oil. It was a composition called "Deisus," representing the Saviour sitting in judgment upon a jeweled throne with the Virgin on his right and St. John the Baptist on his left, pleading for clemency.

I knew that only a short time before the Italian Minister had bought the very same icon, and that his wife, with screams of rage and indignation, had made him return it to the dealer. I went even further. In addition to screaming, I burst into tears, since the idea of dragging a bad painting the size and weight of a door around the world was too much for me.

But John was built of sterner stuff than his Italian colleague. He did not return the icon. He smugly asked, "Have you ever bet on a horse?" I admitted that I had. "I am betting on this icon," John announced. What had interested John was that, while the painting was not old, the wood was very ancient. John called in a Russian expert to find out if there was anything beneath the oil painting. The expert took the icon to his studio and undertook the extremely delicate task of peeling off the oil painting. He discovered that there was, indeed, an older picture underneath, but unfortunately it was very mediocre and the expert decided it was not worth the painful trouble of restoration. I was maliciously pleased. I gloated and sneered that John's horse had broken a leg. Or perhaps it was only a donkey.

Weeks went by. Late one night the Russian expert telephoned in great excitement. He did not know why, he said, but he had scratched the second icon and there was gold leaf underneath. Should he continue? John told him to go right ahead and see what was there. He worked for months, while we waited in mounting nervous tension. Finally one of the greatest icons of its kind emerged. It was the same Deisus on a gold background, painted superbly in the fifteenth century. John did not gloat.

Before Europe exploded, our twin posts of Latvia and Estonia were ideal for me as an artist. There were relatively few social obligations. The Diplomatic Corps was small and not at all stuffy. Both countries were functioning on an even keel. With everything so smooth, I was left with a lot of time for my sculpture.

This is how President John Kennedy entered the Vatican in the guise of an angel. Jack, then a youngster, visited us in Riga while I was doing an altar of St. Thèrése of Lisieux, my favorite sant. The altar consisted of small panels depicting the life of the saint. In one of these an angel leans over her, while she is writing the book that made her beloved even by non-Catholics. I needed a model for the angel, and Jack with his curly hair and his youthful serenity of expression was literally God-sent. He sat for me, patiently, and is rewarded by having the privilege of being the only American President with his likeness in the Vatican, where the altar now is.

In addition to sculpture, we had delightful hours at the beaches, in both Latvia and Estonia. Probably there are no more beautiful beaches than the Baltic strand of these two countries.

John in particular was overjoyed because he had imported from the United States a seagoing, sailing canoe in which he cruised up and down the Dvina and into the Baltic. Weekends, when the weather was warm, we would go to the beaches for picnics. The wife of the Italian Minister had an idea of pure genius. She cut short the legs of a bridge table and stuck them in the sand. It is surprising how much a table can contribute to a beach picnic.

At Narva Jesu, in Estonia, the beach was filled with attractive Estonians. We and the British Minister went there once as the guests of the Estonian Foreign Minister. We all went bathing in a normal sort of way—everybody wearing conventional bathing garb. We did not know that to the right of us the beach was reserved for men, and to the left for women, all in the nude.

After our swim, John and his British colleague started

strolling up the beach, completely engrossed in their conversation. Yes, they found themselves in the midst of the female bathers.

John says there must have been a thousand or so, ranging in age from a few months to antiquity. Among them, of course, were the most lovely-looking girls in Europe. John claims that females in the nude, when seen en masse, look just like females and that there is no seismic shock, no reaction, either exotic or erotic, involved.

Later the same day the Foreign Minister escorted us to the nearby Estonian-Soviet frontier. It was a sinister and threatening sight. The Red Army had cleard about a quarter of a mile of no man's land. There were masses of barbed wire and frequently a high Soviet observation post. In the heavy pine forest one could observe many patches of yellow, where trees had been cut down to make room for gun emplacements. The trees had been stuck back in the earth as camouflage, but when they died and changed color they had casually been left standing. Instead of camouflage, they served to reveal and to remind the Estonians that the big neighbor was malevolently watching them.

Our life would have been so pleasant had it not been for the roaring and raving of Hitler and the ominous, cold monotone of Stalin which, like cuttlefish ejecting inky fluid, darkened all around them.

On the first of September war started.

The German invasion of Poland made clear to me what it meant to be the foreign wife of an American diplomat. There was, and still is, a lot of doubt about the desirability of Foreign Service officers marrying foreigners. When, as a bride, I arrived at the embassy in Moscow, one evening Ambassador Bullitt looked around the dinner table where his staff was assembled and noticed that every single wife was foreign born.

Bill Bullitt, who normally is broad-minded, even international in his tastes, was suddenly engulfed in a fog of nationalism. He telegraphed and inspired the State Department to forbid foreign marriages. That regulation, which lasted a few years, brought so many heartbreaks to so many and so many unnecessary resignations from the service that it was amended. It was naïve to expect Foreign Service officers, living abroad, to be immune to serious love and patiently wait to come home, to be herded into an American matrimonial corral.

Born in Poland, the war for me was not an abstract tragedy. It tore me to pieces. It was then that I understood that there is enough room in one's heart for the love of two countries, but that there is room for only one loyalty. It became quite evident that, however great my attachment to the land of my birth, it was my country of adoption that came first, like an adopted child that becomes as dear as one's own but for whom one adds an extra measure of tenderness. All foreign-born wives must feel the same way, since there has not been one case in peace or war when a foreign-born service wife has not been completely loyal in her allegiance to America.

The United States was, of course, still neutral. Whatever their personal feelings and opinions, the American diplomats had to maintain correct relations with the representatives of all the belligerent countries. I even had to manage to chat amiably with the German Minister while my mother was being bombed in Warsaw. Also, it was not easy to have the Soviet Minister to lunch while the Russians were massacring the Poles and deporting members of my family—but it was done. It was not heroic, since it all responded to a sense of duty, of obligation to my husband and our country. And, as usual, John's sense of humor was the starch when the fabric of my character was getting limp. He told me that when I was passing the salt to the Soviet Minister, I looked more like Lucretia Borgia administering poison than a polite hostess.

Like lightning rods which attract lightning, John and I seem to be always attracting spectacular trouble. We were in Moscow when the purges started, in Vienna when Hitler walked in, and in the Baltic States when the Russians took them over. Luckily we were in a few quieter posts or we would probably have started thinking that we were some kind of a political typhoid Mary.

The Nazi-Soviet nonaggression pact, and the fact that they were not attacked in September, 1939, gave the Baltic States a false sense of security. They hoped to be let alone, neutral, to be able to keep their cherished independence. But it was not to be.

The first move on the chessboard of invasion came in October, 1939, when irresistible Russian pressure forced Lithuania, Latvia and Estonia to grant the U.S.R.R. military bases. Great Red Army garrisons were established so quietly and so politely with iron-disciplined troops that the anxiety of the Baltic people was greatly relieved.

Once, by chance, I engaged in conversation with two young Russian soldiers. They always went in pairs, probably to check on each other. I was startled by one of them saying, "I did not know that they had birch trees in England." The boy had never been told where he was going and he thought he was in England. He was very disappointed to hear that he was in Estonia. Another time I talked to a soldier carrying a big sack. He showed me the contents—it was filled with pieces of stale bread. He explained that he had heard, before leaving Russia, that the people in the Baltic States were starving and he was saving bread to give to the unfortunates. I did not have the heart to tell him that the poorest in this land had more and better food than anyone in Russia. Except for those two instances, we never talked to the Russians, knowing that they were under strict orders to keep to themselves. Yes, I forgot: another Red Army soldier stopped me on the street to inquire where he could find an Orthodox church. He said that in Russia he dared not go to church, but "perhaps here they would not mind."

The Nazis, knowing perfectly well that the Russians' next move was to be the annexation of the Baltic States, made a deal with the Kremlin to evacuate all the Baltic Germans. Most of the German families had been in the Baltic States for centuries and many of them refused to leave.

There are in every European country those strange islands of ghost people who live in pride and poverty. With their future dead, they scorn the present. For them the past is both the present and the future. Their lot is the sadness of nostalgia. They are the old European nobility, the aristocracy that through war and revolution became landless and frequently expatriate. For them all the clocks of the world stopped when they left their ancestral mansions. They have a kind of quiet, stubborn, useless heroism which makes them unwilling to recognize the changes around them. In their inner consciousness the reign of the common man has never happened. The windows of their lodgings, like the windows of their hearts and minds, are closed to the strangely altered outside world.

Such a group still lived in the middle of Tallinn, on a cone-shaped hill, the Domberg, which in czarist days had been a citadel or rather a supremely aristocratic ghetto of the Baltic barons.

One day John told me to visit a very ancient countess who was the uncrowned queen of all the old regime. I was to tell the old lady that she, her family and friends should all go to Germany, since with the Russian invasion they certainly faced deportation to Siberia or worse.

The old lady received me most charmingly in a room where the walls were covered with icons, portraits and photographs of ancestors. She was surrounded by a two-dimensional, un-real-looking family, sitting on straight-backed chairs, like a family group photographed by Daguerre. Very gently I began to hint about the war and the fact that the Russians would certainly occupy the Baltic States. I tried to explain what it would mean for them.

To everything I said the old countess, with a delightful and patient smile, answered, "Yes, it looks bad indeed, but don't worry. Little Ferdinand will arrange everything." And all the daughters, cousins and nieces, like marionettes, nodded their heads and repeated in chorus, "Little Ferdinand will arrange everything." I was in a daze when I left. Only later did I learn from John that little Ferdinand was the late Czar of Bulgaria, a distant cousin of the countess, who had a great admiration and affection for him.

The countess, ages ago, had danced with Ferdinand at the Court of St. Petersburg, and her girlish rapture had persisted until her very advanced years. Alas, little Ferdinand had long since passed away.

XI

O N THE NIGHT OF JUNE 16, 1940, I WAS SUDDENLY awakened from sleep, the last sound sleep that any of us was to have for the next few months. It was John calling from the Chancery to tell me that Soviet troops had crossed the borders of Latvia and Estonia and were marching on Riga and Tallinn. He did not expect any resistance or disorders but he wanted me to be dressed and ready "just in case." I still do not know why John thought I could face machine guns and bombs more easily in a dress than in pajamas. I was tempted, with my love of the spectacular, to put on a ball gown and a tiara and, thus adorned, receive the Red Army. Luckily, I thought better of it. Immediately the door bell started ringing and our Latvian friends streamed in for advice and help. From that moment on they kept coming to us day and night until we left—mostly at night and "never evening wore to morning but some heart did break." All those people who were known as anti-Communists were caught literally between the devil and the deep-blue sea. How to escape the devil and cross the blue sea was the problem. Now the choice was between escape and death or deportation in cattle cars into Siberia or Central Asia.

Fortunately we had marvelous people on our staff. One of them especially, Freddy Rheinhardt, who had been with us in Vienna during the Anschluss, was an old hand in the grim game of outwitting the invader. His kindness and resourcefulness were inexhaustible. John and Freddy would think up the most bizarre schemes to get people out of the clutches of the

Soviets and into safety. Like acrobats, they had to walk a tightrope of American regulations and diplomatic usage.

There had been no resistance to the invading army, but in Riga there was sporadic shooting on the square in front of our legation. I have little courage but a devouring curiosity, so I rigged up a kind of periscope to see what was happening. Crouched under the window of our living room, I could, like an undignified Lady of Shalott, watch the square reflected in the mirror held high in my hand. There was no battle. After a few rounds of machine-gun fire, the crowds dispersed and order was restored. My Polish tradition of fighting any invader, whatever the strength of his army—the tradition of a handful of men staging rebellion against the most powerful despots, the tradition of cavalry charging enemy tanks—made it unbearable for me to see those two valiant countries, Latvia and Estonia, sink with hopeless resignation into slavery like people sinking into a morass. My romantic Don Quixotism hoped for some fierce, desperate gesture. Perhaps there was a more difficult heroism in their silent acceptance of their fate.

Next morning when I went to the Chancery to pick up John I thought the place had caught fire. Black smoke was coming out of the chimney and a thick rain of gray flakes like dirty snow was falling everywhere. We were burning the confidential files that could not be carried out by diplomatic pouch.

Since independent Latvia had ceased to exist, our mission was automatically ended. Silent groups of Latvians were watching this beginning of our exodus, with that hopeless look I had come to know so well in Austria. No born American can understand what America means to a European. We attach so much importance to the occasional "Americans go home" instead of remembering that it is always "Americans don't go" from all who are really oppressed or threatened. A European is sometimes resentful of and often angry at the United States, but in his heart he knows that it is only America that stands for "charity to all and malice toward none."

A so-called plebiscite followed the occupation. It amounted to no more than a mandatory requirement for everyone to present his passport—every Latvian and Estonian carried a passport—to be stamped by the Communists. John and I went to watch this grim proceeding. No election in history could have been a greater farce. The penalty for not "voting" was made clear. Without the stamp, the individual would lose his bread card, his job, and face deportation.

The day after the plebiscite an oversized Russian destroyer docked alongside the President's Palace, which faced the river. Every gun was trained on its windows. Then the Soviet Minister called on President Ulmanis. John got the story direct from President Ulmanis' private secretary, who was present. With great courtesy the Soviet Minister informed President Ulmanis that the Soviet government desired that the President should leave the country. President Ulmanis' reply was "I am a Latvian and I wish to remain in my own country." The Soviet Minister politely insisted that his Government desired President Ulmanis to proceed to Switzerland. President Ulmanis pointed out that, while he had, of course, to comply with the Soviet decision, he had no money with which to undertake a trip abroad. The Soviet Minister assured him that he need give that question no thought whatsoever. He would be given $2,000 for his immediate expenses and in Switzerland his financial situation would be adequately assured.

President Ulmanis, unhappily resigned to his fate, asked if the Soviet Minister would have his private papers examined in order to determine what, if anything, he could take with him. The Minister amiably replied that there would be no question whatsoever of examining his private papers. He could take with him anything he might desire. The Minister concluded the conversation with a directive that the President should be prepared to depart for Switzerland the following Wednesday by way of Berlin. The Minister withdrew.

The next day the Minister returned. "There has been a slight change in plans," he told the President. "Instead of leaving Wednesday via Berlin, you leave tonight for Switzerland by way of Moscow." President Ulmanis replied, "I knew you were a scoundrel."

That night John and I saw the train in which Ulmanis left. A car had been hooked on to the Moscow train, its green shades tightly drawn. No one was visible. But when the train arrived in Moscow, the military attaché of a Western legation in Riga happened to be at the station. By chance, he saw President Ulmanis step off the train flanked by guards. As President Ulmanis passed the attaché, he paused momentarily, gave the man a fixed look and then went on his way.

In one of Ulmanis' last speeches he said, "It is better to die on your feet than live on your knees." Nothing has ever been published so far as we know to indicate what fate President Ulmanis suffered at the hands of the GPU. It is not possible that he could have been charged with any crime or offense. Certainly no public trial was ever held. The lack of curiosity of the American press on that subject has been inexplicable. The same lack of curiosity was displayed about the fate of the Minister of Foreign Affairs, a brilliant young man named Munters, who had been very active in the League of Nations and was well known in Europe.

As the Russians were coming in Mrs. Munters, a Russian, came to me with a plea that we give asylum in the Legation to her two small children. I assured her that we would gladly do so. But a few weeks later when the Russians were already installed in Latvia, she came to tell me that it would not be necessary for us to take in the children. She explained cryptically that "everything is all right for us."

A few days later, as we returned by car from the legation

in Tallinn, we passed the Munters' summer cottage. We stopped to say hello. There was a long garden path bordered by very heavy shrubbery. As we came near the cottage we saw the Munters sitting at a table, on the lawn. With them were the Soviet commercial attaché and his wife. Rumor had it that the attaché, not his minister, was the number one. In the middle of the table was an offering, obviously from the attaché. It was a great basket and, as from a cornucopia, there protruded masses of fruit, boxes of sweets, and bottles of wine and spirits. Unseen, we tiptoed away. That same night the Munters and their children disappeared.

The long trains with curtained windows left every night for Russia. I had thought that in the unspeakable brutality of the Nazi invasion of Austria I had witnessed the depths of horror, but there was something even more nightmarish, more terrifying in watching, weary and helpless, this silent, nightly exodus. The Nazis committed their atrocities night and day; the Russians, more surreptitious, only under cover of darkness.

The GPU arrested and deported people at random as if they were pulling names out of a hat. Members of the Cabinet, lawyers, government officials, doctors, schoolteachers, workmen, suddenly disappeared, never to be seen again.

The Russians broke up families by deporting the husband, wife and children, and then dumping them separately, like unwanted garbage, all over Siberia and Central Asia. They probably planned that by disrupting family unity, they could destroy forever national unity. Until then nothing could uproot the fierce nationalism of Latvia and Estonia. Those two tiny countries, with their small populations, were completely withdrawn from political circulation. For seven hundred years, like a fire banked under cinders, they managed to keep their language, customs, and patriotism. But, then, they were together, on their own soil, with their landscape as their history
104

book. Now they were being dispersed. Being few, they faced national extinction.

After the Russians had been there a week, our doorbell rang in the middle of the night and in came the wife of the Cabinet minister, hiding under a shawl a two-year-old girl. She told us that her husband had already been arrested and deported and that her turn would probably come next. Would we please take her little girl as our own? I took the child and promised to take care of her. John was still in the office, as all were working endless hours, but I knew that even if this was a violation of some State Department regulation, John would approve. When he came back and was presented with lovely, blue-eyed blonde Trudy, he accepted with calm and a smile this unexpected paternity.

The difficulty was that if the Russians knew that we had Trudy, they would make trouble. Since the child was not an American citizen, we would have been helpless. We kept her sleeping in her room during the day and at night we played with her in the garden. As we had a never-ending stream of people coming to the legation, that period has remained in my mind as the "sleepless month." But the GPU never discovered the child.

Trudy spoke only Latvian. After a few days, when she stopped crying for her mother, we conversed in a strange idiom, understandable only to us both.

The serious problem was how to get the child out of Latvia. We tried to adopt her officially, but this would have taken many months, and we were obliged by the Russians to leave within a few weeks. To put her on our passport without formal adoption was against American law. John could not do it as his job was to enforce, not break, laws. We were desperate, since, of course, under no circumstances would we leave Trudy. I had visions of wrapping myself and the child in a large American flag and, thus protected, sit out the war in

Latvia. Salvation came from a very kindhearted Danish chargé d'affaires. Denmark's citizenship laws luckily are more humanitarian and elastic than ours, with much discretion left to their chiefs of mission. When he heard of our dilemma this charming Dane had his housekeeper adopt Trudy, giving her a new surname, and putting her on the housekeeper's passport. She was leaving for Sweden very soon and would take the child to Stockholm. From there, friends of ours would bring Trudy to Washington to meet us.

Trudy's mother was in hiding, but she sometimes managed in the night to sneak into the legation undetected. She did not dare to see the child for fear of breaking down, just stood leaning against the wall with a hopeless look of longing and despair in her eyes. While I was giving her all the news of her daughter and the arrangements for her departure, she would repeat, "Trudy will be so happy with you," as if trying to banish her suffering with the vision of future happiness for the child.

We did not keep Trudy. The night before her planned departure for Stockholm, her mother came and took her away. For weeks, she tried to bear the idea of parting, probably forever, from her only child. But when the moment came she could not. With a heavy heart I watched her leave the safety of the legation with her child fiercely clasped in her arms. She was going to try to get out of Latvia through the "green frontier" into Germany.

In those somber days I learned two lessons. To help the oppressed and the suffering, we must break the glass bowl in which, like goldfish, diplomats live in a safety zone, protected by diplomatic passports and diplomatic immunity. Only then can we do something for the human beings from which we are separated by our special status. I also learned that we must try not to think about the people we cannot help, but concentrate on those we can. Otherwise one becomes bogged down in paralyzing remorse.

This effort at detachment from being hurt by failure to help when help was not possible was not always successful.

I own a black scarf of lovely Chantilly lace, and every time I put it over my shoulders, it is like the wedding dress of Nessus. The scarf is light and soft, but for me it is a hairshirt because woven in the intricate design of human despair is the recollection of my inadequacy, my failure, in keeping a promise.

It had to do with our friends, the Laidoners, who lived on a small country estate just outside Tallinn. A few days after the Soviet occupation, they let us know they wanted to see us.

We drove immediately from Riga to their place. Their three boxers greeted us joyously at the door. The general and his wife were as urbane outwardly as though nothing untoward had happened. The General took John for a walk to show him more than a thousand young trees he had planted. He gave no indication that he did not expect to see them grow to maturity. In the meantime Mrs. Laidoner talked to me alone in the garden.

Women are not soldiers. We do not live by the same code as men, perhaps because we had nothing to do in drawing it up. Our heroism is not in pretending that we do not care and that we are not afraid. When we were left alone, Mrs. Laidoner handed me the lovely black scarf, and said: "This lace has been in our family for three generations. I will never be able to use it again. I want you to have it and to think about me when you wear it." I was taken by surprise and said, "But why won't you be able to use it?" She looked at me with eyes filled with grief and acceptance. "Don't you understand, don't you see that this house, this garden are already our prison, that any minute we will be deported? But, you know, I have had such a full life, such a happy life, I am so thankful for the past that I have to accept any future that is my lot. But I will tell you a secret. I have poison hidden on my person, enough for us both, and if the life we have to face proves unbearable, then there will be a simple way out."

I was stunned. I begged her, "Please don't kill yourself, wait, even when things are bad. We are going back to the United States. I will see President Roosevelt, and he will surely ask Stalin for your release. I promise to help you. When things are very bad, they are never unbearable while there is hope." At that moment the general and John rejoined us and the conversation turned to generalities. When we were leaving she kissed me and whispered in my ear, "I will wait."

We left the Laidoners and returned to the legation. That night they were deported. They entered the Communist darkness at midnight.

It was some months before we reached Washington. I am sure that Mr. Roosevelt did everything he could but to no avail. They were probably already dead. There was no charge, no indictment, no trial. They were simply eliminated, obliterated. General Laidoner's crime was patriotism.

Like the Germans in Poland, the Russians were anxious to get rid of the foreign witnesses to their reign of terror in the Baltic States. They required all diplomats to leave as soon as possible. Half of Europe was already in the hands of Hitler so the State Department instructed us to return to Washington via China and Japan. We had to leave the furniture from the residence—which was our own—in vans on the docks of Riga whence, circumstances permitting, it would be shipped to America by way of Sweden.

The problem of packing proved exceptionally difficult. We managed to get vans and cases, but no one to help. The Russians were trying to prevent the departure of too much movable wealth. They arrested all professional packers. We had to pack ourselves, with the help of our Chinese servants. Since we had little actual experience in crating, wrapping, and the like, it took us more than a week to finish the job.

On one of our last days in Riga I was packing books in the library, with more enthusiasm than skill, when the Papal Nuncio called to say farewell, for he also was forced to leave. I asked his Excellency to excuse me, as I had to go on packing, since time was short. He was talking with John, but I noticed a curious gleam in his eyes as he watched me. After a few minutes of polite conversation with John, he jumped up, rushed toward me in a whirlwind of ecclesiastical robes, crying out, "I cannot stand it any longer; I cannot bear to see you murder those books. I love books too much. Please let me do it." And for hours, with love, care and patience, crouching on the floor, he packed the books for me.

The last days before our departure the legation looked as if it had been hit by a tornado. There were people sleeping all over the place; on sofas, on camp beds, even on packing cases. Among them were Americans evacuated from Poland and Lithuania, awaiting passage home. In some miraculous fashion order was emerging out of this chaos. So long as I was physically busy with the preparations for our departure I tried not to think about its symbolic significance. Presently I realized what the forced exodus of foreign diplomats meant for the Baltic nations. It was a formal acknowledgment of the death of their countries.

Time has not erased from my mind the poignancy of our leaving the Baltic States. Even today, after so many years, it hurts to remember our uneasiness and remorse on abandoning those helpless, desolate people to an implacable fate. It is always hard to break the threads that attach our hearts to the many friends in a post, but one normally has the consolation of hoping to see them again. But when leaving the Latvians and Estonians we knew that to see them again we would have to wait for Gabriel's last trumpet.

XII

WE BOARDED THE TRANS-SIBERIAN IN MOSCOW.

When all the United States watched Daniel G. Farrell with interest to see if human beings could stand being locked in a space capsule on the way to the moon, I did not need a scientist to tell me that it can be done. I know by experience.

Our capsule launching into Siberian space took place in a compartment of the Trans-Siberian Railroad, where we spent twelve days of confinement—temperature 90° or more, almost no water, and great quantities of dust and dirt. The compartment looked like a moth-eaten 1900 sitting room, red plush, gold tassels, mirrors, and red carpets. In those deep carpets, generation after generation of bedbugs had made a happy home for themselves. They would attack us in close formation, but would bite only John, not me. John's explanation was that my immunity comes from a thousand years of insect bites in Poland.

For most travelers, the question of food was simplified by a dining car. But after the first meal, non-Russians suffered acute food poisoning, which took away all desire for nourishment for the rest of the trip. We had heard many tales about this poisonous diner, and had provided ourselves with superb Latvian canned goods, a Sterno stove, and instant coffee. My one great joy was the huge copper samovar in the corridor of the train, where at any hour of the day or night one could make delicious, strong, black Russian tea.

On that trip I learned the psychology of dirt. There was a

most luxurious washroom attached to our compartment but the plumbing was purely decorative, since there was no water. A few cupfuls of water a day was brought to us for our ablutions, which were thus almost reduced to "washing our hands with invisible soap in imperceptible water." For the first few days I tried desperately to keep clean. I used everything liquid I could lay my hands on to wash away the soot that was slowly accumulating over us—eau de cologne, tea, even beer since it was plentiful, but I do not advise it. It sticks. Vodka is better but too expensive. Then, suddenly, I gave up. And, strangely enough, when I stopped the fight for cleanliness I stopped minding. I settled quite resigned in my cocoon of grime and dust, until many days later I got into a real bathtub in Harbin. There, under a shower, with the blunt side of a kitchen knife, I spent hours scraping the dirt off my body.

We, that is, John and I, our Chinese servants, and the wife of our first secretary, took up all of a car, except for one compartment, occupied by a German spy. John knew all about him. He was a blond, Nordic young man from one of the old families of Germany, with excellent and smooth manners. He knew everybody, everywhere, and was on a secret Nazi intelligence mission to Japan and the United States. With his artificial charm, he tried to ingratiate himself, but we were glacially, if politely unresponsive. In peacetime, to be accompanied by a spy throughout Siberia might have created the amusing atmosphere of a whodunit. But with the war on, and with my repulsion for Nazis, I envisaged with dread being cooped up with him for so many days. I was saved by microbes. The German intelligence must have been very poor, as their secret agent did not know about the lethal qualities of the Russian dining car. The second day out he became violently ill of food poisoning.

How right are the Quakers! An unhappy and sick man loses his nationality, even his characteristics, and becomes just another human being who needs help. There was no need on my part for a battle between my repulsion and my pity. It seems that a vomiting and suffering Nazi cannot inspire hate. It was quite natural to nurse and feed him until we reached Manchuria. I did not tell him, but in Harbin, somehow or other, he learned that I was of Polish birth. He looked utterly stunned, not understanding how great a chasm of hate a normal human reaction can bridge even in the worst of worlds.

In Moscow our friends had said to us, "How lucky you are to have your marvelous Chinese with you on such a long trip." Of course I was looking forward to twelve days of rest, lying in my bunk, tenderly rocked by the slow movement of the train, and waited on hand and foot. But fate unkindly had other plans for me. One hour after leaving Moscow and until we arrived in Manchouli eleven days later, Fu and Yui-chen were desperately, continuously train-sick and needed constant attention. Alas, Han, immune to such ills, had gone on ahead to visit relatives in Harbin. Between nursing my poisonous and poisoned German and the bedridden Chinese menage, there was not time for my dream of *dolce far niente*. To make matters worse I was full of antiseasickness pills in order to avoid car-sickness myself. They were almost as bad as sleeping pills.

Perhaps it was lucky that we were kept so busy. The tragedy of the Baltic States had left us so wound up, our nerves so exposed, that I probably would have jumped out of my skin from the dreary monotony of the long train trip. A train window usually offers more variety, more strange and unexpected sights than a TV screen, but not on the Trans-Siberian. There one saw only vast, colorless, melancholy plains like a terrestrial vacuum. For days, framed by the window, there was the same abstract landscape, consisting of two colored stripes, one blue-gray for the sky, one brown-gray for the earth.

I wondered why the railroad stations were so far away from the villages. Only a few times during our whole trip through

Siberia were human habitations visible from a train stop. If the Soviets had built the Trans-Siberian it would have been understandable. But perhaps the czarist regime also had things to hide from Western eyes.

Despite the distance from the towns, the stations were always crowded. They offered an opportunity to buy food and some relief from the dreadful monotony of village life. The deeper we got into Siberia the more bizarre was the variety of races, with Turkomans, Tatars in strong contrast to the Russian muzhiks. The silence of these passive crowds was emphasized by the noisy colors of Oriental garb.

At the stations there were always peasants selling loaves of black bread, and those ugly, wrinkled Russian apples that are delicious. Once in Irkutsk we spotted a woman with a few eggs in a basket. John loves soft-boiled eggs for breakfast and, of course, we had not had any for days. He rushed down the platform and bought the eggs for a ruble each. John's comment was "I have been trying to find out the value of the ruble for years. Now I know exactly: a ruble equals one egg."

Next morning we started a ceremonial breakfast. There was still one clean towel available, and it was procured. John lit the Sterno stove, the water boiled, and the eggs were inserted. With great concentration, John timed the eggs to the split second. At the end of exactly three minutes, the eggs were removed from the boiling water. With a dramatic gesture John knocked off the top of egg number one. It was hard boiled, hard as a billiard ball. And so were the others. We had purchased ancient, hard-boiled eggs.

The days were slowly slipping by in the unending sameness of the prairies, when suddenly, like those Japanese beads of wood pulp which when placed in water open into flowers, the woods and lakes of the Baikal region unfolded before our eyes. As we entered into the green coolness of this fairyland, the dust, the heat, the unending monotony of the past seven days were obliterated. We were glued to the windows of our compartment, like children in front of a shop window filled with toys. We were fascinated by the forests of birches and oaks, the crystal-clear streams, and the navy-blue lakes.

Lake Baikal itself is the largest lake in Asia and the deepest lake in the world. It is also incredibly beautiful. If the Soviets should turn from expansion without to expansion within, it could be turned into one of the world's greatest centers of tourism.

We noticed that every so often when the train reached a river, it would come to a halt. I asked the porter of our car the reason for those frequent stops. He explained that both the engineer and the firemen liked bathing, so they would simply stop the train to have a swim. Our attendant found this completely natural as he had the blissful disregard for time, schedules and efficiency of all easygoing non-Communist Russians. I begged him to let us know the next time the engineer had an urge for dunking himself in the river, since I could not imagine a greater joy, hot and dirty as we were, than to plunge into the cold clean water. But he never did, which was to be expected, since with their suspicious minds the Russians did not let us leave the train, except to walk on some occasional station platform.

Not only could we not leave the train, but periodically throughout the trip our porter, accompanied by a uniformed armed guard, came to our compartment, closed the windows and lowered the curtains, and kept them lowered sometimes for hours. Probably we were going through some military installation, but every time I peeped while the guard's back was turned I saw nothing but the unbroken expanse of steppes and later the beautiful endless forests.

In looking back it seems that we voyaged on the Trans-Siberian express more like packages postmarked Moscow, destination Manchouli, than human beings. These were clearly unfavorable conditions for absorbing impressions of the vast

114

region—larger than the United States—that we were crossing. Nonetheless, some secrets were revealed, some mysteries unveiled. We realized, of course, that somewhere behind the curtain of steppes and the green fog of forests a tragedy was being staged. Under the czars, generations of political prisoners were exiled to Siberia. Under Stalin, people of many races had been deported and dumped there, in the atrocious climate, to starve and die if they were weak and old or to slave if they were strong enough.

But we also saw, the farther we got from the Kremlin, that the faces of people we met—the local inhabitants—became more real and took on some expression, as if the mask of patience and resignation had been dropped. It was as though that part of Russia was slowly emerging from behind the Soviet shadow. We thought we could glimpse the Russia of Pushkin and Chekhov, the Russia of the warmhearted peasants, who by their kindness had saved many deportees. There was another, more prosaic explanation why the people we saw on our journey were not so afraid as their countrymen on the western side of the Urals. Being born Siberians, they did not risk being deported to Siberia.

Past Lake Baikal, we traveled for three days across a mountainous region separating Siberia from Manchuria. The latter immensely fertile and potentially rich region, inhabited by a virile race of Chinese Manchus, had long been dominated by the Russians who, at the beginning of the century, built across it the so-called Eastern Chinese Railroad leading to Vladivostok on the Pacific Ocean. Lenin was forced to return Manchuria to China. In 1932, however, the Japanese seized it and established there the first puppet state in modern history. They called it Manchukuo and erected it into an empire under that most hapless young man, Henry Pu-yi, who as a small child had been the last emperor of China. Of real inde-

115

pendence Manchuria had none, for the Japanese Army controlled it entirely.

On the twelfth day we finished our Trans-Siberian hegira on the Manchurian frontier at Manchouli. It ended on a heated note. The passenger cars were shunted onto a siding, where we waited and waited while the frontier guards of the GPU conducted their microscopic inspection of the train. As part of the ordeal, a guard closed the windows of our compartment. We roasted as the thermometer soared. Then a guard closed the door into the corridor. We were stifling, so John opened the door. The guard closed it. John reopened it. The guard closed it. This dreary ticktacktoe with the door went on and on until John lost his patience. He slid the door open with a violent slam and recited "Mary had a little lamb" with such violence of voice that the guard, the last Russian we came across, retreated in haste. He was probably convinced that John was cursing him in some horrible and evil way.

It was with a sensation of physical relief that we left the train and entered the dingy frontier station. But our relief was short-lived. It was lucky that John had spent hours on our trip in giving me the Coué treatment. Instead of saying "Every day in every way I am getting better and better," he made me repeat, "We are not going to be a diplomatic incident." American relations with Japan being already very tense, John was afraid of trouble with the Japanese in occupied Manchuria and China. And how right he was!

The moment we crossed the border we met with such unreasoned insolence, such brutal rudeness, that if we had not been in a state of hypnosis by repeating "we will not be an incident" we might easily have let ourselves be provoked.

The first unpleasant event occurred when John was walking through Manchouli to pick up our reservations on the Japanese-operated Chinese Eastern Railway, which ran through Harbin and Mukden to Peking.

John encountered three Japanese soldiers on the sidewalk. He stood aside to let them pass, but they gave him the heave-ho into the gutter, a very deep one. John got up, brushed himself off, and went tranquilly on his way. He explained to me that if there was going to be a frontier incident on that particular frontier the United States, so far as he was concerned, was not going to be involved.

The insolence, if not the brutality, continued all through our trip to Peking. One example of studied discourtesy was to make us get up and leave our table in the dining car in the middle of a meal in order to make room for a Japanese general. A small annoyance was the constantly repeated intrusion into our compartment, night and day, of Japanese intelligence agents who subjected us each time to the same long, aimless interrogation. Each interrogation followed precisely the pattern of the previous one. It could serve no other purpose than to annoy us. On every one of these countless visitations John was required to hand over one of his calling cards. Forewarned, John had a stack with him. We have often wondered why this curious passion for calling cards, and what they did with them.

I am very sorry that the initial impact of the Japanese on me came when I saw them as conquerors in a vanquished land. Alien people, seen for the first time, especially as invaders, outside their own background, their own landscapes and homes, even if revealing and interesting individually, do not give any real clue to their lives and culture. They are as puzzling as tourists, in the sense that they are like a sentence out of context.

I was familiar with the art of the Japanese, an art filled with love and understanding of nature, a taste for prettiness, even an engaging childlike sweetness in the objects with which they surround themselves. It was impossible for me to reconcile all this with the people on the train—ugly, with small cruel eyes, spilling undiluted hatred for the foreigner, arrogant, swollen with national pride. Those were the Japanese we saw in Manchuria. I was completely baffled. My deep belief that art always is the true reflection of a nation was beginning to totter. Suddenly I remembered that the Japanese did not only create ethereal screens, sensitive in their beauty, exquisite lacquer objects, and incredibly poetical flower arrangements; they also produced those horrifying, scowling masks that the Samurai, not so long ago, still wore in battle, and the monstrous, grimacing statues which, like demoniac scarecrows, stand in many temples. That part of Japanese art does expose their cruel, merciless concept of war. Alas, it was seen in all its horror a year later.

On our way to Peking we stopped over in Harbin. I vaguely remember the wide yellow Sungari River, flowing lazily across a drab, sad, Westernized city. I was too limp, too tired, too confused to absorb or even to see anything. John, though, with his Scotch-Irish resiliency and his passion for political impressions, was full of energy, and after a nap and bath, rushed to see people and learn what he could.

What I remember best of Harbin was our consul general, George Merrill. Not only for his hospitality, but mostly for the maddening beauty of his house and the perfection of his meals and service. Maddening, because he was a bachelor. It was humiliating to realize in George's well-appointed and well-kept house the truth of the refrain of an old song, "Whatever women do, men can do better."

From Harbin to Peking we were once again on the Chinese Eastern Railway, which was now called the South Manchurian Railway. Under the Japanese the trains were immaculate and beautifully run. The August heat was intense. Because of this heat, although I did not acquire much knowledge of Oriental civilization on this journey, I learned a lot about Japanese anatomy. The Japanese have the startling habit of undressing when the spirit moves them. I was taken aback the first time a Japanese, in correct European clothes, came into our compartment and then calmly proceeded to strip. When he was stark naked except for a kind of G string, he folded his clothes in a neat, precise Japanese way, and sat down with his newspapers. This was not the only episode of the kind.

This Japanese custom of disrobing gave me an opportunity to study both their faces and their bodies. Their form, shape and expression should have been more revealing than words, particularly since they spoke bad English, if any. If there is a misconception in the idea that all Orientals look alike, the truth is that even in their diversity they are undecipherable. On an Occidental face every intimate thought, all actions, good or bad, are written for anyone to read. There is a staggering truth in the story of *The Picture of Dorian Gray*. I have often felt ashamed and embarrassed when making a portrait, to see, so clearly, the real character of my sitter, as if looking through a keyhole or reading surreptitiously somebody's intimate diary. But this was not the case with the Japanese. Their souls, their expressions, seemed to be written in a code to which I did not have the key.

But until we reached Peking the train was always filled with obviously very important Japanese generals. At every station we passed through, massive Japanese honor guards stood stiffly at attention. Whenever a Japanese officer or soldier walked past the awesome presence of the generals, he not merely saluted but went through gymnastic gyrations worthy of the high diving board and the double back-flip. The Japanese concept of military courtesy looked almost as if it had been borrowed from the burlesque stage.

While traveling through conquered China I kept thinking about a story told me years before in Moscow by the Chinese Ambassador, Dr. Chen. Dr. Chen was considered one of the most luminous minds of the world, and, like all great people,

119

he had the humility that permitted me, even with my low IQ, to be happy when talking to him. He had also a very Chinese idea of time. Once in a conversation about great historical cycles I asked him what he thought about the French Revolution. He looked quite shocked and quietly replied, "But, dear Mrs. Wiley, it is much too recent to us to judge. How can one form an opinion of an event that took place only a century and a half ago?"

When we heard about the Japanese invasion of Manchuria and China, we went to see him, to express our sympathy and condolence. We found him quite cheerful. He reassured us: "Don't worry, all will be well. I shall tell you a story which will explain my optimism. Once in a village in China a man-eating tiger came every night. It would steal into the village and kill a man, a woman or a child, and then drag off the body to be eaten at his leisure. The villagers tried in every way to get rid of the tiger. They laid traps and the aroused villagers attempted to hunt him down, but to no avail. Finally the villagers assembled and drew lots. The one who lost swallowed strong poison and went over the village wall and into the forest. Next morning they found the tiger dead by the side of the half-eaten man." And, he added, "China is most indigestible to conquerors."

This eloquent parable showing how China copes with foreign invaders is convincing, but what is lacking is how China will, as China shall, dispose of the conquerors from within.

When at last we arrived at the railroad station in Peking, Bob Smyth, the American Chargé d'Affaires, met us with his staff at the station. He approached John very anxiously, asking, "Do you and your wife have your cholera vaccination certificates with you?" John replied that we did not, that no one had ever mentioned the need for cholera certificates. Bob Smyth turned pale. He said, "There is nothing I can do to help you," and pointed helplessly and hopelessly to a cordon of Japanese sanitary troops. Every single passenger and every coolie received a veterinary-sized hypodermic shot against cholera as he passed into the station. Needless to say, the same needle was used for everyone, without any sign of sterilization or even disinfectant. The outlook was most unpleasant.

John, as usual, was very calm. He said quietly, "Let me handle the matter." John led the procession down the long platform and finally confronted the Japanese major in charge of the sanitary troops. He said, "Here are our certificates," and actually produced two officially stamped certificates, written in Latvian, that testified to the fact that we were members in good standing of the Riga Tennis Club. The major inhaled his breath with exquisite politeness and scrutinized the certificates very carefully, pretending to read Latvian. Then he waved us on. We passed through the gates of the Forbidden City without let or hindrance. Bob Smyth gave a sigh of relief, and so did I.

XIII

SEEING PEKING FOR THE FIRST TIME DID NOT DESTROY my imaginative picture of the city. When facing reality, a reality even more beautiful and spectacular than my idea of it, but different, I sometimes felt a sense of loss for the image that I had created and cherished. But Peking was in fact true to the last detail to my vision, a vision founded on the metaphysical abstraction of the Tang and Ming sculptures, the Sung painting and pictures of their intellectually traditional architectures.

One cannot describe Peking with words. One needs color, form and sound. Especially color. The grays, the beige of the earth, the mad yellows and the burning blues of the temples and palaces of the Forbidden City, the "terre-verte" patina of age and the ochreous dust that covers everything.

Day and night one heard the rustling of the eternally moving crowds, like wind blowing through autumn leaves. There is something hypnotic about the Chinese crowds perpetually in motion and perpetually present. How beautifully the Chinese move, so freely, so gracefully, with an Oriental fluidity in the simple perfection of their long narrow coats. Vulgarity and coarseness are unknown to them. Even the poorest coolie, even the beggars have an aristocratic elegance of movement. One finds the same elegance in their handicrafts.

Unlike Harbin, in Peking one was barely conscious of the Japanese occupation. Peking was too great in itself to change its complexion because of an alien conqueror. Moreover, the diplomatic quarter, a city within the city, successfully curbed Japanese encroachment.

There had been a moment when the Japanese had ridden literally roughshod over the diplomatic sanctuary. Army trucks filled with Japanese soldiers would speed through the crowded streets indifferent to death and injury to the population. The Diplomatic Corps met the situation promptly. "Thank you ma'ams," or ridges in the pavement, were quickly constructed. Japanese trucks would hit them at high speed, bump into the air and bounce Japanese soldiers all over the landscape. From that time on Japanese Army trucks drove with the greatest circumspection.

In Peking itself there seemed to be a truce between the Japanese and the Chinese. Only in the hills around the city, Chinese guerrillas kept harassing the Japanese Army of Occupation and occasional rifle fire could be heard.

Some of John's friends and colleagues in the embassy differed with John when he referred to the Chinese guerrillas as Communists. They were described as "agrarian reformers." John replied, "Someday they will kick you out of China." The answer was "Just as long as we are not kicked out by the Japanese, it will be O.K. with us." John thoughtfully drank a gimlet.

Our stay in Peking was made perfect by the generous gesture of Bob and Jane Smyth. Bob was the Counselor of the embassy at that time and as such had a lovely, small house in the embassy compound. They were leaving for a long vacation and invited us to take it over, together with their Chinese servants during their absence. Like the good fairy in Cinderella, they changed an uninspiring pumpkin of a cosmopolitan hotel into a delightful and lived-in house. What might have been a dreary sightseeing touristic life became a real life in a new world.

Without the Smyths' hospitality our stay in China would

have been entirely wasted on me. I have none of the tourist's delight in glimpsing monuments, landscapes, and local color. I have to live in a place, a nonhectic, unrushed life. I have to watch it in all its moods, get to know it patiently, not in its obvious beauties but in its small everyday manifestations. The Don Juanesque attitude of delight in new experiences, new sights, is alien to me. I enjoy a place more and more the longer I stay in it, the more I get to know it. That is why I dislike being a tourist but love being a diplomat's wife. I can watch leisurely the changes of seasons without having to rely on museums and other forms of instant art.

By moving into the compound we were immediately at home. The routine of running a house, with normal everyday chores, the people and the landscape became immediately a part of our life, instead of a stage filled with actors in exotic costumes and an Oriental backdrop, into which we had blundered by mistake.

This kind gesture of the Smyths was not untypical of Foreign Service life.

There is a lingering legend that the Foreign Service is like a select, stuffy, restricted club, whose members are inflated with self-importance, wear spats and striped pants, and are filled with pompous dignity. True, among our saints we may have an occasional sinner but what conglomeration of people is without them, except perhaps a monastery. And those few snobs, for whom a diplomatic passport is a coat of arms, a *laissez passer,* a sign of their importance, and whose Bible is the Almanach de Gotha, those misguided creatures are the ones that have distorted public opinion. Actually I doubt very many of this category survive in the service. Few in numbers, they have probably become extinct.

The Foreign Service is not like a club. It is much more like a large family or perhaps a tribe. We have so many tribal characteristics. Always nomadic and always surrounded by

124

alien people, we have a certain tribal instinct of loyalty to each other.

The Smyth gesture was an illustration of that solidarity. We had never met them before, they had no obligation of friendship or service toward us beyond meeting us at the station, which is a pleasant unwritten law in the service.

One afternoon at the studio of an American sculptress I met a man with a most beautiful, subtle, and fascinating face. He had golden, inspired eyes and looked like an eagle, the challenging fierce eagle of St. John. And his mind was as inspiring as his face. He was the Rev. Father Teilhard de Chardin, a French Jesuit, a paleontologist, and one of the discoverers of the Peking man.

In the mosaic of all the people I have met—monarchs, princes, statesmen, artists, writers or anonymous people with great souls—never until I met Father Teilhard did I so deeply feel the truth of the words of Genesis: "So God created man in his own image, in the image of God created he him."

John was not with me that day, as he carefully avoids tea or cocktail parties whenever possible. But I could not stand the idea of his not meeting Père Teilhard immediately, and so I invited the father to dine with us that night. To my great joy he was free and accepted. When I came home and told John that we were having a Jesuit priest for dinner, he was not pleased since he had looked forward to a quiet evening alone. I promised him that immediately after dinner I would see to it that the father left, knowing perfectly well that the impact of Père Teilhard on John would solve the problem. It did. Sunrise found Père Teilhard and John walking up and down the sitting room, with me curled like a pretzel in the corner of a sofa, listening with reverent ignorance to their metaphysical discussions. When he left John said, "This man may well be the Roger Bacon of the twentieth century."

We saw a lot of that marvelous man in the next few weeks.

I cannot forgive myself for not having written down every one of his words. Without scientific and theological knowledge, I could hardly follow him in his spiritual and scientific itinerary. But such was his greatness of soul that even without understanding them, one could feel his burning fervor and sense the glow of his words. His new vision of the universe, illuminated by scientific knowledge and mystical experience, was a revelation even to one so uninitiated as I. He would often talk about the spiral of evolution, about the fact that consciousness has never ceased to increase in human beings; about God penetrating the universe like a ray of light piercing a crystal; about love being the highest form of radial energy. In his thinking there was no contradiction between spirit and matter, no boundary between religion and science. "Christianity should be both horizontal and perpendicular," he would say.

When we were leaving for the United States, Père Teilhard appeared with an imposing manuscript of his latest book. He asked me to take it to America, knowing that war with Japan was inevitable. There was no assurance that he would escape alive from Peking. He asked me to keep the manuscript until I heard from him, failing which I was to forward it to a friend of his. During the months of the voyage home, while in Japan, and crossing the Pacific and America, the manuscript never left me. Like a king's messenger, I guarded it as a world-shattering message. I kept it for two years, until we were transferred and left Washington; then I entrusted it to the keeping of the friend of Father Teilhard.

We had no news of him except for this one letter:

Peking, February 2, 1941
Musie Hoang-Ho-Pi-Ho
Tientsin

My dear Mrs. Wiley:

For six months now since you left us, I have often thought of the hours we spent together. The primary purpose of this letter is to thank you once again for the confidence and comfort afforded to me by your delicate sympathy, an élan that always endures.

I would also like to tell you that I am afraid of burdening you with the manuscript which you were so good as to take in your charge. Weeks ago I finally decided to write to Rome in order to enquire where and how to have the book "revised," but the reply has not yet been received. Can you keep the three notebooks for a few weeks more? As soon as Rome gives me a solution, I shall let you know. In the meantime, if for one reason or another you wish to be relieved of the manuscript, here are two addresses of friends in your neighborhood. . . .

Nothing new here, only that the circle of friends has greatly diminished since your departure. Without the rather unexpected arrival of a certain number of Frenchmen at the Embassy, it would be almost reduced to nothing. Personally, I keep busy with ancient rocks and extinct animals, but my thinking is much more with the future of the earth. I would like to feel myself freer to preach a new "crusade," one that would unite Christians and non-Christians, all those who believe in the enormous forces of the spirit still to come out of man.

Remember me to your husband.

> Respectfully and faithfully,
> P. Teilhard de Chardin.

Then, years later, one morning in New York, when leaving church after Mass, I heard a voice calling "Irena." It was Father Teilhard, who was then working at the Vendegreen Foundation. I asked about the fate of the manuscript. At that time it had not yet been published.

It was destined to appear after the death of Father Teilhard under the title *The Phenomenon of Man*.

After two months in China we left for Japan on our way home. We arrived in Tangku, where we had to transship from a river boat to a Japanese passenger ship bound for Yokohama, a sturdy little vessel built in Scotland ages before. The storm that later became a typhoon had already started.

The Japanese sailors had put a narrow gangplank from one ship to the other. As the waves in the river were very high, one had to wait until the plank was horizontal for a split second and then race furiously across before it again reached an impossible angle. It was terrifying, since a false step would throw one into the boiling black current. I was helpless and paralyzed as in a nightmare. If not for Yui-chen I would still be in the river boat. She was seasick, terrorized and refused to move.

My own special brand of courage appears only in the presence of others who are afraid. When with brave people I am usually a coward. That is why John is never a help to me in moments of danger. He is always so completely calm and relaxed.

John had already made the trip twice from boat to boat, walking on the dancing plank as if it was a red carpet, bringing each time one of our Chinese boys to safety. But Yui-chen was my responsibility and would not budge without me.

With a lightheartedness I did not feel I told Yui-chen not to worry, that it was very simple, even amusing, that she would cross with me. As she is very small and light it was easy for me to hold her by the shoulders and propel her across. I am also a retrospective coward. I still shiver when I remember that episode.

We were the only Europeans on the small, crowded vessel and for us alone European meals worthy of the Ritz were prepared. Three times a day, with a big smile and a polite, inhaled hiss, elaborate, printed menus were presented to us and to us alone. Not only was the food excellent but, luckily for us, so was the seamanship. Excellent, though reckless. Only a few hours after we were at sea we were struck by the typhoon. With visibility zero the ship's speed was never reduced and finally we plowed sightlessly full speed ahead through the Inland Sea of Japan. With the blind fury of the

128

winds, liquid mountains fell upon the ship and it was like being inside a frantic cocktail shaker.

One of the sailors tied me with a thick rope to my bunk to prevent my being tossed around like a ping pong ball. It had suddenly turned very cold and the only coat I owned was a red brocade coolie coat lined with ermine that John had bought for me in Peking. I put it on, establishing, I think, a precedent on how to dress during typhoons. I must have presented a strange sight, wrapped in ropes and ermine and half doped with antiseasickness drugs, reading detective stories, and pondering over Père Teilhard's manuscript.

John is a magnificent sailor. He has such sea legs that even during the typhoon he refused to be tied down, and he was the only perpendicular passenger in the storm that lasted forty-eight hours. John resents very much that I am such a poor traveling companion as most of the time on sea I look and act as if someone had just hit me over the head. I am sure he often wishes he was a Moslem and could have a spare wife for sea voyages.

Limp and soggy as a dunked doughnut, but right side up, we arrived in Yokohama and then went on to Tokyo. At our embassy in Tokyo a telegram from the Holy Father was awaiting me. Before leaving Riga I had sent the Vatican the altar of St. Thérèse that I had sculptured.

When that telegram reached Tokyo it created tremendous confusion. It was handed to Ambassador Joe Grew, who could not figure out why the Holy Father was sending him his blessing and his thanks. He was desperately trying to remember how he could have merited the papal blessing, when someone on the staff suddenly noticed that under the name of Ambassador Grew, was written "For Wiley."

If we had come to Tokyo on a pleasure trip I would have been inclined to ask for our money back. But being there out of necessity, I contented myself by simply disliking everything about it—from the frigid, disdainful politeness of the Japanese and the hopeless monotony of Tokyo's streets, to that squatting monstrosity, the Imperial Hotel.

The great Frank Lloyd Wright, for whom I have an extravagant admiration, produced in Tokyo a most architecturally pretentious, uncomfortable hotel. And as John says, it was, alas, built in such a way as to withstand even the most shattering earthquakes.

It took us nearly a fortnight to learn our way from the lobby to our small suite. It was summer and terribly hot. To aggravate matters the Japanese staged a series of air-raid drills. Our windows were literally sealed. All the electric light bulbs save one were removed. The remaining bulb was covered by a lamp shade draped with black felt. Instead of *nuits blanches* we had *nuits noires.*

I should not write about Japan, as during our stay I was like a fly in amber, congealed and paralyzed by the atmosphere of hatred that surrounded us. How tangible hate is! Like fear, it impregnates the air you breathe. Like a fog it distorts all you see.

Before Pearl Harbor, the Japanese did not try to hide their malevolent hostility toward Americans. It was with a sense of escape, but also with anxious foreboding about the future that we boarded an American ship for the voyage home. We had been for the last few years under various dictatorships: German in Vienna, Russian in the Baltic States, and Japanese in China. Probably no one who has not lived under a system of Government where everything that is not forbidden is an obligation, a system under which the only positive reaction is fear, can realize what it meant to us to be once again under the American flag.

Our arrival in San Francisco on a cold, rainy October day presented a startling sight. All our trunks had disappeared when we crossed Siberia. We only had a few summer clothes

130

that were in our handbags. John in a white linen suit looked like an extra escaped from a Hollywood tropical film. I was in a cotton sun dress, in sandals, coatless, as if I belonged to some strange sect.

We would probably never have seen our belongings again had it not been for the press. We were interviewed a lot on our arrival and we never failed to mention our vanished trunks. It was in all the newspapers and perhaps influenced the Russians. They returned them to us after six months, beautifully repacked, quite unlike my careless handiwork.

XIV

WHEN JOHN WAS APPOINTED AMBASSADOR TO COLOMbia in 1944, all my friends who had been stationed there told me what a dismal life I would lead. During the war there was a regulation forbidding wives to travel on military aircraft. There were few commercial planes. Railroad facilities in Colombia were rare and roads were often unpassable by car. So the wife of an ambassador was virtually a prisoner in Bogotá, the mountaintop capital.

As the role of an unwilling Penelope did not suit me, I went to see President Roosevelt, whom we knew quite well personally. I asked him, "Do you approve of our marriage?" The President looked astonished. He replied, "Of course I do." "Then how would you feel if through your fault John abandoned me for another woman?" The President's eyes took on a glazed look. "I would be very upset," he replied very seriously.

"Then why do you send John to a post where he has to travel so much, exposed to all kind of temptation, while leaving me behind?"

"What do you want me to do?"

"Please write an order saying that Mrs. Wiley can accompany her husband on all Air Force, Navy, Marine Corps and Coast Guard planes."

I thought of them all, I was taking no chances. Happily, the President was in a magnificently good humor. He immediately wrote and signed an all-inclusive order. Very amused, he handed me the precious document with his hearty, contagious laugh. I still treasure it.

I have used it in many parts of the world. Curiously enough, it is still valid. A presidential order can be revoked only by a president. It never has been. I shall never forget the look of utter amazement that would come over the faces of Air Force officers whenever I proudly displayed it.

Another victory with another president helped to make my stay in Colombia such a happy one. In many South American countries the wives are still in a kind of vague "purdah." It is not entirely the man's fault, since Latin-American women have wisely chosen as their lot the three Bismarckian "K's": *Kinder, Kirche* und *Küche*—children, church and kitchen. Today the young women are much freer and more adventurous in their lives. But in 1944, the men went on trips, stag weekends, shooting parties, expeditions, while the women stayed contentedly at home doing the "divinely ordinary things."

When for the first time the President of Colombia asked John to go with him on a stag weekend to the coast, I rang him up. I told the President that he would have to invite me also in order not to violate the law under which John and I were married. I explained that under French law the husband has to protect his wife, but the wife has always to follow her husband. And I could follow John only with his permission.

The Bogotanos have a great sense of humor. The President roared with laughter and from that time on I was invited on all expeditions.

Sometimes I wished I had stayed at home, especially during the rainy season when on mountain roads our car would slither perilously on the brink of bottomless precipices. It was terrifying and one can easily understand why Colombians usually make their wills in anticipation of a journey.

Once on such a trip, almost like the Light Brigade, we had a landslide in front of us, a landslide back of us. We were boxed in on a deserted mountain road far from anywhere and, to make it worse, under a tropical downpour.

We were sitting in the car in frustrated helplessness. I was already visualizing our bleached bones being discovered after many months, when suddenly farm hands appeared from neighboring fields and led us through primeval slime to a railway station in a small town.

The news spread rapidly that the American Ambassador and his wife were there, stranded, and the entire population of the pueblo came to greet us. The people were friendly and generous, a little too much so. One of the *campesinos* put into my arms a brown and white mongrel puppy and, after a passionate burst of protracted oratory, announced "Her name is Miss America. I love her and I love America. Please take her as a token of gratitude from the people of Arauca." And the five-week-old Miss America, unweaned and unwanted, remained in my arms for the next twenty-four hours.

Miss America was in my arms while we were propelled to another village on a hand car, as no train was expected in Arauca for another week. She was on my lap when we reached another village, one that had an airfield, which we reached in a dump truck with the floor boards almost gone, the doors fastened with a thin wire. I was holding tight to John with one hand and to Miss America with the other in the hope that nobody would fall out the door or through the floorboards. Needless to say, Miss America was as unhousebroken as a leaky hot-water bag. She would protest with the most tragic voice when I tried to put her down. She also insisted on sleeping with me on the narrow army cot in the air force guest house where we spent the night while waiting for the plane from Bogotá. Every time I moved, she fell out of bed with a loud plop and ear-shattering yelps. Miss America did not grow up to be quite as beautiful as her title would imply, but she became a very respected member of the embassy.

The fact that Colombia is nearly all up and down, with communications consequently very difficult, has given aviation tremendous importance. Indeed, aviation is indispensable to the Colombians. It was probably quite natural that Colombia should have been the birthplace of what we now know as commercial aviation.

Our memory of Colombia is vividly associated with flying. When we were leaving for Bogotá, our Air Force kindly offered to fly us to our post. John accepted with alacrity. Several days later, we suffered a grievous disappointment. A telephone call announced that on further investigation it had been learned that no four-engine plane had ever landed at Bogotá and the pilots considered the trip too risky. Our faces fell and we started making plans to proceed by a commercial airline. Then the telephone rang again. Yes, there was a pilot who had volunteered to make the flight. Did we still want to go? John gave an emphatic yes.

The trip was incredibly beautiful. We had marvelous weather and the mountains were breath-taking. And the plane was so big that we were able to take with us everything necessary to set up housekeeping immediately. As John put it, we were "operational" within minutes after we reached the embassy residence. And we needed it too, as the day after our arrival we gave a lunch for thirty people in honor of visiting senators.

Our arrival at the Bogotá airport, however, was a tragicomedy for me. It was then that I understood the girl who dreamed she was at the Court of St. James's in her Maidenform bra. I did not dream it, it was not a bra, but all the qualities of a nightmare were there. Though neither the pilot nor the navigator had ever flown in Colombia before, we landed on the precise minute of our schedule, without even circling the field. When we taxied to a standstill, we saw a multitude of people awaiting us. There were, of course, dignitaries of the government, the embassy staff, our military mission, the press, and a mass of curious people who had come for the sight. They got it in generous measure.

The ramp, that is, the usual platform and steps, was rolled up to the plane. Alas, it was equipment for unloading two-engine planes that were like midgets compared to our Goliath. But the Colombians had nothing else. They were not prepared for us. Then the door of the plane was opened. We looked down in fright. The gap between the door and the ramp was enormous.

Every eye was on us. First, Pushkin, our black poodle, jumped out. John then, as he put it, bailed out without a parachute. Happily, he landed on his feet without losing his hat or much of his decorum. Then it was my turn, so I bailed out, but with parachutes. My skirts billowed out and then went right over my head. Movie cameras were grinding away, press cameras clicked their shutters in unison. From a photographer's point of view, I was overexposed. When we descended the ladder, we were greeted with dignity and charm. Not a leer lit up a single face.

One thing touched me very much after our arrival. Not a single Colombian paper published a photograph of my strip-tease descent from the plane. Impressed by the delicate discretion of the Colombian press, I asked John if the American press would have shown me the same consideration under equal circumstances. He replied, "Certainly not. You would have jumped into national prominence with but a single leap."

I read somewhere that when Robert Louis Stevenson was a child he once said to his mother, "Mother, I've drawn a man, shall I draw his soul now?" So often have I thought about this remark when arriving in a foreign country with a different civilization and culture, since one is so apt to miss the spirit of the people when one is blinded by the external differences in racial types, customs, costumes, and living habits.

When we arrived in Colombia, my first experience with

136

South America, I felt as if I were at the other end of nowhere. I had read her history, studied her art, but I soon realized the difference between merely reading about people and knowing them at first hand. It was then that after much groping I discovered the three essential elements in understanding the inner life, the individual life of foreign people. One is religion, another is climate and environment, while the third, the most obvious of all, is the language.

For instance, it is impossible to understand Colombia if one does not know what it means to be a Catholic, catholicism being an organic part of their nature. An experience I had in the mountain village of Chiquinquirá showed with amazing vividness one aspect of a religious formation. In that village there is a Shrine of Our Lady of Chiquinquirá to which is attributed miraculous powers. Once a year there comes a great stream of pilgrims walking barefoot, often hungry. The poor campesinos save all year, depriving themselves of even the very necessities, to be able to visit Chiquinquirá. I was there for one of the feasts of Our Lady and, moved by a deep curiosity, I asked many of the destitute pilgrims what favor they were seeking of the Virgin that would warrant all their sacrifices. Was it money; was it health; was it a job? I got only one answer from them all—"Por una buena muerte," which in English would mean for a death in a state of grace. How curiously Spanish that attitude. Those *campesinos,* the vast majority full-blooded Indians, were the spiritual descendants of St. Teresa de Avila, who said that "life is like a bad night spent in an uncomfortable inn."

The influence of climate and landscape is so obvious that one cannot fail to notice it. But in Colombia, on the coast, the sun and sea produce gay, carefree people, while the forbidding, cold plateaus of the Andes breed melancholy introverts. It is easy to see that the sun and sea, the skies and mountains do not merely make a scenic background.

As for language, even a grammatical knowledge of Spanish is not quite enough to dissipate the film of incomprehension between us and Latin America. Some words represent ideas we do not have, and frequently the same words will have a different meaning for them than they have for us.

I recall a conversation John had in Bogotá with the President of Colombia. John had been instructed to urge a certain line of action on President Lleras Camargo, who is probably the outstanding Latin-American statesman of the century. When John finished his argument, the President replied, "Tal vez si," which literally translated means "Perhaps yes." John wanted to pin the President down so that he could accurately inform the Department of State. He said, "Mr. President, you speak perfect English. How would you translate 'tal vez si' "? President Lleras smiled and answered, "I would translate it as 'Certainly not'."

One of the first readjustments I had to make was in punctuality. The Colombians are not slaves of "whistle, clock or bell." It is a marvel that their casual, erratic attitude to time does not create chaos. On the contrary, it was rather John's punctuality that would produce confusion. But we soon became attuned to the clockless rhythm of their lives.

This disregard for the tyranny of the clock that one finds in Latin America is not necessarily a Spanish inheritance. For instance, Charles V of Spain relinquished the most powerful throne in the world in order to seek seclusion. In a monastery he diverted himself by trying to regulate two clocks so that they would both keep time with identical precision. He found this impossibly difficult to accomplish. According to Havelock Ellis, he finally turned in exasperation to a member of his entourage, exclaiming, "To think that I attempted to force the reason and conscience of thousands of men into one mold and then cannot make two clocks agree!"

As in Colombia, no such problem bothered the Peruvians.

When John was in Lima, every morning he would leave the embassy for a coffee break in a nearby café where he met his Peruvian friends. At these friendly little gatherings all the gossip of the day was ventilated and appraised. As they chatted, an earnest young lieutenant would stride purposefully by. Then, sharply at high noon, a cannon shot was fired from a hilltop to signal the hour. All of Lima would quickly check their watches.

In the window of the leading jewelry store in Lima there was an impressive chronometer. One day while making a purchase John asked the proprietor how he verified the accuracy of his magnificent timepiece. He answered that he never failed each day to check the chronometer with the noonday cannon. He added proudly that there was never a discrepancy between them.

The next day, at the morning reunion, John told the story to his friends. Then, as the lieutenant ambled by on his return from the hilltop, his mission accomplished, he was intercepted. How did he know the precise instant to discharge his cannon? "Quite simple," he replied: "as I pass the jewelry store each morning, I set my watch by the chronometer to the very second."

What Charles V needed was a cannon.

Colombia was a revelation to me. It was there that my heart understood the words of the psalm: "I have loved, O Lord, the beauty of thy mansions and the places where thy glory dwells." When one lives always in the same place, habit, that terrible, blinding word, covers with a gray veil what is around us. It is so much more difficult to react with passion to your own tree, in your own backyard, even a beautiful tree, a tree that for your diversion and joy becomes tenderly green, then flaming red, then stark, then snow-laden white. And one so rarely looks at the sky coming home from work or going to the grocery.

That is why we, the Foreign Service wives, are in such a lucky position. You have to look up when you are under the Southern Cross. You can't be indifferent in the Colombian llanos or unmoved by the desert of Saudi Arabia, where the "pillars of sand walk before you in the day and the pillar of fire at night." Traveling all over the world as we do, it also becomes clear that the same hand studs the skies with the stars, the same hand paints the Aurora Borealis, the same hand puts His seal on a flower and carves the Himalayas. And what other explanation but a divine joke has made emerald the color of the wings of the immense butterflies that circle slowly around the emerald mines in Muzo, Colombia. Nowhere else can those butterflies be found. Each wing is about the size of a hand. The underpart is grayish brown, the color of the rocks where those stones are found. The top looks as if it was enameled with translucent emerald dust.

It was in Colombia that nature first tugged at my sleeve whispering "Look at me." I always felt that "above the electric lights, there shone the stars," but it was a religious experience, not one of aesthetics. I am a citified creature, and up to then only the "urbi" impressed me and the "orbi" never got a glance. I loved and still love the smell of asphalt, the stones, the bricks, the marble, the concrete, that make a city. The variety and perhaps the freakishness of the Colombian landscape was what at first attracted my attention. Ferns the size of oaks, oaks the size of ferns, an Easter lily plant big as a cherry tree, entirely covered with white lilies. That tree is called *arbol loco,* the "mad tree." There is a superstition that if one sleeps in its shade one wakes up demented. And the jungle where everything is out of focus like some paintings of Douanier Rousseau. He had never seen the jungle and when he wanted to paint it, he used as models the plants in his studio. But he made them into trees, and thus created strange, mysterious forests.

140

Colombia did for me what the discovery of commercial ultramarine did for the painters of the end of the nineteenth century. In a soda factory in Alsace a chimney sweep, after having cleaned the chimney, came out blue from head to foot. As all the research people had been for years on the lookout for commercial blue—the only one in existence was the very costly lapiz lazuli—they saw their opportunity and discovered that ultramarine was the by-product of soda. And it was that unlimited, cheap supply of blue color that permitted impressionists to paint air and to open for us windows on landscapes.

Nature in many of the South American countries has not the discretion, the unassuming beauty, the half tones, the politeness of European and North American landscapes. It hits you like a blow between the eyes. I had looked at without really seeing the rosy grayness of the Ile de France, the silvery olive trees on the hills of Tuscany, and the lacy pattern of birches in New England. The operatic beauty of the tropics, the primeval strength and passion of jungles was what I needed to make me see. There is something even *nouveau riche* in the landscape of that part of the world. Too much green, too much blue, too much sun, too many mountains, too many trees, as if a drunken decorator had been told to splurge, to show off, to go ahead and use everything there was and a lot of it. This terrific blaze of color, the strange shapes of mountains, the unending prairies, are like an immense symphony orchestra with all brass and drums. It could not be ignored and, while the chamber music landscape of Europe went unnoticed by me, this visual blast woke me with a start. It opened a floodgate of new joys, new experiences. It makes me shudder to think that without the impact of Colombia I probably would have gone to Asia blindfolded, would have missed the iridescent air, the dead desolation of the desert, the mountains like "solid darkness" in Iran, the haze of a pink Lebanese city.

When we were stationed in Colombia we used to spend weekends at a friend's finca in the country. A lovely, primitive house without doors or windowpanes, where at night one was visited by all known and unknown species of insects and small animals. The jungle was all around us. It was a losing battle trying to prevent it from taking over the garden, where reigned thirty thousand orchid plants, shaded by poinsettias.

One day while indulging in our agreeable habit of walking barefoot in the morning dew, my husband and I came upon a large, purple Cattleya on which rested a cobalt and emerald hummingbird. Carefully, slowly we approached it. The bird never moved. It never moved when we were one step away from it. And it never moved when I extended my hand and stroked its back with my finger. It even looked pleased and turned its head toward us. I stroked it several times. Then gaily it took off, leaving us in a state of dazed amazement and strange happiness.

The strangeness of this experience is that, though I have a Hindu respect and love for every form of life. I have no magnetism. I have been bitten by dogs, scratched by cats, sneered at by horses, even attacked by a pelican on the beach of Pontevedra.

At another finca where we were staying a large crocodile got into the swimming pool one night. When the water was let out the poor thing was a prisoner. He was shot, to my sorrow. I did not like a sitting crocodile being killed, but he was very dangerous.

The fun in Colombia is that in the morning one can be in Bogotá, the most cultured city in Latin America, with bookstores in every block, and at night in the *tierra caliente* with all the exotic life of the tropics. The transition is fantastic from the literary salons of Bogotá, with their high standard of intellectual conversation, in two hours by plane to the land of the

Guajira Indians who, though peaceful, have never been conquered.

As John felt it essential to visit all the cities and provinces of Colombia, and since the embassy had a plane, we decided not to miss the Guajira. Few foreigners have ever been there, and few Colombians for that matter. It is completely isolated from the rest of Colombia and from neighboring Venezuela as well. There was a minor Colombian official in a tiny village and nothing more except salt flats. No roads, no doctors, no schools. Our plane landed in a clearing that served as a landing strip. We were at once surrounded by Indians, all males. Their idea of haberdashery was unique, they wore topside an abbreviated version of a cotton undershirt and a turban-like headgear, and nothing else. We never found the reason for this modesty in reverse. It was a startling sight which required a little time to get accustomed to. They were magnificent creatures, cheerful and laughing. We amused them as much as they interested us.

Later, ghostlike, appeared the women, not an inch of their bodies showing, in long togalike garments made of nine yards of cotton, their faces covered with gray clay and streaks of color, black eyes shining out of the curious make-up.

We spent a charming day, talking to them, drinking tea and rum and drawing them. We heard many strange tales. I think their mentality comes out best in the story of the young doctor.

Some years before our visit La Guajira was swept by an epidemic of pernicious malaria and it is said that twenty thousand of the Indians died. The Colombian government decided that it would be highly desirable to have a doctor in the area. Since there were no medical volunteers, the government thought up a bright idea—to educate a Guajira Indian for the job.

The government persuaded one of the caciques to turn over one of his young sons, a particularly bright boy. In Bogotá

143

the boy was put through school and college. He ended up with a perfectly good medical degree and the great moment had come.

The embryonic Dr. Schweitzer was put on a plane and duly dispatched to care for his people. The plane arrived, the young medico debarked. He promptly threw away his medical gear, took off his pants, and went into the business of buying and selling women and cows, which is the only form of commercial enterprise in La Guajira. A woman, depending on her sex appeal, is worth from one to twenty cows. John says it was the quickest economic survey ever made.

When we returned to the plane to take off before dark for Cartagena, we found that something was the matter with the starter. While waiting for it to be repaired, I got out my sketch-book to draw one of the small Guajiran Indian boys who had been following us around. When I tried to talk to him, using an apple as a lure to get him to approach the plane, he ran away. As he spoke no Spanish, I asked one of the other small boys around why the boy was so afraid of me. He said, "He is afraid of you, señora, because he thinks you will buy him and take him off in the plane." I will never forget the shock of even the thought of buying a child. I questioned the Colombian Army captain accompanying us about the "buying and selling" of children. He answered casually, "Oh yes, they sell the children here." But then he explained that this so-called slavery consists of a form of "apprenticeship," that the boys who are bought from their families live in the patron's house more or less like one of the family until they are grown up. Then they leave.

In Colombia the trips I enjoyed the most were the ones to the jungle, even if my love for the jungle is an unrequited love. So much is said about the indifference of nature, but there is no indifference toward man in the jungle. There is hate—hate, malevolence, cruelty. Flowers poison, bushes prick and tear, the rotting earth gives way under every step. The only way to bathe in a jungle river or pool is to wear a coat of mail, and even that might prove dangerous as one might be electrocuted by encountering an electric eel.

In poetic Greece long-haired, gay naiads guarded the streams, but in South America stingrays, which afflict most painful wounds, and carnivorous fish, which pick your bones clean, are the montrous sentinels that guard the waters.

I have heard that if a man was lost in the jungle without a shotgun he would die of starvation. Not a berry, not a root, not a leaf is edible.

And the crazy variety of vegetation—vegetation reconciled to live in the darkness and vegetation determined to find the sun and fighting its way to enormous heights in its quest! Mahogany, cedar, flamboyants, and a thousand varieties of palms. One of the variety is a slender tall palm tree. Once on an expedition our guide warned us against contact with it since it was invariably infected with a breed of red ants that give a painful bite. At the very moment of his admonition he absent-mindedly leaned against such a tree and gave an immediate and visible proof of the truth of his statement, followed by a scream of anguish. In a split second ants swarmed over him.

On that same trip, which was our first jungle expedition, we were preceded by a guide who with a machete cut the trail. There is an oppressive heat in the jungle, no breeze, the leaves motionless and a cathedral quiet, shattered only by the occasional screeching of monkeys. As we walked on we came to a stream, crystal clear and cool. As we made our way across it, it became knee-deep and I gave way to an irresistible temptation. I sat down. Never have I been so refreshed nor did I see people more shocked. The kind and dignified people who escorted us did not anticipate seeing an ambassadress, garbed in sloppy red denim pants, act with such lack of decorum. I was promptly warned about the dangers of stingrays and urged on my way. And dripping I went, realizing too late that once more I was a traitor to my official dignity.

My next diplomatic fiasco, sartorial this time, happened when I accompanied John on a visit to the United Fruit plantations on the Caribbean coast.

By that time I should have known better than to be dressed in a cotton shirt, slacks, sandals, even when going to the jungle. On the small landing field a reception committee was awaiting us. Already, when circling the airfield, I saw to my horror that the women were all dressed up as for the Queen's garden party, stockings, high-heeled shoes, gloves, and of course hats, and all that in a temperature of 100° in the shade.

They were too nice to show what a letdown it must have been for them when, instead of a glamorous, Dior-dressed, Paris-hatted ambassadress, a female hobo appeared from the plane. But I noticed that at the reception they disappeared, one by one, into the ladies' room, and then reappeared having shed their stockings, their girdles, and—hats. From that time on I always carried a skirt, stockings, gloves, all the paraphernalia of my profession. When from the air I saw a welcoming committee I would do a quick change and appear looking reasonably official and presentable.

Colombia is like a gigantic Whitman's Sampler. It has samples of everything, of snow-capped mountains, of steaming primeval forests, of grass-covered prairies, of temperate zones overflowing with fruits and flowers. Every town has a different character, a different atmosphere. From the sad, cold, intellectual Bogotá, with its faceless houses, black-dressed people, its rigid, conventional eucalyptuses, to the orchid-festooned Medellín, to the gay, smiling, naked, white and blue Cartagena.

Cartagena is our great love. We spent many happy vacations there. We love it for the incredible beauty of the city built by the Kings of Spain as the great citadel of the New

World. Its people, the clean, carefree, friendly, democratic Cartageneros, have no equal. We made friends with the poor, with the rich, with the blacks and the whites, with the alcalde and his beautiful green-eyed wife, with their aunts, uncles, cousins, nieces, with the Colombian naval officers stationed there, with an old woman selling shells on the beach who once, on seeing me after a long absence, exclaimed happily, "What a joy to see you so fat and rosy"—and that at the time when I was desperately trying to lose weight! We made friends also with a young Negro musician, Rodo, who introduced us to the cumbia. The cumbia is a dance which came from the depths of Africa with the first slaves. There is an official cumbia danced during carnival all along the Caribbean coast, even sometimes in Harlem. But there is another ritual cumbia danced only in the darkness of the night and rarely seen by whites. The official cumbia is to the real one what a plaster cast is to the Elgin marbles. We wanted very much to see it but our friends gave us little hope in arranging it. But Rodo said he could and he did. It took a long time, but one day when we arrived in Cartagena Rodo told us, "There is a cumbia tonight in a pueblo on the island of Tierra Bomba, and I have permission to bring you, but don't tell anyone."

In great secrecy we reached the little fishing village, where we sat under trees and waited. There was no sound, no light. Slowly, silently from all sides crowds began to gather, leaving a space in the middle of the plaza. Suddenly, shattering the deeply tropical night, there was the first beat of a drum. Then the African music started, powerful and mysterious as if announcing some supernatural occurrence. And out of the shadows two by two came the dancers, each woman holding in an outstretched hand a bunch of lighted candles. They danced in pairs, facing each other but never with contact of their bodies. Undulating like reptiles, the dancers began a slow rhythm. Then the rhythm became feverishly accelerated

147

till great shivers shook their bodies in mad gymnastics. For hours they went round and round, with closed eyes, the women oblivious to the hot candle wax running down their arms, in some kind of ardent lascivious frenzy, but with the dignity of a solemn ritual. One by one the candles guttered out. As silently as they had come, the dancers disappeared in the night.

It was so strange to see those deeply Catholic people sweep away all moral sense, all Christian civilization, disintegrating for a night into a primeval dark instinct and next day revert to a gay, simple, God-fearing life.

I also found this paradoxical approach to religion among the Negro population of Haiti. When I asked a Haitian if I could see a voodoo ceremony while we were there, he answered in a shocked voice, "We do not have voodoo during Lent."

The people of Cartagena love pageantry and it is mostly in religious fiestas that they can give rein to their colorful imagination. They are deeply religious in a warm personal way. They are not just hatched, matched and dispatched. Like the juggler of Notre Dame, religion is ever present in their lives. Their special devotion is to Our Lady of Candlemas, otherwise known as Our Lady of the Popa. La Popa is a hill in the shape of the prow of a boat that dominates Cartagena. On the top stands a church built by the Spaniards, within it a miraculous statue of the Virgin and Child. An ancient legend has it that when the church was built there was no statue of Our Lady, none to be found in all Cartagena and no sculptors to carve it. One day while the priest was in his church, in came a stranger who told the priest to follow him. He led him down to the city, into a house where on a table stood a small beautifully carved statue. He gave it to the priest, who carried it to the Popa and placed it on the altar, where it stands to this day. When next day the priest returned to Cartagena to thank the stranger, there was no house. He found only some old ruins.

Many miracles have been attributed to the Virgin of the

148

Popa. When the Cartageneros are in trouble or in joy they climb the long and tortuous road up to the church to lay at her feet their sorrows or their happiness.

The most delightful manifestations of their devotion come on the night preceding Candlemas. Starting on February 2 at midnight the whole population, young and old, rich and poor, each with a lighted candle, makes its way to the dawn Mass at the shrine. The candles in the dark tropical night give the road a look of the Milky Way. All are on foot, only the babies are carried in large baskets suspended on the sides of very small gray donkeys. Everybody is singing, playing the guitar, and drinking rum. "They dance as they walk, they walk as they sing, they sing as they think," as in an old Spanish poem.

There is nothing solemn about this procession, and probably a Puritan onlooker, dry-cleaned of *joie de vivre,* would be shocked by this exuberant mob. But then he would miss the whole beauty of the relation of those people to religion. Our Lady is not to them a vague abstraction but a Mother, a Friend, whose anniversary is the occasion for joyous celebration and they visit her with presents and gaiety.

My strong dislike for walking never prevented me from joining the procession, as I also have a great devotion to Our Lady of the Popa. How rewarding it was when, after two hours on a stony road, in the pink dawn, I would find myself in the little church. Swallows and bats were flying in and out the open window. On the altar, laden with flowers, surrounded by countless candles, as inside the Burning Bush, stood Our Lady of Candlemas. She was like the Morning Star of the litanies and seemed to be smiling and listening to the unending chant of prayers.

And it was those simple and trusting pilgrims, with their love of God, of life, of their neighbors, that taught me that love is contagious, that being loved makes one capable of love, and that it is impossible to love God without loving those He loves.

XV

From Colombia we were transferred to Portugal. When we arrived in Lisbon, that charming, civilized city, I thought that at last I could peacefully squat under a tree and calmly contemplate my navel. No household problems, no medical problems, no strange climate to adjust to, no alien civilization to absorb. My submerged, but unconquered, sin of sloth was getting ready to take over in an orgy of laziness. But I soon found out that *dolce far niente* is not in the dictionary of an ambassadress. There are always people to meet and entertain, places to see, languages to learn, and mentalities to fathom.

When as a young girl I went all over Europe I always traveled horizontally, on the surface, never into the depth of a country. But an ambassadress is not a schoolgirl or a tourist. Because life in Portugal does not present obvious or exotic problems, it was where I found the importance of the basic ones. For example, learning the history of the country. How could one begin to understand Portugal without knowing that once it was a vast empire. How incomprehensible the Emanuel style which decorated the cathedrals and palaces with ships, ropes, anchors and compasses if one did not know what fierce and imaginative sailors the Portuguese had been. And how puzzling is modern Lisbon's architectural past, which starts in the eighteenth century, if one does not know of the terrible earthquake of 1755 which destroyed the entire city. John has

150

a theory that in that earthquake, together with all the past of stone, perished also the Portuguese will to be a great power.

When we first come to a new post we travel all the time, since John does not believe that a capital explains a country. He always wants to know how people live, what they think, and what and how they eat, in villages, in industrial cities, and in rural areas. No one can give you that information. You have to see, to hear, and to interpret it yourself.

We found a marvelous guide in the Minister of Foreign Affairs, Caero de Mata, who was not only gay and charming, a great scholar with forty learned books to his credit, but also full of loving knowledge of every inch of Portugal. He took us to the Alantez in the spring, where as far as one could see there was only the vista of white apple blossoms, and told us the story of the King who planted those trees so that his bride, a northern princess, would have them as a substitute for her country's snowy fields, and feel less homesick. He took us to a fishing village called Nazareth, where at sunset women all in black, silent, motionless, anguished, stand on the beach waiting for the fishing boats to come in. And the arrival of the fishing fleet is like a ballet, with the fishermen in tight, violently colored plaid pants and shirts, jumping off the boats with the agility and grace of dancers—the boats unchanged since the days of the Phoenicians.

We went with him to see the Cathedral of Alcobaça, where stands the touching tomb of King Peter I and his wife Inés. On their sarcophagus their recumbent effigies are placed feet to feet, at the command of the King, who desired that the first object seen on his resurrection should be his beloved wife.

He also showed us the sadly picturesque pine-covered hills in the north of Portugal; the vineyards whence comes port wine; took us through the cork forests, where the red trunks of the trees with the bark partly stripped away made them look like bikini-garbed creatures with bare midriffs. We even went through sardine-canning factories, efficient and immaculately clean.

Portuguese sardines, especially fresh, when fried make a delicious meal and were a source of my unending feud with the cook of the embassy, Luis. Luis was, I think, one of the great master chefs in Europe, knew it and behaved accordingly. He also got used, with the long succession of very rich noncareer ambassadors in Portugal, to serving only lavish meals; the word "economy" was anathema to him. Luis was a very nice human being, but could not work for service people like ourselves, people who could not afford a bill of $4,000 for food, which was the bill presented to us after our first month in Lisbon, and which upset our finances for months to come. I put him on a budget, but his nervous system could not stand the strain, and he quit.

The sardine battle went on as long as Luis stayed with us. John and I are very fond of fresh sardines, but since this was a very cheap and common food in Portugal, Luis thought that it was below his dignity ever to serve sardines and he always pretended there were none in the market. Sometimes I outwitted him, when from the windows I saw fisherwomen carrying huge baskets on their heads. I would then rush down into the street, buy the sardines, and triumphantly present them to Luis.

The way Portuguese women carried everything made John say that Portugal was certainly one country where women really used their heads.

The bond I share with the Portuguese fishwives is our common hatred of shoes. I am happiest when walking barefoot, and so are they. I would see fisherwomen walking along the streets, straight backed, long necked, and on their heads those immense baskets filled with silvery fish, and perched perilously atop, a pair of shoes. There was a law in Portugal obliging everyone to wear shoes. When a fisherwoman would spot a policeman, with lightning speed the shoes would come off their perch. Without removing the basket from her head or spilling even one sardine, the woman would put them on and hobble a few steps until the policeman was out of sight. Then back went the shoes where they really belonged—on top of the fish basket. I watched them going through that act with the agility of circus acrobats, sometimes two or three times in a city block.

The bull ring in Lisbon also is a show place for the remarkable agility of the Portuguese. Shamefully, I must confess that I am an *aficionada*. Yes, I know, the poor horses of the picadors, the poor badgered bull, but if nothing is more hideous than a bad corrida, a good one is a most beautiful, most exciting spectacle.

I never missed a good bullfight in Lisbon, but I had to go without John, who had tired of bullfighting. John had been a great aficionado in his younger days in Madrid, and it is said that he once played a bull in a bull ring in the early hours of the morning while still in his white tie and with an opera hat on his head. A ribald friend of John's once explained how John withstood the charge of the enraged animal; he breathed the fumes of champagne into the bull's angrily distended nostrils and the bull passed out. Of course, after this experience at sunrise, any other corrida would have been an anticlimax.

I used to draw a lot of bullfighters. They are such marvelous models with a capacity for immobility, but an immobility never congealed but vibrant and alive. Living as they do under the ever-present shadow of death gives even the youngest of them a great dignity.

There was a young torero, José, who had just started on his career, whom I used frequently as a model and who gave me a revealing explanation about courage. I asked him one day if he was afraid when the bull rushed into the arena. "No, señora," he said earnestly, "I am never afraid, but my feet are."

It was an encounter with the great Mexican *espada* Aruza, which shattered my belief that the wife of an ambassador, as Caesar's wife, is above suspicion. I asked Aruza to sit for a portrait. He arrived flanked by his manager. After a few minutes of polite conversation in the drawing room, I asked Aruza to come to my studio. The manager said, "I am coming too." I explained to him that it disturbed me to have anyone present while working. I was met by a stony stubbornness. The manager was going to accompany him or Aruza would not sit for me. Like an idiot I did not realize at first what it was all about, until suddenly it dawned on me that Aruza was fighting a big corrida next day and his manager was there as a dueño to protect him from the *femme fatale*. He probably thought that plastic art was just a veiled excuse for the art of seduction. Vastly amused, I took the dueño into the studio, where he sat in a corner for the next few hours drinking cokes and watching me constantly and suspiciously while I worked. He only relaxed when he saw the finished drawing, which at last convinced him that I was a professional artist.

For decades Portugal has been overshadowed by the mysterious, enigmatic personality of Salazar, who rules as perpetual prime minister. John used to see him quite often, but I met him only once when he asked us both to tea.

I had watched him from afar at a solemn Te Deum, and had been impressed by his extraordinary self-discipline. Except in the ballet, I have never seen anyone with such a control over his body. During the service, which lasted an hour, he sat without a single visible movement. If not for the few instances when he had to rise or kneel with the congregation, one would have taken him, with his pale ascetic face and his long white hands, for one of the many Gothic sculptures that filled the cathedral.

154

In Portugal, where to be without servants is a mark of extreme poverty, it was astonishing to find none present when we went to see him. He opened the door himself and served tea that was already set on a table in a neo-Louis XVI salon. And what an inhospitable room it was. Every piece of furniture was rudely shouting "Get out." Not a chair, not a sofa that corresponded to the human anatomy. The physical discomfort of sitting in a cramped position on hard, contorted chairs was heightened by the severity, the abstract politeness that emanated from our host. Never in my life have I felt as much of an interloper in spite of our host's perfect amiability. It was like intruding into a monk's cell while the monk was in contemplation.

This visit would have been an ordeal if not for the fascination of watching every one of Salazar's movements, his pouring tea, serving cakes with calm and slow gestures as if performing some solemn ritual, and for the mysterious magnetism of this man who is a puzzling blend of dictator, pure spirit, and mystic. Frail of health, he has always taken perfect care of himself. He neither smokes nor drinks and eats sparingly. His capacity for work is said to be fantastic. His strength seems to lie in his aloofness from personal motives. He wants nothing material for himself; he practices no nepotism. He fits nowhere into any conventional political pattern.

We spoke French, but it is characteristic of that visit that I cannot recall a word of the conversation. The visit remains implanted in my memory like a stifling, silent movie.

John saw much of Salazar in connection with the Azores, which at that time presented great interest to American strategic interests. Indeed, without the facilities for an air base in the Azores, the subsequent airlift to Berlin would have been impossible.

John found Salazar curious and difficult. He had views as tightly laced as the high black shoes he habitually wore. John's job was herculean. He had to convince Salazar, deeply suspicious by nature, that the United States was not engaged in some devious scheme to rob Portugal of an important and cherished colony. Once John had succeeded in this, all was well. Salazar demonstrated great and wise statesmanship. Instead of following the universal practice of mercilessly shaking down Uncle Sam, Salazar granted everything with great elegance, as an act of cordial, generous grace. He did not stoop to a *quid pro quo*. The story of the Azores is rare in the chronicles of international collaboration.

In many ways Lisbon society was as straight-laced as Salazar. The manners and forms of traditional social usage have been preserved to an extent unequaled elsewhere in Europe. It explains why society rocked and reeled through the disrespect of protocol of an American ambassador. The Ambassador, a political appointee, was a man of charm, wealth, and a bachelor. He had also a complete disregard for protocol and at official dinners would always sit pretty girls next to him, announcing "beauty before rank." And notwithstanding his age and dignity, he had a roving eye.

The Ambassador was one day honored with an invitation to dinner from one of Lisbon's greatest hostesses. He accepted the invitation "with pleasure." He arrived at this very formal dinner in an impeccable white tie and with a lovely young creature on his arm. To the hostess he blandly announced, "I accepted with pleasure, and here is Pleasure," and thus he introduced the young lady. She was a lovely model from Paris who had come to Portugal in a fashion show and had caught the Ambassador's fancy.

This is an extreme example of the complications, the anarchy that can result from a debonair and independent approach to the accepted ways of diplomatic life. It was a very funny incident but the Ambassador never realized what trouble it was for his hostess to reseat the table, reshuffle the place cards, and conceal her embarrassment when he brought an uninvited and unwanted guest.

John and I always had a sneaking admiration for the old gentleman. Actually, on the whole, this particular ambassador represented more that was good than what was bad with political appointees. In any event, one cannot deny that he had imagination. Of the others so many were so bad.

I must complain bitterly about political appointees to ambassadorial posts. There are, with of course some magnificent exceptions. But many have been unprepared and conceited couples, their posts obtained in a shocking and shoddy political traffic. Then they are obliged to play a game of which they know neither the rudiments nor the rules. When the political appointee does have aptitude and application, about the time he is really worth his salt, political change removes him and the dreary task of attempting to educate the new politico and his wife begins all over again.

I agree that a man of high quality, with political talent even without service training, might very well be sent abroad to do a job, but this auctioning of posts to the highest bidder regardless of the capacities has always shocked and astonished me. And we are the only country in the world where ambassadorships are on sale in the political bargain basement. Not even Abdul Hamid the Damned stooped to such a practice.

Receptions, formal dinners, lunches, and ceremonies marked the state visit of Evita Perón to Lisbon. Ten-course banquets were the order of the day. She would appear every night dripping with rubies, emeralds, and diamonds, looking like a Byzantine empress, carved in ivory and encrusted with jewels. Doubtless already very ill of the disease that killed her a year later, she had a translucent pallor, without color, just like a lighted alabaster lamp.

She would sit through the interminable dinners not eating a thing, visibly in pain, but always smiling and courteous. I

157

could not help admiring her courage and discipline—a discipline verging on stoicism—which so often is the inheritance of the poor.

Except for that characteristic, there was no sign in Evita of her having been born and raised in abject poverty.

What actresses women are! How quickly and well they learn any role they have to play. When, for instance, a man of modest origin is knighted, he remains a simple man with a title. But when a barmaid marries a duke, she acquires the genuine veneer of nobility in a short time.

And so with Evita. She behaved like a born *grande dame* with a built-in *habitude du monde* that was most impressive.

For some strange reason she took a liking to John and me. The relations between the United States and Argentina were at a very low ebb at that time, but, notwithstanding, during a most formal dinner at the Spanish Embassy, Evita raised her glass to John to toast the United States. She talked at length to me, showing what seemed to be deeply sincere interest in the welfare of the underprivileged and concern over the misery and illiteracy of the Argentine workers. When she complained bitterly about the lack of funds which prevented the Argentine government from helping its people, she was completely oblivious to the incongruity of this, coming from her, while bedecked with the wealth of Croesus in fabulous jewelry.

Perhaps Evita Perón was right, and there was no contradiction. Coming, as she did, from the lugubrious slums, she wanted to tell her people, "I am one of you, but look at me now; look how splendid, how adorned I am." Perhaps she knew the deeply rooted desire of people for beauty, for color, for luxury. Evita's unconventional attitude toward the welfare of the destitute was very similar to the one we encountered in the mountains of Colombia. In that desolately poor village where everything—the people in gray ruanas, the adobe huts, the muddy streets—was drab, colorless, unsmiling, stood the

158

gayest, the most wildly exuberant Spanish baroque church. The church held a great treasure, a gift made in the eighteenth century by a Spanish grandee. It was a monstrance, beautifully gold and green. Clusters of emeralds in the shape of grapes and diamond kernels of wheat were embedded in a sunburst of gold.

The priest who was showing us the monstrance told us that some months before a jeweler from New York had come to see it. He offered to buy the monstrance for a staggering sum of money. The priest submitted the proposition to the people of the village. He explained to his parishioners that the money would improve their lives, build a school, a hospital, and the much-needed road which would permit commerce to develop. The answer was unanimous. It was "No." Under no circumstances would they let the monstrance leave the village. And they were not moved by a superstitious fear of offending God, by taking away something that belonged to His house, but by love of beauty. They even secretly concealed the monstrance lest the priest might sell it against their will. It was restored to the church only after the jeweler left.

Love of beauty, after all, is not the privilege of the rich alone.

John was once given a cigarette box bearing a map of the world, a tiny precious stone marking each one of our posts. The most precious of all stones marks Portugal. Not because it is a charming country with delightful people. Not because John had most interesting work there, not because he was able to negotiate successfully for our bases in the Azores, for which he received commendations from the State Department and the armed forces. But because it is where I had the shattering experience of seeing a miracle.

There have been many saints who were diplomats, but diplomatic life to my knowledge has never produced a saint—

though it is probably as full of miracles as any walk of life, full of private miracles kept in the secret places of the heart.

I witnessed this miracle in broad daylight, together with thousands of people. Since I do not want to be like the nine lepers in St. Luke who incurred the reproof of Christ for not proclaiming the miracle they had witnessed, I will tell what I saw.

Some ninety miles from Lisbon, near the small Portuguese village of Fatima, "A Lady all in white, more brilliant than the sun, dispensing light cleaner and more intense than a crystal cup full of crystalline water, penetrated by the rays of the most glaring sun," appeared to three shepherd children, Jacintha, Lucia and Francisco. On a moor where sheep were grazing, by a small evergreen bush, she appeared six times, asking each time for the world's penance and prayers, for the consecration of Russia to her Immaculate Heart, as only then "Russia will be converted and some time of peace will be granted to humanity." This happened in 1917 on the eve of the Russian Revolution, which she foretold. But she promised that if the world would follow her wish for intense prayer for peace, Russia would be converted and "if it is not done the errors of Russia will spread through every country in the world."

A basilica has been built in Fatima, a hospice and the Bishop's quarters. There also is in the square a fountain whose water is the source of health to many sick people. Otherwise the little village is unchanged. No hotels, no shops, no vendors of objects of piety, no commercialized religion which often diffuses and disturbs the atmosphere of meditation in places of pilgrimage.

When with my nieces Betsy and Barbara we decided to go on a pilgrimage to the Shrine of Fatima, we were told that there was no food, no sleeping accommodation in the village, and that I would better let the Bishop know of our arrival. I did not think that it was the right spirit on a pilgrimage to be pampered and fussed over because of one's official position, and decided to go incognito. Portugal was my second post as ambassadress, and I still believed in the possibility of anonymity. Of course, nothing came of my plans to be unknown and unnoticed. A few hours after our arrival in Fatima, the Bishop heard about it and most graciously offered us a room in his palace. It was a beautiful room dripping with crimson and gold, red brocade on the walls, red silk curtains, and a huge gilded bed. I was busy helping in the first-aid station during the night, but Barbara and Betsy and two young Portuguese girls slept most comfortably in the four-poster bed.

When we arrived the village was already overcrowded. The pilgrims to Fatima did not consist only of the sick, the afflicted, or the petitioners. No, most of them came to Fatima as a gesture of love for the Mother of God. It was the first time I understood what democracy could mean, when I saw this crowd made up of royalty, fisherwomen, the rich, the poor, the intellectuals, the workers, and the beggars. The rich and the mighty had left behind their fortunes, their titles, all the identification of social position; the poor, their just resentment. All had kept only their humanity. I saw there a queen with her crippled little daughter, and nothing distinguished her from any other sorrowful mother, not even her clothes, as nearly all the women wore a scarf on their heads and the same dark undistinguishable clothing. The only hatted woman was an old aristocratic lady who came into the dispensary at three in the morning. In a black taffeta dress, tightly corseted, a black toque with velvet flowers perched on the top of her head, a silver-handled umbrella, and high laced shoes, she had walked the ninety miles from Lisbon, sleeping at any house where the night would find her, as on the road to Fatima all doors are open to pilgrims. The old lady wanted to rest. She refused to lie down, remaining seated on a hard chair. I noticed that her

161

legs above the tightly laced shoes were very swollen, but she would not let me take them off, saying that she would never be able to put them on again. She told me that she was nearly eighty, but that four times a year she walked to Fatima to pay her respects to Our Lady, as she would visit her queen. She sat on the chair till it was time for the early Mass, when straight as a ramrod, on her swollen and bleeding feet, she marched off to church.

That night when the flow of patients was at a low ebb, the doctor in charge of the dispensary told me the story of his conversion, a conversion dating from October 13, 1917, when in the midst of seventy thousand people he witnessed the miracle of the spinning and diving sun. He told me how at that time he was a student of medicine, not merely skeptical of but even hostile to religion, and for whom Mary was a myth, a legendary figure. With a group of his friends he decided to go to Fatima when the news spread that Our Lady promised to appear again to the children. They expected to be able to debunk the supposed apparition in which they saw only mass hypnosis. He stood for hours in the immense crowd, waiting and watching the tree under which the children were kneeling. Suddenly at midday he saw the sun begin to rotate like a wheel and, gyrating, plunge toward the horizon. In the same manner it returned to its former position. He told me how he fell on his knees, suddenly knowing that he was not in the presence of a phenomenon scientifically explainable, but of a supernatural sign.

Since that day this doctor, one of the great ones in Portugal, comes to Fatima every thirteenth of each month to look after the sick pilgrims.

In the morning, with Betsy and Barbara, we went to the Mass of the *doentes* that was held in front of the church. After the service, there was a complete silence, a silence charged with indescribable tension. As if caught in an invisible net of

162

hope and expectation, we watched the priest descend the steps of the church, holding high the Sacred Host in a monstrance. He walked into the square, where, as around the pool of Bethesda there "lay a great multitude of the sick, blind, lame and those with shrivelled limbs." The priest passed between the rows of stretchers, of camp beds, of kneeling people, stopping in front of every one, holding the Host before their eyes and imploring God to heal them.

On a stretcher a few feet from where we stood was a paralyzed young woman with an inoperable cancer of the spine. She was lying motionless, no expression on her waxen face. Someone had crossed her arms on her chest and entwined a rosary around her fingers. We had noticed her because she looked so young, so pathetic, so hopeless.

When the priest stopped in front of her, even before he finished the short prayer, the girl suddenly sat up, stretched her arms toward the Host, and in an agonized voice screamed, "I am cured, I am cured!" She jumped off the stretcher and ran sobbing into the arms of her mother, who was standing nearby.

I stood petrified and felt as if the marrow was melting in my bones. There was a moment of dead silence. Then suddenly, like the surf of a stormy sea, a thundering roar of aves rose from the crowd. The joy, the delight of the pilgrims in the miraculous healing of the young woman, the lack of envy, of bitterness, the fact that all gave a hosanna of thanks and none said, "Why not I?" "Why not *my* child?" was the second miracle of that memorable morning.

XVI

WE HAD BEEN IN PORTUGAL LESS THAN A YEAR WHEN John was transferred to Iran. John's orders were the only unperemptory ones that we had ever received from the State Department. They read in substance that John could decline the new assignment and remain in Portugal "without prejudice." The State Department indicated that it would, however, like him to go to Iran. All in all it was a marvelous telegram. Of course John decided to go.

I was overjoyed, since all my life I had wanted to see the country that had given to the world jasmine, roses, tulips, Hafiz, and Avicenna.

But my joy was short-lived.

When she heard the news of our transfer the wife of a Dutch diplomat, who had spent two years in Persia and hated every minute of it, came rushing over in the hope of changing our minds. She spent hours telling me gory stories of dreadful Asiatic diseases, diseases that are ready to pounce on every foreigner the very minute he sets foot on Iranian soil. The list was endless—the Baghdad boil, which eats out large holes in one's face, preferably on the nose; trachoma, which blinds; dysentery, which leaves one weak and shaky for months. She told stories about the polluted water, the dirt, and the utter lack of sanitation. I kept repeating stubbornly to myself "jasmine, roses, miniatures, Ispahan" while thinking "Baghdad boil, trachoma, dysentery."

We had served in the tropics and in many other unsanitary

places. In the course of years I had developed a fatalistic attitude towards disease, the knowledge that hypochondriacs suffer more than the sick and that a brave man dies but once; but trachoma scared me. When we first reached the Middle East and I saw in the streets so many inflamed, pus-filled eyes, I became like a nonmurderous Lady Macbeth, washing my hands all day long, opening doors with my elbow, never touching anything without gloves.

It was becoming an obsession, until one day a secretary of our embassy remarked that he had contracted trachoma in New York City, presumably from hanging onto a strap in the subway. On hearing this, my silly panic suddenly vanished. For the rest of our stay trachoma became one of those things one should watch but not worry about.

I did learn though to diagnose it by rolling the eyelids on a match stem to see if there was granulation. This I did periodically to the people who worked for us, since it is very catching but easily cured if diagnosed in time.

Teheran, which I had imagined in the form of an Oriental dream, looked in reality like a European nightmare, a mud-colored provincial German city, filled with people rushing around in nightgowns. It was Reza Shah Pahlavi, the father of the present Shah, who in his desire to turn Teheran into a modern city had imported German architects. They succeeded only in robbing it of its Persian dignity by creating a town with neither character nor sense.

But who should blame Reza Shah for cutting big avenues through the maze of dirty, narrow streets, which even if they had attraction for tourists had nothing to commend and everything to condemn them? Who can blame him for his desire to wipe out slums, no matter how picturesque they were, in order to build decent houses? His mistake was that he was in too great a hurry to destroy the past, too eager to convert Teheran into an impressive national capital. The results were

165

jerry-built modern buildings, now crumbling away in the same remorseless fashion—but with less charm—as the few remaining old ones; and a town that had lost its memory without acquiring either beauty or the glaze of modernity.

But still there is beauty in Teheran, as the aberrations of the human mind could not destroy the splendor of the iridescent sky, of the austere, serene, detached, snow-capped mountains that surround the desert plateau on which Teheran stands. One immediately gets the impact of the dramatic extremes and contradictions are so characteristic of Iran—the blazing sun and the cool shades, the dusty desert, and the green elms and willows that grow wherever there is a little water.

And an apotheosis of blue everywhere. A French writer called Iran the "queen of the blues." How right he was. The blueness is everywhere from the intense sky to the most humble object. Indigo blue are the roofs of the mosques, cerulean the tiles of the fountains, pale blue the cloth of the peasant, and turquoise blue the beads draped around the necks of the donkeys.

Our embassy in Teheran stood in a huge compound filled in the spring with wild hyacinths and little striped tulips. It was surrounded by a high wall and guarded by seventeen Iranian gendarmes who stepped straight out of *The Pirates of Penzance*. Why they were there and what they guarded us against has always been a mystery to me.

The gendarmes slept, cooked, ate, dressed, bathed, and prayed quite publicly in two open tents just inside the gate. They also amused themselves by throwing stones at our poodles. In revenge, Polita, the matriarch, formed her numerous, benign, gentle offspring into a ferocious poodle pack. They pursued the gendarmes relentlessly. From that time on I was constantly busy replacing gendarmerie khaki pants that were literally torn off them by the poodles and furnishing first

166

aid for countless bites and scratches. Oddly enough, the gendarmes took it very philosophically. They never complained.

The gendarmes also cultivated a large patch of white and pink poppies. The first few months we were in Teheran, in my innocence, I impressed American visitors with the love of the Persians for flowers, using as a graphic example how the tough gendarmes worked so hard to be able to enjoy the beauty of poppies.

My illusions were shattered when a friend of mine who had lived years in the East showed me that each poppy had a deep incision from which trickled a white goo. It was, of course, a crude form of opium, which the gendarmes dried and smoked.

The one-storied embassy residence, with its collapsing ceilings, floors and walls adorned with long, ominous, zigzag cracks, looked like a Charles Addams house. For more than ten years emissaries from the Foreign Buildings Office of the State Department periodically inspected the building, shook their heads in dismay, and reported in alarm "unfit for human habitation." But the Department, always short of funds and rather like the Catholic Church in its patient approach to the passage of time, did nothing about it. And until fairly recently the doomed chiefs of mission kept on living in the shadow of imminent danger.

There must have been a special guardian angel delegated to see to it that the living room was empty of people—as it happily was—when the massive plaster ceiling crashed down like an Alpine avalanche and, miraculously, supported my bed, with me in it, when the rotted floor in our bedroom collapsed. We seemed always to escape calamity but not embarrassment. Embarrassing, indeed, was the moment when the kitchen ceiling gave way right over the stove and buried under the plaster and debris was our luncheon, just as it was to be served to an array of official guests. (We all sought refuge in a restaurant.)

Embarrassing also was the melting wall in my bathroom. The walls of the embassy, as was customary in Teheran, were made of adobe. After a severe winter, when the thaw set in, the walls started to go. Every day the hole got bigger and bigger. In the Orient one lives by the proverb, "Hurry was invented by Satan," so before we could get anybody to repair it, I had to sit on the floor, chattering from cold, to do my ablutions in order not to be seen by the passers-by.

The plumbing, too, was very ancient, but devoid of the charm of antiquity. The water closet was strangely capricious. There was either no water or there would be sudden cascades inundating the bathroom. Once we nearly drowned a charming, elderly senator who was staying with us. He suddenly found himself in the dilemma of a man going over Niagara Falls, but without the conventional barrel. John used to explain that we really had hot running water since the servants used to run from the kitchen to the bathrooms with huge pitchers.

Living abroad, we learn not to take too many things for granted. Such as water, for instance. Every time I turn on the tap and crystal-clear water comes pouring out instead of mud, sand or leeches, I bow my head in thankfulness. I know what a divine gift water is. In Iran, *ab,* meaning water, is said to be the most important word in the Persian language. The water in Persian towns used to flow in the streets through *jubes* or open sewers before it got into kitchen or bathroom. As people in the streets used it to wash themselves, their clothes and their horses, it was not very clean by the time it reached the house.

The more fortunate people in Teheran had a *qanat,* a miniature subterranean aqueduct. It was usually three feet high and two feet broad and ran for many miles from a mountain stream. The inclination and flow are perfectly calculated. How? It is apparently an ancient hereditary genius that permits Persians to work like moles, sometimes several hundred feet underground, with such exquisite skill. The *qanats* are supposed to be beautifully pure, but when John had the water of the one running through the embassy grounds analyzed, it was found to be full of virulent bacteria. A sweet story was told us by a previous ambassador. Our *qanat* flows through a room called a *zerzamin,* and its cool water makes the room deliciously fresh in summer. One afternoon, when guests were sitting in the embassy's *zerzamin,* the Ambassador proudly declared that *qanat* water was so pure it could be drunk without boiling. At that very instant the startled guests saw a dead dog come floating by!

Fortunately a new and modern water system is now being completed in Teheran.

The embassy servants consisted of a cook and two vague, inefficient but amiable and friendly menservants. They could not read or write but, with the prodigious memory of the illiterate, knew by heart not only the Koran but also the great Persian poets. One of the servants, Iskander, used to recite different poems for different chores—Omar Khayyám when dusting, Saadi when starting the fire with little pieces of kindling in the iron water heater in our bathroom, and Hafiz when waiting for the guests to arrive. This approach to housework did not help very much to make the embassy spick and span, but it created a delightful atmosphere of unreality. One can never train Persian servants; they have too much imagination and too much individuality to do the same thing twice in the same way. But as soon as I gave up hope of efficiency or fixed routine I enjoyed having them around and the housework was always done sometime and somehow.

Three servants in a large embassy were not very many, but it worked out all right due to our two personal Chinese boys and to what I used to call the "miraculous multiplication" of the servants. Every time we gave a party, masses of young and old people would materialize, for all I could tell, from outer space. One would find them scrubbing, peeling potatoes, making sandwiches, etc. They were never paid, but I was told they had the privilege of taking the leftovers home and after a large party there never was even a grain of rice left. It was as if a plague of locusts had descended on the buffet. I think it was a very fair arrangement, but all the time we were in Persia we could never put to use a very important French cookbook called *The Art of Accommodating Leftovers*. All the foreign housewives who fought the battle of leftovers were always defeated by this same silent and stubborn erosion.

Our cook Mohammed Ali was a cheerful rascal escaped from the fabulous pages of Hadji Baba. He had a charming personality always illuminated by a smile of white teeth. His talent for cooking and his spectacular dishonesty were proverbial in Teheran. He had been, off and on, the Embassy cook for many years. Conscious that he was the only great chef in town, he did not care if one discovered the outrageous discrepancies in his market bills. He did not pad his bills. He created them, as you would create a work of art entirely based on imagination. I had a sneaking fondness for Mohammed Ali since there was nothing mean or underhanded in his dealings. I used to fire him periodically. Then he would come back saying how sorry he was. And, of course, I would take him back. He knew that if he asked for forgiveness I had to pardon him.

It is a creed in Iran that, whatever the offense, you must forgive once forgiveness is asked. General Schwartzkopf, at that time American head of the Gendarmerie Mission, told me about an American lieutenant who was rude to an Iranian colonel in Schwartzkopf's house and was put in jail for the offense. The offended colonel would come every day to General Schwartzkopf asking him to forgive the lieutenant since he had begged for forgiveness. That, under the circumstances, Schwartzkopf insisted that the lieutenant be punished worried the colonel more than being insulted by a junior officer in the presence of foreigners.

I heard another story from the general about one of his Iranian friends who, while playing poker, lost $200. He discovered that the winner was cheating. The outcome was typically Iranian. The friend explained that, "He confessed to cheating but asked my forgiveness, so of course I had to forgive him." The delightful part of the story is that the money was not returned. The ritual is for the offender to kiss the right shoulder of the offended and all sins are forgiven.

Poor Mohammed Ali was very suspicious of and unlucky with electrical appliances. One afternoon he burst into my room screaming with pain and fright. The pressure cooker had exploded and had thrown ground coffee in his face. The fact that for a year we had told him repeatedly never to use the cooker for preparing coffee probably added to his panic. Of course, it would happen in the summer, on a Friday, the Moslem Sabbath, a day when all doctors are in the country or unreachable. The cook's eyes were full of coffee grounds, and it took me two hours to clean them out with an eye dropper and a solution of weak tea. My special medical guardian angel must have stood by my side, as my ministration worked and he recovered.

As the electric current was not strong enough for a washing machine, all our laundry was done by hand by an elderly woman. The washerwoman used to arrive at daybreak wrapped in her *tchedor*, with a corner of it between her teeth to conceal her face. The *tchedor* is a large cotton sheet which transforms Persian women into eerie ghosts. It covers them from head to foot with only one eye peeping out. In the old days the law requiring women to wear veils was strictly observed. But Reza Shah tore the veil off their faces by imperial decree, a decree which led to a lot of divorces since many a husband did not mind the ugliness of his wife as long as he was the only one to know about it. Now the women of the people again wear the *tchedor,* not always from a desire for modest concealment but as a conveniently cheap garment and also as a sop to religious superstitions. It trails in the dirt of the streets behind the woman, who often believes that it erases her footsteps so that Satan cannot track her down.

The system of washing clothes had not changed since biblical days. It consisted of rubbing the soiled linen between two stones. It efficiently removed the dirt, but the fabric disappeared with it. I got our washerwoman a washboard and detergents, but neither reproaches nor cajoling could persuade her to abandon her ancient manner of doing the laundry. To save my lingerie from being massacred, I used to hide it, so as not to hurt her feelings, and wash it myself when the household was asleep.

My *badji,* if she knew the history of the Middle Ages, must have thought that I was like Queen Guinevere, the one who made a vow not to change her chemise until her husband came back from the Crusades. If she had known that I did my own washing, she would not only have been hurt but I would have lost face.

I fully realize that some well-intentioned persons would object to this expression which, according to them, smacks of the past colonial era. But those who imagine that in Asia democracy is demonstrated by dressing shabbily, riding streetcars and bicycles instead of in motorcars, and doing manual chores, are sadly misinformed. In the traditional Asian societies with their background of ancient civilizations, the people have a great sense of what is appropriate and fitting. An ambassadress does not cook, wash or sweep the floor. Her role should be decorative and matriarchal. She is there to help, to console, to take part in the joys and sorrows of the people who work for her. They do not want mediocrity in egalitarianism, but understanding and love.

172

The way to show the reality of democracy is to dry-clean ourselves of our Western arrogance, our superiority complex when in countries with cultures other than ours, or else it will be regarded as a proof of our intellectual imperialism. One must have respect for Asian people's religion, customs and sense of values and not fling at them, as we do, the dogma that our high standard of living makes us superior to them.

What perhaps proved that John and I were right in thinking in that way were the many deep friendships we made in Iran with people from every walk of life. The greatest compliment that was ever paid to me came from a group of beggars in Teheran.

I used to go on Sundays to Mass in a small Italian church. At the door of it there was assembled a group of beggars; they were always the same group. I am sure they had some kind of informal concessions, as each church had its own cluster of beggars. During the two and a half years we spent in Iran I got to know them very well. There was, for instance, an old man with whom I had a standing feud. The first time I saw him on a very cold winter day, he wore a shift so full of holes that he was practically naked. I rushed home and brought him a warm woolen shirt. Next Sunday he was back in his old one, having sold the other. I gave him another one and some money and sternly made him promise to keep the shirt at least till summer. He kept his promise for a week or two, then the old worn shift reappeared. He laughed and said that he had torn the shirt I had given him, and would I get him another. It was a game we played throughout my stay.

One could help some of the young beggars by finding them jobs but many of them, women and men, unskilled and old, one could not really help. One could only alleviate their poverty by gifts of food, clothing, and money.

When we came back on a short visit to Teheran five years later I went on the morning of our arrival to an early weekday

Mass. When I was entering the church, I suddenly heard a voice screaming *"Khanum-i-safir-kabir,"* which means ambassadress. I turned and saw one of my beggar friends, an old woman with hennaed hair escaping from under her *tchedor*. She kissed my shoulder, telling me how happy she was to see me back and hoping that we could stay in Teheran. We had a little talk and then I went into the church. When I came out, I found that she had rounded up all the beggars I had known years before. They were waiting for me with flowers in their hands and chanting in a chorus *"Doost-i-azia,"* dear friend. Since it was a weekday, I could not imagine how she managed to find all of them so quickly. But there they were, embracing me and making me welcome. To be remembered after so many years by people who should only have bitterness and resentment toward someone who did not share their poverty and for someone who was a stranger, an "infidel," was a great example of real friendship.

The notion of "infidels" has survived in some Moslem countries still faithful to the blind religious fanaticism of the past. In Iran the church I went to in Teheran had once been the chapel of the Italian Embassy in the times when Christian churches were not permitted. It had become a real publicly attended church under Reza Shah and remained so under the present Shah, who is broad-minded in questions of religion. This transition has undoubtedly been helped by the devotion the Moslems have always had to the Virgin Mary, whom they call Myriam, and lately to some of our saints. I often saw veiled women praying in our little church and lighting votive candles.

Some of these Moslem people travel spiritually in their own strange ways, showing that baptism is not a visa on a passport. There is a curious story which illustrates it. A priest who ministered in another church in Teheran told me that one day when he was in the refectory he suddenly heard coming from the church the most heartbreaking, anguished bleatings. He rushed over and saw an old Moslem, complete with turban and the henna beard of the pilgrims to Mecca, cutting the throat of a sheep, whose blood was flowing in front of the statue of St. Thérèse of Lisieux. When the priest tried to stop this strange procedure, the Moslem, bewildered and puzzled, explained that he had asked a favor of St. Thérèse and when she granted it he decided out of thankfulness to sacrifice a sheep for her in the Moslem tradition. I have always wondered what St. Thérèse thought about this unique offering.

The possibility of friendship with Moslem upper-class women came to me as a surprise, for I had expected them to be lazy, haremlike creatures with whom no conversation was possible. I mistakenly patterned them on the wife of a Moslem ambassador on whom I made an official call at the very beginning of our stay in Teheran. During this visit, after the first salaam, the conversation went this way:

The Ambassadress: "Have you any children?"

I: "No."

She: "Is your husband still young?"

I: "Yes."

She: "Is he going to take another wife?"

I: "I don't know, but I don't think so."

She: "What strange men, those Americans."

End of conversation. And for the rest of the thirty minutes of the call we consumed a great quantity of gooey sweets in a smiling silence.

So it was a great joy for me to find many sensitive, intelligent, educated women in Iran, totally unlike my Moslem fellow ambassadress. I remember with affection and admiration my many Iranian women friends as each one of them was not only a friend but an interesting human being. Among them was the older sister of the Shah, the green-eyed Princess Shams, who stood aloof from the many unavoidable intrigues of the imperial court. Another Persian lady with the same attributes of kindness and beauty, the wife of our marvelous embassy doctor, was prophetically called Malek, which means angel.

She introduced me to the delight of the *hamam*. We Westerners have an erroneous idea that with our daily scrub, bath salts and deodorants, we are the cleanest people in the world. I thought so too, until my first visit to the *hamam*. The Persian *hamams* are different from our Turkish baths. They are like a beehive with tiny rooms covered with tiles, each with steam pouring in. Then there is a marble slab and a shower. You sit there for hours in the steam, until a *badji* appears in a *tchedor,* which she immediately discards and, stark-naked, takes you in hand. First she puts henna on your hair and nails and then, armed with a hard horsehair *loofah* and a white soft stone, she starts rubbing your body. The first time I was under her ministration, I saw in horrified fascination, gobs of dirt roll from under her *loofah*. I stopped her, exclaiming, "Your washcloth is dirty. Please get a clean one." This was received with delighted laughter. "It is not the washcloth that is dirty, it is *you.*" And she was right. I had never realized how much dirt can accumulate in one's pores that no showering or bathing can get at. A lot of my Western superiority was sweated out of me that day. It gave me also a new understanding of the much-advertised Oriental dirt. Poverty too frequently covers their bodies with filthy, torn garments, but their bodies are often clean, as even the poorest manages sometimes to get to the *hamam* and be steam cleaned.

No country has the cult of "body beautiful" more than Persia. It comes probably from the harem tradition, where women had nothing to do but invent new ways of improving and keeping their looks. I cannot understand why our beauticians don't learn from this magic. The *rishur,* a white hard substance that leaves the skin velvet soft, then the *some,* a mixture of nut oil and some other mysterious substance that makes the eyes luminous and languorous, and of course a mass of different depilatories as hair anywhere on the body is considered not only ugly but dirty.

There is one method of depilation that I do not advise except to masochists. One day Malek sent me an old woman who was supposed to give my legs the appearance of Aegean marble. She looked like the deadly Fate, Atropos, when she sat cross-legged on the floor with a long white thread between her teeth, which with an incredible dexterity she would wind around each hair, pull, and out it would come. I do not know of a slower and more painful process, but, like a juggler's act, it was fascinating to watch.

The husband of Malek, Dr. Radji, took care of us in all our illnesses, together with another prominent physician, Dr. Egbal, who has since been prime minister of Iran. The general standard of the Teheran medical practitioners was high, due to the intelligence of the Iranians, who when given the chance to study abroad make first-class doctors. Alas, when we were in Iran few could afford it. The medical corps was very small and mostly concentrated in Teheran, thus leaving large areas of the country without medical help. Even with the many doctors, in Teheran on the Moslem Friday (which is like our Sunday) in the summer none could be found. They would all disappear somewhere in the country. One of my girl-scout ventures was due to that doctorless day.

Late one night an excited Arab arrived at the embassy announcing that his master was dying, would we help. It was the servant of the Saudi Arabian Ambassador, who spoke only Arabic. He had called on John a few days before and developed a great liking for him. So in his emergency he turned to him. We had a list of doctors and John tried to reach them one by one by telephone. But it was Friday and none could be found. We were getting more and more anxious, since from the vociferous and hectic description of the messenger, the Ambassador was practically at the Pearly Gates. John woke up one of our secretaries who spoke Arabic and had him come over. He told me, "Irena, go to the Saudi Embassy, take a look and take some penicillin along, and ring me back, I'll keep on trying to get a doctor." So off we went. The eerie and strange atmosphere of the completely dark house with Arabs clad in burnooses sleeping on the floors and stairs. One had to step over them like walking on a battlefield to get to the Ambassador's bedroom.

In the bedroom in a large mahogany bed in a spectacular nightgown lay my patient. His face was bright red, his eyes were glazed with fever and terror. I took his temperature. 104! Then the routine questions started. "Does your stomach hurt?" "No." "Does your right side hurt?" "No." "Are you nauseated?" "No." My rudimentary medical knowledge permits me only to diagnose pneumonia, appendicitis, food poisoning and measles, and that only when the symptoms are glaring. I was completely baffled until I suddenly noticed that he had a swollen cheek. New questions: "Does your tooth hurt?" "Oh, yes, very bad yesterday, but not today." "Have you seen a dentist?" "No." So an abscessed tooth looked like the answer.

I told the Ambassador that he was not going to die, that he needed a shot of penicillin and a dentist, that John was trying to find a doctor but if he did not, I would give it to him myself. The joy and relief in his face was really touching. But he said that he did not want a doctor, that I was his doctor, and that he wanted only me to give it to him. But I did prefer to have a doctor do it, especially as I felt sure the emergency was not great. In those days penicillin was still in wax and had to be injected in the place in the back where it loses its polite name. My knowledge of protocol had not prepared me for handling that situation. By then it was three in the morning and I de-

178

cided to wait another hour. The pressure of the Ambassador became such—"You my doctor, no other doctor"—that I decided to give it to him. I was boiling the needle when there appeared a doctor whom John had finally managed to find. So my modesty was saved. It was an abscessed tooth after all. The Minister's gratitude was such that at every party he always rushed toward me in his flowing robes to greet me with "Salam, my doctor, salam." He even wrote to his king and I was given the rare privilege of going to the capital where women are seldom admitted. Perhaps some day I shall go.

The friendly and understanding attitude so characteristic of the Persians prevented making a catastrophic fiasco of our very first official function.

Have you ever, dressed in a white Dior evening gown, delivered seven puppies while giving your first official dinner in a new post? That combined role of ambassadress, veterinary, and midwife fell upon me. It left me looking like yesterday's gardenia and nearly a nervous wreck.

At that time we had two poodles, one a black male called Pushkin, perhaps the greatest gentleman in the canine world, and his wife, Polita. Polita had a brown fringe over yellow, dissipated eyes and was utterly ferocious. She was also in an advanced state of pregnancy, which made our trip from Lisbon to Iran, via Rome, Cairo, and, oddly enough, Saudi Arabia, slightly difficult, as Polita was suffering car, sea, and air sickness morning, noon and night. It sometimes became most embarrassing, especially when it happened on the new light-blue velvet upholstery of the car of our ambassador in Rome.

When we finally reached Teheran, I found to my dismay that there was no veterinary in the whole city. Also, there had apparently never been a poodle in Persia. But our two poodles had such success that telegrams immediately went from the Shah's palace to Paris, and Air France planes began importing poodles for the court and cosmopolitan Iranians. After a year the place was swarming with poodles. We felt very much like the man who brought the first couple of rabbits to Australia. Luckily, poodles do not breed quite so fast or so copiously, but John spoke often of the rising tide of poodles.

We had always had male dogs, so I was without experience in *accouchements,* and the lack of a vet was most disquieting. Luckily the charming wife of a member of the British Embassy, Lady Screen, was an expert. She even opened the first animal clinic in Teheran. Lady Screen patiently instructed me in the procedure of delivering puppies, and also asked me to call her up for advice at any time, day or night, when the great event was taking place.

A few days after our arrival, John having presented his credentials to the Shah, we gave our first official dinner for the Cabinet. That day John came down with a high fever (it turned out to be sandfly fever) and the doctor made him stay in bed. So I had to receive the guests alone. When I was all dressed, waiting for them, Han, our Chinese major-domo, came running into the sitting room announcing, "Polita has started to have puppies." I rushed Polita into the basement, where I had prepared her delivery room, and waited. When the first puppy appeared, I fed her warm milk as Lady Screen had instructed. Then I rushed upstairs to greet the first distinguished arrivals. For two hours I kept rushing into the basement to help Polita, then rushing back to attend to the guests and to telephone Lady Screen for additional advice. And so I would get up from dinner, murmur a feeble excuse, and deliver another puppy. After the sixth, which I thought was the last, I relaxed and tried to be amiable. But at the dessert Han whispered in my ear, "One more puppy is arriving." After each excursion to the basement, more spots and more creases appeared on my dress, which by the end of the evening looked like an abstract painting. I tried to drape, to pull my skirt so that the ravages would not show, but all my contortions were in vain. One of the lessons I learned during that hectic night was not to wear a white satin dress when serving as midwife.

I have often wondered what my Persian guests thought about my strange behavior on that occasion, but now that I know their philosophy of life I am sure they probably found a most charitable explanation for their flushed, vacant-eyed, disappearing hostess.

That was the only time Polita ever chose the dinner hour for giving birth, which was fortunate as she had many more litters while we were in Teheran. She would choose the middle of the night instead. She was an independent creature who did not sleep in our bedroom but would roam the house and the compound. But when her time came she would creep into our bedroom, pull off my bedclothes and nuzzle me until I woke up and came down with her to the basement.

Poodles must have a Chinese respect for the male sex, as neither Polita nor Pushkin (who always slept in our bedroom) would ever wake up John when an emergency arose. They always awakened me while John slept blissfully on.

The official parties in Teheran have less *taedium vitae* than in many other posts, since the winter is short and for the rest of the year one entertains in gardens. It never is so bad when the ceiling does not reverberate the cacophonic noise of many voices, when you can look at trees and flowers, when people are relaxed due perhaps to the murmur of the ever-present fountains. Relaxing also are the multicolored carpets invading every surface.

The charming Persian habit of putting carpets everywhere, on the grass, on the roads, on the street, in gardens, the fact that every Persian, even a beggar, owns a carpet, is probably due to the dead desolation of the desert around them. In that country, where water is so scarce, where cultivating a garden is a privilege of the very few, a carpet is the nearest approach to a garden. A Persian rug, with its stylized roses, leaves, cypresses, is like a tiny portable garden. That is probably why I have seen poor people sitting on their small carpets on the sidewalks of dusty, dirty, sandy streets with the same enjoyment as we would sit on the flower-studded grass in our back yard. Sometimes illusion awakens the realities of life.

I liked all about Iran except the fact that I rarely saw John. The hard-working ambassador is a product of this century, to judge by the description of the leisurely life of diplomats before World War I.

Early in the morning John would disappear in a whirlwind of telegrams, visitors, reports, and meetings, and I would see him only at night while, like quick-change artists, we would jump into our evening clothes. Sometimes I would catch a glimpse of him across a flowering centerpiece at an official lunch. It was not very satisfactory, so you can imagine how happy I was when one morning for the first time in months John announced "All is quiet. There is nothing on the agenda that can't wait. I have decided to take a day off and we can go swimming, walking or just do nothing." It seemed marvelous to have a whole day together without interruption or interference. We went for a ride, a swim in our water reservoir that served as a pool, and after a leisurely lunch and a siesta, we settled down to a game of gin rummy. It was all so peaceful. The servants were somewhere taking their siestas, when suddenly the door of our sitting room was thrown open with a crash, and into the room burst Bochram Shabrok, Iranian Director of Propaganda screaming "Hadjir has been assassinated." And thus tragically ended our one day of privacy.

We very much liked Hadjir, who was then the powerful Minister of Court. We were naturally deeply shocked—so horrified we rushed to the hospital where they had taken him. There, under the cruel light of a naked bulb hanging from the ceiling, on a little narrow iron bed in a room jammed with

182

people, we saw Hadjir. He was dying and knew it. But in the great tradition of the Persians, or perhaps of all deeply religious people, he showed only dignity and courage. When he saw us, he smiled, took my hand, and with that exquisite Persian politeness that had not deserted him, even in his agony, he whispered "How kind of you to come, it gives me so much pleasure." He died a few hours later.

I could never understand why Persians who have a great respect for human dignity have none for human life.

Political assassination dates from "the Old Men of the Mountains" nearly 1000 years ago. Always, hashish, which is the origin of the word assassin, plays a great role. An eminent mullah told a friend of mine "Give me a young man for one night and I will make an assassin out of him."

Not even the Shah's life is respected. After we had been in Iran a few months an assassin in the guise of a press photographer approached within a few feet of the Shah during an official ceremony. He fired point blank at the Shah and five bullets hit his person. Three went through his military cap, one through his cheek without hitting a tooth, and one through his shoulder without touching a bone. He had a miraculous escape.

The Shah's physical courage is superb. In the pandemonium that followed and covered with blood he calmly turned to one of his aides and remarked, "What a bad shot."

I always greatly enjoyed receptions at the royal palace, as the Shah has that rare gift of keeping Persian tradition in a modern frame. He seems to follow the dream of the great Alexander to blend the East and the West, and certainly he achieves it in his social life. But it created in him a Hamlet-like duality. So often I have noticed how he was prevented from acting out the role of an Oriental potentate by his Westernized conscience.

His parties were sometimes delightfully unexpected. One evening, during a diplomatic reception, the Shah's pet leopard wandered in, switching his tail and slowly stalking through the ugly neo-Louis XVI salon, a room redeemed only by its honey-colored alabaster floor. With considerable effort we all pretended we were unafraid and took it as a matter of simple course. Personally, I was so startled that for a moment I was convinced I was having hallucinations. To the relief of all of us, the beautiful animal sauntered quietly out.

The imperial palace, alas, had very few objects of ancient Persian art. When once I almost rudely asked the Shah why there were so few of the superb things of his own country in the palace, he answered, "Because they are all in the museums of Paris, London and New York." And he was right. For hundreds of years conquerors, merchants, kleptomaniac tourists, and diplomats have been removing from Iran all that they could grab, taking advantage of the poverty or indifference of Persian people.

Even the treasures that escaped the foreign grasp have by process of democratization, by the trend to ungild the imperial splendor, been taken away from the court. The crown jewels are now in the prim, modern National Bank vault as a guarantee for the stability of the currency of the country.

The crown jewels are a fabulous show. Showcase after showcase with diamond crowns, tiaras, brooches, rings, seals; casks filled with uncut rubies, diamonds, sapphires. On the walls, dangling casually, ropes and ropes of priceless pearls. In a corner an immense globe made of pure gold, with oceans made of emeralds and continents of a mosaic of precious stones. Strangely enough, there was nothing dazzling, nothing joyful in those fabulous gems. On the contrary, the general impression we received was one of sadness, of forlornness, as if the jewels felt neglected and unloved, if jewels can be said to have such anthropomorphic qualities. They were like ghosts of jewels, without life, without sparkle. In this melancholy accumulation of the gems of the Orient there was only one object

184

that gave me joy to contemplate. It was a three-inch box made of ten flawless emeralds held together probably by magic. Like a green burning fire, it blazed with its own, not a reflected light. I felt it would scorch my fingers if I touched it.

There was enough Oriental décor and enchanting tradition left to give magic and fictitious beauty to the Shah's parties.

One of the most spectacular was the one given by the Shah of Iran for the King of Jordan, Abdullah Abdul, who was assassinated shortly afterward.

His Majesty was receiving his guests in the Mirror Room. The strong lights of the great chandeliers changed into a cascade of diamonds the walls which were entirely covered with a mosaic of fragments of mirror. On that resplendent background the Shah would have looked out of place in an unadorned military uniform, but with an Oriental sense of splendor he had covered his uniform with gold braid, pinning on decorations in gold, silver, enamel, in the shapes of stars, moons, suns, with the wide blue ribbon of the grand cordon. In that way he changed a simple army garb into imperial regalia.

From the ballroom a broad stairway guarded by two stone sphinxlike lions, painted, alas with some kind of silvered aluminum paint, led to the garden where the reception was held, and into fairyland. There were flowers everywhere. Flowers bloomed on bushes that lined the garden path. Patterns of crushed flowers on the carpets were spread over every inch of the lawns. Flowers climbed around the gigantic crystal candelabra standing every few steps, the lighted candles of which seemed like reflected stars of the green night. And fireworks showered over us abstract wreaths and bouquets of flowers from the dark sky.

The beautiful Persian princesses with their large dark eyes, their multicolored gowns, scintillating with jewels and the white flowing robes of the retinue of the King of Jordan, helped to create an Arabian Nights atmosphere.

Something amusing happened at this party. The pretty young wife of our naval attaché unwittingly put herself in an embarrassing situation. Only a few days before her husband and she had been burglarized—everything had been taken out of their house. She was telling the story to one of King Abdullah's aides, saying that now they had a fierce dog to guard their house, and she added, "But it is locking the barn after the horse is stolen." Hearing that, the aide in distress told her, "Your horse has been stolen? How terrible! I will send you a horse from Jordan." She tried to explain her figure of speech, but with the aide's sketchy English he did not understand and kept insisting that he would have a horse delivered to her. The poor girl was desperate. What on earth could she do with a horse in a three-room house? However, the party was over, the next day the King departed, and the aide could no longer be reached. A couple of weeks later a thoroughbred stallion did arrive to Teheran and was brought to the naval attaché's door. It was placed in a stable outside the city and discreetly given to an Iranian friend who was breeding horses. Embassy ladies were advised never to use the dangerous metaphor when chatting with their Arabian acquaintances.

Gala events like those of the Shah are now getting rare, for the West is imposing its conformity on the East and dissolving its old customs. Noisy cocktail parties are replacing serene, slow evenings in gardens; air conditioning is taking the place of the soft breezes from the mountains; harsh electric light has exiled the soft illumination of candles. I have always deplored that our mass-produced goods, our gadgets, our comics, our chewing gum and cocktails take such a hold on some alien cultures while our laws against child labor, our five-day week, our preoccupation with public health and hygiene find so few followers abroad. Why, for example, do the Persians try to copy us when their culture is so much older? Why do they imitate our way of dressing when theirs is so beautiful and so well adapted to their climate? Why do they copy our mannerisms when they have their own traditional politeness?

At the palace, however, much of the old tradition survives, even at unofficial parties.

The Shah frequently asked John for lunch alone, but from time to time I was included. I enjoyed these long friendly lunches which usually lasted three to four hours, as the Shah would throw off the burden of his own importance and become a relaxed and gay companion.

It was the lunches in the summer palace that I selfishly liked the best even if they were torture to John. The meals were served on the lawn under shady plane trees. A white lace tablecloth was spread over a large Persian carpet. Gold and crystal glasses, golden plates engraved with the imperial crown were set as for a formal dinner and we sat on brocade cushions on the ground.

To sit on the floor is no hardship for me. It is even my favorite posture. I do most of my art work sitting cross-legged and I am the only student in the whole existence of the Art School in Vienna who cut her big toe while wood carving. But John is not the lolling type and with his long, long legs it was an excruciating experience. He would look like a suffering, unwilling yoga disciple and his being able to talk sensibly for hours while aching in every joint was an example of mind over matter.

The servants passed the large platters of food, circulating on their knees. Writing about it, it seems shocking, to be served by people on their knees, but in the palace garden it seemed so unservile that one noticed it only to admire their incredible agility in carrying the huge platters, and especially in backing out in that position, since one cannot turn one's back when leaving the presence of the Shah. Besides, there was an excellent technical explanation why the servants remained on their knees, for they could not possibly have served the cross-legged company while they were standing, and to squat alongside of the guests would look ridiculous and undignified.

At those lunches the Shah would often jokingly say to me, "Mrs. Wiley, find me a wife." Then we would half-seriously discuss all the nice Persian girls, but usually discover that some were too Westernized to be able to play the role of a Persian empress and some too Oriental in their upbringing, too harem-minded to be a real companion for the Shah.

Being happily married myself, I have compassion for those who are not and I am usually try to do something about it. As John says, I am my brother's keeper with a vengeance and often without discretion. This preoccupation with the affairs of others led me to take to heart the Shah's loneliness and prompted me to try to arrange an imperial marriage.

One day when leaving the palace I asked John if it would not be possible for the Shah to marry a girl from one of the great semi-independent Persian tribes. I had already had the opportunity of meeting and admiring the broad-minded, hard-riding, gay tribeswomen with their free nomadic way of life. They seemed to me more interesting, much tougher than the submissive creatures of Teheran society.

John thought it might be a good idea, since it might help finally to settle one of the long-standing feuds between the palace and the tribes. The United States was interested in having Iran as united and free of internal strife as could be achieved. The green light from John was all I needed to start meddling in something that was none of my business. Enthusiastically I got in touch with a friend of ours, a high-placed Bakhtiari tribesman and asked him if he had a cousin, niece or sister, about seventeen, beautiful, intelligent, and with some Western education. He was very curious to know why I wanted such odd information, but of course I did not tell him. A few days later he replied that, yes, he had a cousin who corresponded exactly to my specifications. She was beautiful, young, had a German mother and, like the Shah, had been educated in Switzerland. Her name was Soraya.

At our next luncheon the Shah again jokingly said, "Mrs. Wiley, find me a wife." I answered, "Your Majesty, I have found her." He was visibly surprised and interested. "She is Soraya Bakhtiari." The Shah threw up his hands and curtly announced, "I will not marry a tribeswoman." And for the rest of the luncheon the subject was not mentioned.

I was very disappointed by the cold reception of what I thought was a splendid idea. And by the apparent failure of my mission. Just as I was saying good-by, the Shah asked, "What did you say her name was?" "Soraya Bakhtiari, your Majesty," I answered.

The episode took place just before our final departure from Teheran. I learned afterwards that, after reflection, the Shah dispatched one of his sisters to Switzerland where Soraya was studying. She came back ravished by the beauty of the girl, and advised her brother to marry her. Six months later they were married.

I wish they had lived happily ever after, as befitted a royal fairy story, for no one more than the Shah needed and deserved a loyal companion in his lonely job. The fates decreed otherwise. But that is another story.

When writing these lines I cannot help remembering a poem Victor Hugo wrote a hundred years ago. Its first two lines were "The King of Persia, worried and feared, lives in Ispahan in the winter and Tiflis in the summer." Just changing Ispahan for Teheran and Tiflis for Shimran the picture today is still the same. As in the poem, the present Shah is not always certain whom he should trust. He does not—or did not—even know whom to love. It is glorious but very, very difficult to be Shah of Iran.

XVII

I WOULD PROBABLY NEVER HAVE KNOWN WHAT REAL politeness was if we had not lived in Asiatic countries and countries of Spanish culture, where politeness is not a social form but a *Weltanschauung*. It is religion, courtesy, and philosophy all mixed together. In the Islamic world the words "thank you" are never used in addressing people. They are reserved only for God. To people, instead of "thank you," they have other forms of expressing appreciation: "May God give you big pockets," "May your hands be always full," "May your shadow never grow less." The last one is most appropriate for the Near East, where the burning sun and desert are the ferocious enemies of man, shade is the great gift, the lifesaver. Shade and shadow are one in Arabic, and also mean protection. That is why when going on a journey "Go under the shadow of God" is the parting phrase. In the Middle East politeness is paramount, except when tempered by assassination.

Humility and dependence on the will of God are the foundation of Asiatic character and behavior. Never will they say "I will do this or that" without adding *inshallah,* "If Allah is willing." If by any chance the speaker forgets to use these conventional words, the people around him will say "May God's forgiveness be on him." One can never understand the biblical patience, the heroic acceptance of a life deprived of even bare necessities of the people of the East without the

"This is the will of God," which is not just an empty phrase but a deep creed.

Once when meeting the chief of a small tribe in the north of Iran, I said that we hoped to come to visit him. He bowed very low and said, "Come and walk on my eyes." As eyes are so precious, they are referred to very often. For example, instead of "yes," one hears *chasm,* which means "my eyes are yours."

My first encounter with tribes was in Lebanon, where an experience with a tribal chieftain taught me a lesson in true politeness, the one the French call *politesse de coeur.*

Whenever the pressure of work slacked during the summer months we would leave the heat of Teheran to spend a few days in Beirut, the capital of Lebanon. The blue sea, the dark-green hills were so restful, so refreshing after the dust, the heat, the fierce sun of Teheran. There is something of the radiance, the luminosity, the greatness and simplicity of the New Testament in Lebanon, where time does not move since it remains always under the shade of holiness. When one goes to Sidon or Tyre one walks on the same stones that our Lord walked on. The shape of the boats has not changed since the Holy Fishermen were casting their nets. The past is so close to the people of that coast that once in Baalbek, a local guide with complete seriousness and conviction showed us a small stone hut and said, "This is where Adam lived, after he was chased out of Paradise." He found it as natural to have Adam's house preserved as an American guide would when showing a place where Washington had slept.

There is a conglomeration of races and creeds in that small corner of the world—Arabs, Druses, Maronites, Moslems—but in 1951 "the wolf dwelled with the lamb, the leopard lay down with the kid, and they did not hurt or destroy each other." The Communist yeast was already there but active fermentation had not yet begun. The strife and conflicts were in the past or were to come much later.

The Druses in particular intrigued me. I had seen them walk with detached serenity in the streets of Beirut and became possessed of a great desire to draw them.

I was told by our embassy and by my Lebanese friends that it was impossible, since the Druses keep to themselves in their mountain villages and never see foreigners. But luck was on my side and an unexpected friendship with a cab driver named Naim, who turned out to be a Druse, helped me to fulfill my wish. When he found out that I wanted to make a series of drawings, he promised to get in touch with the head of his particular tribe and ask permission. The permission was granted, but for me alone. So one morning at daybreak, armed with drawing pads, paints, and a thermos of tea (a thermos of tea being a part of my anatomy on a trip), Naim and I started on this strange excursion. We drove for hours into the hills until we came to a large brick house. We were led into a big room without furniture, only cushions on the floor. From one of the cushions there rose to greet us with great politeness a most beautiful, spectacular, aristocratic-looking old man, very tall with a white flowing beard and flowing robes made of homespun wool streaked with broad stripes of white and black, an eagle nose and light-turquoise blue Crusader eyes. He moved with the grace and dignity of a mountain cat.

We sat on the floor and I started drawing him while my cab driver friend sat respectfully in the corner acting as interpreter. The chieftain was very interested in America and asked a lot of questions. Curiously enough, not one question was about material things. Not one question about all our technical progress that makes life easier. Only questions about spiritual things that make life more difficult—our religions, our beliefs, our education. For the first hour we were alone. Later one man after another came into the room to greet the chieftain, to sit down and be served a cup of coffee. I noticed that when they were greeting the old man, some would kiss his hand, but he would kiss the hand of others. I asked my friend the reason for this strange protocol. He said: "The chieftain kisses the hand of the poor, and the rich kiss his hand." And with that one silent, courteous gesture, the erratic caprices of fortune were momentarily corrected and justice was re-established with exquisite politeness.

I tried, on my part, to find out about their religion, innocently asking prying questions. With great amiability the chieftain would invariably reply as though he were unveiling deep secrets to me. He confided to me that the name of this strange and mysterious tribe comes from their spiritual leader, Ismail el Doraz, who nearly a thousand years ago brought a new variation of the Islamic faith from Egypt to Lebanon. He told me how Druses marry only Druses, that they do not convert, neither are they converted. Their sect is divided into three groups—the Uninitiated, the Aspirants, and the Wise.

I also learned that an aspirant Druse may revert to the uninitiated but is liable to death should he tell what he knows. The uninitiated do not see sacred writings nor do they know where these documents are. The wise must be modest in their dress and must not swear or use obscene language. They are not allowed to drink or smoke. They are not permitted to dine in official circles or with people who might be suspected of dishonesty. The analogy between the two is odd, or perhaps in Asia it is not.

I was so proud, thinking that I was treated practically as an Aspirant, and that my Slavic charm and ability to paint—the chieftain having been delighted by my sketches—had permitted me to invade their impenetrable secrecy. To my chagrin I learned on my return that all he had told me was common knowledge, was in every book on the subject. He had disarmed me with politeness.

There are a few more things known about them and one, perhaps the strangest, is that the Druses believe that when a

193

man dies a child is born at the same instant. What makes that idea so uncanny is the fact, established by census, that the Druse population in recent centuries has neither decreased nor increased. Well, there are "things on earth and in heaven also."

After we had left the chieftain's village my friend said to me: "There is another village in the mountains, but that is completely taboo for any outsiders. They would stone or shoot any foreigner who would come in. But you are tall and dark, and if you want to see it, I will take you there and explain that you are my cousin from Syria and that you are deaf and dumb. But you must promise not to say a single word all the time you are there."

It is almost too much for me to sit through a whole evening with people talking all the time on the stage and not be able to take part in their conversation. I knew it would be a great hardship, this long silence, but the temptation was so great that I promised and, what's more, I kept my promise.

Why I wanted to go to that village was to draw the Druse women. It was not permitted. I could not do it in the chieftain's home. But when we got to the small village, lost in the mountains, I was taken to a friend's house and one by one, women and children were brought in for me to draw. The women would appear and disappear without a sound, ghostlike under their white veils. Those veils enveloped their heads and fell in graceful draperies to their waists, and long-sleeved, high-necked cotton dresses reached to their feet.

Only one friend of the cab driver, to whose house he took me, knew the secret. While I was working he stood guard outside the house so that no one would come in and see that the women were sitting for me. From time to time he would call out "Attention." With lightning speed I would push all my working implements under me and sit on them cross-legged, pretending to be relaxed.

I could not draw for very long as the news spread that Naim was here with his cousin and everybody wanted to see us. So for the rest of the stay we went from house to house drinking coffee and eating marvelous bread and honey. Three things stood out strikingly in Druse character, cleanliness, dignity, and politeness. Even the poorest house was spotless, even the poorest Druse offered you coffee in a broken cup but with a gesture which would inspire a queen. And not a beggar in the village. No one has ever seen a Druse begging—and that in a part of the world where at each step one is painfully, remorselessly reminded that half of the world is hungry and homeless. All my impressions of this village were, of course, only visual. I did not know their language and since I was pretending to be deaf and mute, no translation was possible.

My second encounter with tribesmen was in Iran.

I have always been fascinated by what I read and heard about Persian nomads and their tribes. I liked to dream about their fierceness and freedom, their galloping horses and uncrowded horizons. I never thought that I would have the opportunity to meet some *in situ*.

Such an occasion presented itself during our stay in Iran, where several nomadic tribes survived the gradual settling of the population on land and preserved their centuries-old way of life. In Teheran we met some highly educated and distinguished members of the tribal aristocracy and were enchanted to accept an invitation to visit the Ghashghais.

The Ghashghais tribe, the largest and most cohesive in Iran, has been dynastically ruled by one family for countless generations. Their system of government is as strange a hybrid as a mermaid or a centaur. It is a feudal democracy.

There are no beggars in the tribes, no degrading philanthropy, only a brotherly spirit of sharing. It might seem contradictory that the four brothers—Nasser Khan, Malek Mansur, Hossein, and Khosro—who are at the head of the tribe, are all powerful and invested with the prerogatives of sovereigns. The love of the brothers for their people somehow miraculously replaces the Magna Charta or any democratic slogans. It is a curious phenomenon to see the respect and obedience to their chiefs coming from these free and proud tribesmen.

The Ghashghais' winter home was in Shiraz in southern Persia and that was where we were going. When our plane started circling over Shiraz, I felt like a teen-ager on her first date. Some names have magic, names that are like windows opening on mysterious and beautiful worlds. Since childhood the sound of words like Sidon, Tyre, Samarkand, Ispahan, Baalbek, and Shiraz had stirred my imagination and given me what the Germans call *Sehnsucht nach Süden,* which can be translated as nostalgia for strange southern places and warm sun.

However, my first impression of Shiraz from the plane was glum and melancholy. The city is built entirely of bricks and adobe, all beige in color. From the air the blue-green enameled domes of the mosques looked as if someone had carelessly scattered a fistful of old turquoises on a heap of rubble.

The introvert character of Shiraz, as of many old Persian towns, is very depressing at first. The houses have no windows. The marvelous gardens filled with roses are behind high walls, and from the outside nothing can be guessed of the life of the people within. Coming from a country of picture windows, this secrecy makes one feel unwanted and lonely. Only after one has come to know the Persians and has been enveloped by their warm hospitality does the nightmarish quality of the faceless cities disappear.

We felt that unparalleled hospitality the moment our plane

196

landed and we were met by one of the four famous brothers, Malek Mansur, whose name means "conquering king." Like all the Ghashghais, he is tall and dark, with a handsome, curiously egg-shaped face, hazel eyes bigger than life size. This young man, a perfect illustration from *The Thousand and One Nights,* was educated in the rarefied atmospheres of Oxford and Heidelberg, knew London, Paris, and even Hollywood. Then he had dedicated his life to his people, riding with them for months on their great annual migration. With his wife and children he joyfully led the primitive tribal life. He took us to the family mansion, to which, in the Persian way, he always refers to as "our garden." For him, as for all Persians, the garden is much more important than the great house itself. The garden in Persia is the soul of the dwelling; the house just a convenience.

The residence of the Ghashghais is not a fairyland palace. It is simple, sober, full of light, its modernization redeemed by the old parts left from the original palace—for example, a wide loggia facing the cypresses, and on the top floor of the house one great room open to the world on all sides. From that room we could look down on a stylized garden, a garden so lovely that I understood why in the Near East Paradise is always a garden. Masses of dahlias and black roses bordered a pool, running its whole length. A small blue-domed summerhouse at the far end also was surrounded by roses. These black roses are a triumphal achievement of the Ghashghais. Malek Mansur told us how, a long time ago, a tribesman found a bush of dark, dark roses in the wilderness. He brought back a cutting and, after years of grafting and pollenizing, the spectacular, deep-black roses were born. They are not sadly black, but have a deep, warm velvety color, as if a thin coat of China ink had been spread over on an underpaint of vermilion. The pride of Malek in this achievement endeared him to me forever. The love and understanding of nature is characteristic of Persian tribesmen. I imagine that Malek was happier in creating a new rose than he would have been in launching an earth satellite.

The tribesmen have a complete indifference to the rest of the world, no desire for military or scientific conquest. Their unveiled, free women share their gregarious life. And how gregarious they are! Perhaps it is because after centuries they are still strangers in a foreign land, speaking a different tongue, that they hold so closely together.

Everything is an occasion for a joyful meeting of the tribe. It may be a wedding, to which thousands of guests come from miles away, or the summer hunts for gazelles, partridges and mountain goats. Their great gathering is during the migration, which they love so passionately that they even bury their dead by the roadside so that the dust of the migrating tribe will fall on the graves. In that way the dead will still be with them. Of course, there is much dust. Immense herds of livestock move with them in their quest for green pastures.

I knew little about the tribal etiquette when, on our arrival, a huge, fierce-looking tribesman was delegated to take care of John and me. As there were no locks on any doors in the mansion, and knocking is unknown in Persia, he had the habit of suddenly materializing in our bedroom, like a genie of Oriental tales, and at the most unexpected and embarrassing moments. I learned very quickly to dress and undress in bed under the covers, since I never knew when he would appear. This lack of locks complicated also the process of going to the bathroom, until I worked out an arrangement with members of our party to act as sentinels at the door. In Persia, women have a wing to themselves. I was, I think, the first female who stayed in the main part of the Ghashghais house with the men, and they were not prepared.

Apropos of bathrooms, in Persia, the principle of a w.c. seems to be more sanitary if less relaxing, than ours. The toilet has no seat. There is just a hole in the floor, with two

198

depressions for the feet, one on each side, in order to facilitate squatting. In wealthy houses, as for instance in the Ghashghais, all is covered with tiles and there is quite modern plumbing.

To come back to our big tribesman, he took marvelous care of us, bringing us tea, sweets, flowers, whenever he knew we were in the room. One morning I asked him in my primitive Persian for fried eggs for breakfast. He appeared with twelve of them on a large dish and was heartbroken when I ate only two. He was so upset, asking me if they were not prepared the way I liked them, and would not believe me when I explained that my appetite was small.

However, there was nothing small about my appetite that first evening in Shiraz. I was delighted when the double doors of the dining room were opened and we went into the large white room with a painted ceiling. We sat at a long table covered with silver, gold and pewter dishes and magnificent china. There was delicious Persian food, including two whole stuffed lambs. The unpleasant eyes of one glared balefully at me, until eaten by a courageous guest. Lambs' eyes are considered a great delicacy. There were also rice dishes of all colors and tastes, preserves, game, spices, walnut sauce, and delicious fruit sherbets in golden cups.

And above us there was a most spectacular ceiling, so exquisite and humorous at the same time that, hungry as I was, it took my mind off the superb food—like reading an interesting book during a meal.

The ceiling was really a glorified, gigantic miniature, painted during the period of Fath Ali Shah, that fabulous king with his rosebud mouth, his black beard in which pearls were strung, and his passion for jewels and women. (We once saw his portrait on which he had written "I and my hundred favorite sons.")

Every inch of the ceiling was covered with elaborate Persian
199

scenes, stylized flowers, trees and birds, all in the splendid technique of that period.

Most startling in that orgy of Oriental ornamentation were the four large medallions at the corners of the ceiling, painted in a sober realistic way. They represented the Elephant and Castle Inn in London, Clapham Junction, and two others of London's early railroad terminals, one of them being the Vauxhall Station, all built in the 1840's. An ancestor of Malek Mansur's had felt compelled to switch from an Oriental fairy dream to the prosaic Occidental dawn of mass transportation and asked a traveling Dutch artist to depict the four London sights among birds and flowers.

Another charming fantasy on the ceiling was a sumptuously curved and unveiled houri, stretched voluptuously. From her navel descended the magnificent crystal chandelier.

Late that afternoon, at the moment of a most dramatically beautiful sunset, under a heavy sky of vermilion and Chinese black, Malek Mansur took us to see the tomb of Hafiz, the great mystical poet, at whose spiritual well the Iranians still drink deeply.

A friend of ours, the director and curator of the Art Museum in Teheran, Monsieur Goddard, once wrote: "Iran is the only country in the world that puts her great monuments to the memory of her poets and philosophers and marks only by a stone, in a forgotten cemetery, the tombs of her kings."

A few miles outside Shiraz, in a garden of roses, cypresses and orange trees surrounded by marble pillars, in a black marble sarcophagus sleeps the great Hafiz "of the mystical tongue." How true is the German saying that "whoever wants to know a poet must go to the poet's land"!

As we were standing next to his tomb, Malek Mansur turned to us with a shy smile and said, "We have a curious belief that when a man is clean of heart, he can visit the tomb of Hafiz once a year, open the great book of his writings, at random, read the first verse on the right-hand page and he will be given a message of guidance. I will do it now if you permit." One of Malek's aides handed him the book and a silver bowl filled with white rose petals. Solemnly, with closed eyes, Malek opened the book, covered the pages with petals which he then brushed gently onto the sarcophagus. Then he started reading.

In the deep stillness John, our political officer Jerry Dooher, and I, all Americans, watched with deep interest. We saw that suddenly his hands began to shake and in a voice hoarse with emotion he translated for us the paragraph he had just read. "If Christians will come to visit you, all will be well with you." It is the only reference to Christians in the immense book of Hafiz.

The Ghashghais tribesmen call themselves Moslems, but they have none of the fanaticism nor the fatalism of that religion. There is something pagan in their art of living, in their vitality, in their approach to nature, to all things alive. As so often in ancient civilizations, esoteric religion is left to the leaders. We saw that Malek's ritual by the tomb was not performed as a popular superstition but as a manifestation of his belief in God and His mysteries.

We drove back to the Ghashghais mansion in silence, deeply moved in a way we could not quite understand. Our friendship with the Ghashghais, which has continued over the years, surely stems from that moment.

Next day we went to Persepolis. We motored through a monotonous, unending desert, in clouds of turquoise dust, with many tribal tombs on both sides of the road. Suddenly like a mirage, unbelievable, protected and surrounded by this desert, rose the great marvel of the earth, Persepolis, the City of Kings.

When I first saw, black on the luminous sky, its dramatic columns, I realized that progress does not exist in art. Material civilization is based on scientific progress—faster planes, more efficient machinery, better mousetraps, better bathrooms. There is a big difference between a Roman chariot and a Cadillac, between a witch doctor and a modern M.D. But is the Empire State Building more beautiful than the Pyramids or the Cathedral of Chartres? Is Shakespeare greater than Homer? And what, with our modern technique in building, have we achieved that compares, if compare we must, with Persepolis?

When I started writing I had determined never to become guidebooky, but with Persepolis the temptation is irresistible. Not only because of its beauty, but mostly from the sense of vanity as so few have had the chance to see it. All the many annoyances, all the many hardships of a life in the Foreign Service are royally compensated for by such moments. They seem to be a small price to pay for all the beauties of the world that are revealed to us.

Persepolis is one of them. Persepolis, site of a great palace built by Darius and added to by various descendants, later burned in the time of Alexander the Great and thus saved from complete destruction. The legend has it that Thais, the girl friend of Alexander, threw a burning torch into the draperies of the palace. Little did she know that she was conserving the bulk of its ruins for posterity.

The palace was made of stone and marble, but the ceilings and many columns were of wood. To cool it, the roof was covered with great quantities of earth, perhaps up to two yards thick. When the fire consumed the great cedar beams, the roof caved in. The entire palace was buried under an avalanche of earth. The wind, blowing sand from the desert, completed the job. Thus Persepolis remained hidden away from man's vandalism and fatal erosion by the elements until excavated by archaeologists at the beginning of this century.

The key to Persepolis lies in the words of Darius carved on

his grave: "When Ahura Mazda saw the world in trouble, he gave it to me, and made me king." Ahura Mazda being God, it established at once the divine right of kings.

When in 518 B.C. Darius started to build Persepolis, he was at that time the absolute ruler of the greatest Empire that had ever existed. His guards of 12,000 men had their spears tipped in gold. One can still see them, inscribed in profile in a long hieratic procession on the reliefs that border the great flights of shallow stairs, up which a squad of cavalry could ride abreast. Those stairs, with their height of rise and breadth of conception are the earliest known example of their kind.

There are yards and yards of those friezes, carved out of a dark-gray basaltic kind of stone. Some of them also show long series of processions, clearly religious in character, with priests bearing gifts and sacrifices, both animal and vegetable. Others depict parades of slaves and representatives of subject nations bringing tribute and symbolic emblems of submission to Darius. All the various types of races and the civilizations whence they came are so clearly portrayed that even modern barbarians, such as we are, could not fail to get the point. It is curious that in all this wealth of sculpture representing all types of humanity there is not a single figure of a woman.

We were shocked to see that on some of these carvings and pillars, with incredibly bad taste, tourists had inscribed their names. Amazing enough, Lord Curzon was one of these. His name is carved more deeply than the others.

The plateau on which the Persepolis palace is built, supported by a high retaining wall of squared stone blocks, faces south and west on to a great plain—steppe is probably a better word—vast, serene, quiet, and apparently endless, as befits one's idea of Asia.

Behind, on the east and north, a stark, desolate, brown barren mountain rises sheer—practically out of the palace wall so close does it lie.

All of Persepolis is on a scale that dwarfs even the Egyptian architectural counterparts into insignificant little bungalowish structures.

Slave labor, of course—but what fun Darius must have had in planning and seeing his ideas materialize. It was all done in something like ten or fifteen years, I was told; the Darius part, I mean.

His son Xerxes continued the work. It was he who carved on the gateway—a gateway guarded by two giant sentinels each with the body of a winged bull and a man's face: "Xerxes, great King, King of Kings, King of the land of many races, King of this great earth far and wide, who by Ahura Mazda's aid made this gate 'All Lands.' What now has been built and seems beautiful, all that we did was by the will of Ahura Mazda."

Nothing in Persepolis touched my heart, nothing moved me emotionally except perhaps the pink anemones that grow in the cracks of the gray basalt and the heavy emptiness of the landscape. Its art is too logical, its symbolism too mathematical and its mysticism too unbelievable. What is breath-taking, overwhelming is the vertiginous conceit that emanates from those silent ruins. The self-apotheosis of the "I Darius" and the "I Xerxes" was perhaps the origin of the Nietzschean Superman.

It has nothing of the devil's favorite sin, "pride that apes humility." It is filled with boastful pride, of self-glorification, and belief in the greatness not of mankind but only of the chosen few—The kings, the initiated, the highborn, the elite that monopolized the knowledge of the gods. I was so impressed by the fabulous achievements of a fantastically high ancient civilization that for the first time in my life I doubted, for a brief weak moment, my hitherto unshakable conviction that "all men are created equal," and that perhaps it was as it should be to have the elite possess all knowledge and share only a selected part of it with the rest of the people.

This solemn glorification of kings still has a deep meaning in Persia. The present Shah, who is only a second-generation dynast, is still the King of Kings. His European upbringing, his love of fast planes, racing cars, his modern life have not weaned him from the concept of the divine right to rule. And when we entered the Hall of the Hundred Columns we almost believed in it ourself. The magnificent and unbelievable palace of Persepolis is perhaps the greatest surviving monument of the earthly splendor of kings.

We spent the whole day walking between the fierce winged bulls and the noble profiles of the kings, up and down the shallow stairways, resting on the fallen column. I wanted very much to spend the night in the remains of Darius' harem, which, strangely enough, had been arranged as a guest house by the bounty of Doris Duke. From Darius to Doris so much and so many centuries have intervened.

Unfortunately other plans had been made for us and we were obliged to return to Shiraz. But we stayed on far into the night and saw the moonlight, with its miraculous capacity for camouflage, restore and revive the dramatic ruins of Persepolis. And in that mysterious light we could almost glimpse in the Hall of the Hundred Columns the "white, green, and blue, hangings, fastened with cord of fine linen and purple to silver rings and pillars of marble . . . a pavement of red, and blue, and white, and black, marble" described in the Book of Esther.

XVIII

A MOST FANTASTIC AND DYNAMIC MYSTERY APPEARED along the horizon of known things during our assignment to Iran, the case of the fabulous American secret agent, Major Roger Throckmorton Lincoln. This superspy escaped the nets of his enemies because, like the little man on the stairs, he was not there. And yet, like the Scarlet Pimpernel, "he was here, he was there, he was everywhere."

Among the thousands who followed the exploits of Major Lincoln throughout the Middle East, there were many who thought of him as nonexistent, a phantom, a product of John's rich imagination. There were also many who still consider him to have been a real person, one of the ablest and most elusive secret agents who ever served in American intelligence.

The truth of the Lincoln saga is simple. In fact, it is almost unbelievable in its simplicity. Major Lincoln was conjured out of the blue by Radio Moscow, then brought into the world by John, and eventually given substance by him and his political officer, Jerry Dooher. The circumstances of his arrival on the scene, and his subsequent career, require a word or two of explanation.

From the time of Peter the Great the czarist regime had coveted Iran (then called Persia), both for its value as a borderland and for its strategic position in the traditional Russian aim to encircle Turkey, reach India and dominate the Persian Gulf. The Communist regime of Moscow inherited this geographical objective and made a vain effort to extract Hitler's promise of a free hand in November, 1940. After the war in 1946 it required the hue and cry of the General Assembly of the United Nations, backed by President Truman, to induce the Red Army to withdraw from Iranian Azerbaijan. Stalin, however, continued to place obstacles in the way of the stabilization of Iran and to oppose Iran's links of friendship with the West, especially with the United States.

The Soviet propaganda war reached fever pitch during our official stay in Teheran, in a period of hot and irritable peace along Iran's whole northern frontier. The political pot, at certain moments, threatened to boil over. To watch for every sign of unrest, every movement of troops, every blast on the Soviet radio or in the Communist press of Iran, was like following the zigzag course of the fever chart of a patient in a hospital.

The embassy monitored, of course, the broadcasts of Radio Moscow. A Persian employee of the Chancery, named Reza, was assigned to listen to Radio Moscow's program in Persian, broadcast at night. He was a curious creature and John would find on his desk in the morning a summary of Soviet propaganda beamed on Iran, supplemented by Reza's own little comments. For example:

PLEASE NOTE: The Night Bulletin was *totally* not heard at this post. 3:30 A.M. to 4:40 A.M. no trace of it. 6 A.M. onward no trace of it. Believe aurora borealis existing. Eats the signals off. Reza
END BULLETIN

PLEASE NOTE: I got up a little late and consequently lost some 5 pages of news. Sorry. I am very shortly going to give up one of my outside jobs to give me more energy and rest. Reza

PLEASE NOTE: Feeling a sudden pang of thirst and burning stomach. Can't go on. No beer could be found downstairs. So boiled some of pump water. Now time 0025 A.M. Some news missed. Going to continue reception from NWB. Sorry. Reza

207

Needless to say, Reza's monitoring bulletins were not limited to such footnotes, for he was a conscientious worker. Together with others, people listening to the Persian program of the Soviet radio, he could not help noticing repeated allusions to the dangerous activities of Major Lincoln. I, too, made the acquaintance of this figure, for as I did not have pangs of thirst or an outside job, John made me also listen to the programs of Radio Moscow.

I soon found out that dictatorships closely resemble each other: Soviet propaganda was so reminiscent of the late Dr. Goebbels. The daily Soviet programs followed a consistent line of attack and vilification directed against the United States.

Like a dentist concentrating his drill on an exposed nerve, the Soviet radio centered its attacks on the infamous exploits of an utterly nefarious American secret agent, Major Lincoln. He was built up into a supremely dangerous representative of American capitalism and colonial imperialism. Yes, he was a dark and sinister character, a sort of evil Lawrence of Arabia. On the old and familiar premise that if a lie is repeated often enough it will be believed, the Iranians were becoming concerned over the activities of Major Lincoln.

Of course, there was no such person as Major Lincoln. He was the creature of the crudely inventive and aggressive Soviet propaganda. Someone in or near the Kremlin had rightly observed that impersonal attacks against American imperialism did not cut much ice with either the unsophisticated Iranian audience or the well-informed Iranian government. To invent a character who could play dangerously with war and peace, to endow him with a famous American name, and to link his supposed activities with the problems of the day must have seemed a stroke of genius to some experienced Soviet propagandists. There was no doubt that many simple Iranians came to believe in the existence of the superspy, a belief which was shared by certain members of Iranian officialdom.

John faced quite a problem. It was necessary to destroy the phantasm haunting the Iranian airwaves. But how does one exorcise a radio ghost? To have denied officially the fact of his very existence would have served merely to give substance to his ectoplasm. Talleyrand stated repeatedly during the French Revolution that the only reliable information was that which was officially denied. To deny Lincoln's existence would have served no useful purpose to us. What to do?

"If you can't lick 'em join 'em" is a method known to save one in baffling situations. But how does one join nonexistence? John worked it out. Since he could not get rid of Major Lincoln, the only thing left to do was to treat him as having substance and real existence. Aided by Jerry Dooher, who has inherited the wit and quick intelligence of all the kings of Ireland, a simple program was worked out.

A curriculum vitae was concocted and secretly "leaked" to the public in Iran. John immediately rechristened the spy, Roger Throckmorton Lincoln, to give added dignity to his already historic name. He was supposed to be a major of the United States Army, born in Slippery Rock, Arkansas on October 10, 1909. In his early days he was a riverboat gambler, but had redeemed himself by daring and important espionage missions during World War II.

Lincoln first gained worldwide notoriety more than a decade before when he roared through Central Asia frightening friend and foe alike by his erratic, unorthodox, and highly individualistic methods of thwarting Communist advances. He was said to have organized the most effective espionage apparatus operating in the Middle East. Among his top collaborators were Colonel Coleman B. Cole, renowned for his mastery of seventeen Central Asian dialects; Magda Obolensky Brown, Lincoln's companion of lighter moments; Admiral Ritchard

Wright Wrong, known as the Tiger Shark of the Caspian; Hei-Lung Hung-Lo, the brilliant Tibetan statistician mentioned in Lincoln's official biography; and the distinguished Congolese ornithologist, Dr. Stanislaus Livingstein-Kredo. Major Lincoln was often identified flitting in and out of airports. He was to be seen in native garb at tribal convocations. On one momentous occasion, a very eminent American, while visiting the Kurdish tribes, actually saw and briefly conversed with the major, who was then in tribal dress and mounted on a white stallion.

Major Lincoln was reported to be intriguing with the government and against the government. And of course he sent and received messages in secret codes which, by the local law of gravity, fell at once into the hands of Soviet intelligence. They were probably the only coded messages in history that successfully defied the Black Chamber. Gibberish in cipher makes a code hard to break.

Those nonsensical telegrams, sent by John to Major Lincoln care of the various consulates in Iran and at other addresses, were easily intercepted by Soviet intelligence officers. They created an atmosphere of uneasiness in the Soviet Embassy. Many Soviet officials in Iran had not been previously informed by their superiors that Lincoln was a fictitious character. They took quite seriously this invented figure of their own propaganda. A meeting of Soviet consuls was called. All were upbraided for not being able to track down Major Lincoln. Soviet intelligence agents, like puppies, furiously chased their own tails. To crown it all, the Soviet Ambassador went so far as to demand that the Iranian Foreign Office expel Major Lincoln. He refused to believe that the superspy could not be found anywhere in Iran.

I also became very attached to the major and followed with excitement every mention of him in the press, every rumor coming from the bazaar. I even did his portrait, pretending that he had sat for me on one of his lightning trips to Teheran.

Many ready minds joined in the amplification of the Lincoln saga. It became a crazy *commedia dell'arte*. American senators, justices, generals visiting Iran would gleefully help to improvise new exploits for the major. They even reported meetings with him. The story was getting bigger and better every day, with the Soviets getting more and more worried and flustered.

Then the Department of State, never having understood the nature of the phantom major, reacted via the cables. John received a stinging rebuke. The department does not like frivolity in any guise. John was in a quandary. To kill off Major Lincoln in a dramatic, imaginary accident seemed the most facile solution. But I intervened. I had developed a soft spot for the major. So, due to my pressure, John promoted Major Lincoln to the rank of full colonel and exiled him to Tibet.

The net result of John's adoption of Major Lincoln was that Soviet agents wasted much of their time chasing a ghost, trying to track down an invention of Soviet propaganda. Major Lincoln was finally taken off the air by Radio Moscow. The case was closed.

While the flow of anti-American vilification from the Soviet Union, all based on flamboyant falsehoods, was being poured on Iran, John had to make his official call on the Soviet Ambassador. The Ambassador received him in the imposing Russian Embassy, a great building surrounded by a high wall. It was in the same embassy where President Roosevelt was lodged by Stalin during the Teheran Conference. On the wall of the great reception room, where Roosevelt and Stalin had conferred, there was a white marble slab, on which the text of the Four Freedoms was inscribed in gold like an inscription on a tombstone.

Over a glass of Caucasian port and a plate of cookies, John conferred with the Soviet Ambassador and, among other things, he referred to the inexactitudes of Soviet propaganda. John is basically polite. When he talks to Russians he invariably attributes to their great poet Pushkin any pointed remarks he may invent. John told the Soviet Ambassador that he had noted with great interest the emanations from the Soviet radio on the subject of the United States and American spies and continued, "To quote your great Pushkin: may veracity never pinion the wings of your genius." The Soviet Ambassador was, of course, unable to refute a quotation from their own great Pushkin, particularly one that, like Major Lincoln, was an invention. He was taken aback. The Ambassador met the situation by inviting John to visit the magnificent park of the Soviet Embassy, noted for its streams, lakes, trees, shrubbery, and lovely flowers.

We encountered Major Lincoln afterwards only in occasional articles in the American press, which had become interested in his life and exploits. Our last glimpse of the famous major, I mean colonel, was, oddly enough, in Caracas.

We started out on a flight around South America with General Vandenberg, then chief of staff of the Air Force. It was Sunday morning. The local newspaper contained a comic section. One page was devoted to Colonel Lincoln. May he rest in peace. He served his country well.

XIX

WHEN OUR TOUR OF DUTY IN IRAN CAME TO AN END, we returned to Washington for a brief assignment. John was put in charge of the lend-lease negotiations with the Soviet Government.

John headed the American team. Panuskin, the Soviet Ambassador to the United States, was in charge of the Russian side. They were the only two spokesmen at the conference table. When the first meeting was held, the press photographers requested permission to take pictures. John, of course, immediately agreed, but on one condition: that there be no request for a handshaking picture. The condition was accepted. The photographers entered the conference room with the mad haste of the Keystone Cops. "Mr. Wiley, shake hands with the Soviet Ambassador," rang out in commanding tones. John, annoyed, replied, "This is not a prize fight." There was no handshaking picture.

So far as I know, nothing of any importance came out of this meeting or from any subsequent lend-lease conference. John told me one incident during his long drawn-out debates that recalled Gogol's *Dead Souls*.

At one moment in the negotiations, John had apparently maneuvered Ambassador Panuskin into a corner. Suddenly, Panuskin exclaimed, "The American army ran like rabbits in the Battle of the Bulge." It was impossible to get the conversation back on the rails for hours.

In *Dead Souls*, there is a lawyer named Tchitchikoff who says to his client:

As soon as you perceive that the affair is approaching a solution, and that it is ripe for settlement, do not endeavor to justify and defend yourself, but simply try to introduce fresh issues, which have no connection with the case. . . . That is with the object of . . . producing confusion, nothing more: you must introduce side issues, extraneous circumstances, into the case so that other people may become involved in it; the object is to render the matter complicated, neither more nor less.

When John's unprofitable assignment to the Department of State ended, we left for Panama where John had been appointed Ambassador.

When our ship docked in the Canal Zone at Cristobal we immediately had a blueprint of the duality of life in Panama.

Arriving as American Ambassador to a foreign post, it was a little startling, if pleasant, to be greeted by the strains of "The Star-Spangled Banner" played by an American Air Force band and being met by American generals and other high officials. The Canal Zone is not a colony. It is a piece of America dropped into the tropical, Panamanian jungle, like a small southern community that has gone astray.

Accompanied by the American delegation we crossed the isthmus in the train that runs from the Atlantic to the Pacific. When we reached Panama City we were ceremoniously handed over to another reception committee, Panamanian this time. After many handshakes and *tanto gustos* we finally reached the embassy residence, which was to be our home for two and a half years.

I had hoped to write this book so that I could merit the epitaph on an ancient sepulcher mentioned by Van Gogh: "Blessed be Thebes, daughter of Telhui, priestess of Osiris, who never complained of anyone." I would probably have achieved my goal if John had not been appointed ambassador to Panama.

One should go to Panama as a missionary, as a doctor, or

as a teacher—not as an ambassador. One should go only in a capacity that brings one together with the underprivileged and not the upper, ruling class.

There is a strange significant distribution of bounties in Panama. The rich have the money, the luxuries. The poor have the great qualities of heart and soul. Except for a few unusual families, I have never seen anywhere a ruling class more selfish or more conspicuous for icy indifference to the sea of poverty that surrounds them, more unconscious of anything but themselves, or more governed by a "get rich and stay rich" attitude.

It is strange to find such deep materialism in a Latin country. In Latin countries, being Catholic, even when religion is just a habit of faith, there is usually found at least a sediment of charity, as charity and faith are inseparable. But in Panama he that hath giveth only to Caesar.

Probably they deserve more pity than censure. Who am I to judge? But I would get very angry at the daily evidence of rampant neglect and injustice. I could not, even if I had wanted to, wrap myself in my ambassadorial cocoon, pretend all was well, because the poignant poverty was even on our own doorstep, an ancient, enduring poverty of which even Pizarro complained.

For instance, one morning my maid wakened me at daybreak, in tears, to tell me that her eight-year-old boy, one of her seven children, had suffered an attack of acute appendicitis in the night. She had taken him to the charity ward of the municipal hospital and was rudely turned away: "There are no beds free. Come back in a week."

I wakened John, who in turn dragged the head of the hospital from his bed with such fury that the child was operated on within the hour. If the maid had not had influential friends to turn to, the boy would surely have died. I could quote case after case of that type of callousness, but shall relate only one more typical instance.

As I agree with Cecile Sorel, who when asked what happiness was replied, "To have those you love in good health and to discover new talents," I got very interested in Francisco, a boy of eighteen who showed promising talent in painting. He came from the poorest of the poor, but had such a determination to become a painter, such desire for knowledge, that he had managed to learn a lot. With great difficulty I arranged to get him a scholarship, with everything paid for two years of study in France. Francisco was delirious with joy. The boy's wardrobe consisted of two cotton shirts and a pair of jeans, so with the help of the American wives of Canal Zone officials we assembled for him a warm and elegant trousseau, suitable for the European climate.

All was ready for his departure when the tragedy hit. The French Ambassador, a decent, warmhearted man, came to see me. With an expression of anguish on his face, he explained that in order to give Francisco a French visa he had to have a statement from the police, who declared that the boy had a criminal record. The Ambassador had, in consequence, been obliged to refuse the visa.

I was thunderstruck. Having known Francisco for many months, I could not believe that he had done anything really bad. As usual, in emergencies, I enlisted John's help. John asked the Chief of Police if he could see Francisco's police record. The chief, a friendly man, showed it to John, and we saw what was Francisco's crime. At the age of twelve he was arrested and jailed for stealing a loaf of bread.

I saw red. To think that a hungry child, with no one to turn to, would have his life ruined because he had been driven by hunger to filch some bread, made me furious.

I rushed to see President Remón. The President, who had just come into office, was a man with a deep interest in his people who passionately wanted to raise their standard of living. (It is probable that his assassination a year later was the result of his severe anticorruption measures.)

The President was as deeply shocked as I and immediately picked up the telephone, got in touch with the Chief of Police and had Francisco's crime erased from the record.

It was, alas, too late for the boy to receive his French scholarship. The harm had been irreparable. But he no longer had a police record.

Francisco's reaction was characteristically Panamanian. When I learned that he was not going to France, I spent a sleepless night, not knowning how to give him such shattering news. When, with a heart as heavy as a lump of wet clay, I finally told him that he had lost his scholarship, he looked at me with a smile and softly said, "Don't be so unhappy. It is the will of God. I must accept it."

In Panama there is, of course, a lot of organized charity, all "scrimped and iced in the name of a cautious, statistical Christ," but the least said about it the better. Where there is no compassion, charity is zero. What is lacking in Panama's upper classes is compassion, even though sometimes there is good will. One could clearly discern there that charity is not what we give but what we are. I must add in all fairness that I have also known patriotic, humane, deeply concerned people in Panama, but they were the exceptions, and their outspoken clamorous efforts for social reform were but voices in the wilderness.

It was in Panama that I first *really* understood that poverty per se seldom provokes revolutions. Poverty seems to break the spring in people, to pulverize independent thinking, to tame rather than drive to revolt. All attempts at revolt that I witnessed in Panama (and there were some bloody ones) were instigated by students, indoctrinated by the Communists. Communism does not appeal to Panamanian workers and *campesinos.* But one must not forget that proletarian revolutions are generally sparked by the intelligentsia. In Panama the people are too kind, too religious, and too downtrodden to initiate organized revolt. Of course, when there is an uprising they may join in, the way they would a procession or any other manifestation—more in the spirit of excitement than of class revenge.

An example of their kindness was manifest during an attempt to overthrow the government. The mob stopped rioting and calmly went home during the political upheaval, saying "One can't overthrow the President today, his mother died last night. He has enough sorrow as it is, *pobrecito.*" How can one help but love such people!

Notwithstanding this attractive trait of character, the inflamed mob in Panama, as elsewhere, can be frightening, dangerous, and destructive. Street disorders usually, as I said before, stem from the university.

Political tension was high and it was interesting to see how Communist techniques were employed to exploit the situation.

In Germany long ago there was a considerable class of permanent university students, called *ewigs studenten.* These students loved university life and probably feared the competitive struggle they would encounter outside university walls; so they stayed on year after year, accumulating and hoarding knowledge as a pretext for existence.

This same class of perpetual students was in the University of Panama, but, alas, there was nothing idyllic or innocent about their academic careers. They were either Communists or, still worse, crypto-Communists. Their sole goal was to gain influence as student leaders and they were well-trained for the job. When student demonstrators flooded the streets these hard-core Communist students master-minded everything. And when one of them would harangue the crowd, it was always a young man who was the identical counterpart of the

218

Communist youth leaders we had seen in Riga and Tallinn; the same impassioned voice, the same impassioned face, glaring eyes and waving arms. The words were the same; only the language was different.

I was impressed and greatly shocked in Panama by the use the Communists made of teen-agers, and even of boys only ten or twelve years old. Well-trained and practically immune from police brutality because of their youth, they were very effective in the Communist science of street fighting. One day at a street corner near the Foreign Office I saw two very young boys sedately approach a policeman. In a flash he was dis-armed and the boys had disappeared. These boys had been highly trained.

The next day, during street rioting, the mounted police went into action. Normally the Panamanians were frightened by the mounted police, perhaps just as the Incas were terrified by the Spanish conquistadores on horsback. But on this occasion three youngsters attacked a horse and his rider. One boy held the horse's head, a second grabbed the policeman's leg, while the third held up the horse's tail, plying the poor animal's hind legs with a stick. The horse tripped over the curbing and in an instant horse and rider went sprawling over the sidewalk.

Oddly enough, a horse will not kick if his tail is held up. A Panamanian boy would not know this unless he had been specially taught and trained. In any event, these three boys dissipated mob fear of the mounted police and put quite a scare into the police as well.

During this same period of unrest, John was sitting in the library of the embassy. Through the window he saw the Min-ister of Education arrive in his car, ring the doorbell and hand a letter to a servant.

John liked the Minister, whom he regarded as a man of unusually high standards and great integrity. Moreover, he played an important role in Panama, since about one third of the budget was dedicated to education. So John rushed out and intercepted him with an invitation to come in for a drink.

While they were chatting, John asked the Minister why he bothered to bring a letter personally to the embassy. "I have no one in the ministry I could trust to bring you a letter," he replied. "Moreover," he added, "when I have anything of a confidential nature to be typed I have to take it home and have my wife run it off."

If Panama is a pattern of Communist infiltration in Latin America, we have a lot to fear.

Another thing that fills one with savage indignation is the lack of development of the country's potentialities. It is a constantly gnawing thought of how marvelous Panama could be were it not for the insensitive selfishness of the ruling classes. The underdeveloped mineral resources, the virgin soil, the great forests, are there waiting to be exploited for the cause of a higher standard of living. But greed, indifference and sloth—these stifle real development.

Even with my primitive knowledge of economics I could see that there was "something rotten in the state of Denmark." For instance, with two oceans and one sea, why do Panamanian merchants import and sell fish at such high prices? And while driving through miles of orange groves we would often see thousands of oranges rotting on the ground, in a country where the price of oranges in the cities is exorbitant and where they are denied to poor children.

Perhaps in Panama I was too impatient with other people's sins. Instead of merely condemning them, I should have made a greater effort to find out why they were committed, what was the background that led to them. I do not think that sinful acts appear ready-made like Pallas Athene from the head of Zeus. They are usually the end result of circumstances, environment, and mental climate. Looking back I can see that the shocking behavior of so many Panamanians could be explained by the history of their country.

Panama has always been the crossroads of the world. It is difficult to develop a sense of patriotism toward a railroad station. For instance, even loving the United States it would require a lot of imagination to sacrifice one's life for Grand Central Terminal. The lack of patriotism can also be explained by the fact that so many of the ruling classes are first- or second-generation Panamanians. They came from Europe for the building of the canal or for business purposes. When emigrants come to a new country with the desire to take roots, to start a new life, often in one generation they become real citizens. But those who come to foreign lands with the idea of getting out of it all they can in the form of riches keep the mentality of "owners of souls without passports." Many Panamanians remain tourists in their own country.

The history of Panama is a story of transit and tragedy. It starts with an old Indian trail going through the jungle from sea to sea. During the Spanish conquest that transisthmian route became the *Camino de Oro,* the "Accursed Way," paved with gold and drenched in blood, serving to bring the treasures of South America to the sea and then to Spain.

The gold pouring into Spain established the power of Spain over most of Europe. But in the process the local Indian population perished as beasts of burden. Very soon, to replace them, black savages were shipped in from Africa. They brought with them their superstitions, the drum, the poisons, and the ritual of the African jungle. Their voodooism, brought hundreds of years ago from Africa, still survives in many places of the isthmus and is an integral part of Panamanian civilization.

When long after came the canal, in spite of its humanitarian purpose its building cost thousand of lives, not only in accidents of work but by yellow fever, malaria and dysentery.

And with the building of the canal a new mixture of peoples

spilled over the isthmus—French, Germans, North Americans. This time it was an "Ubi panem, ibi patria" crowd, who left their mark on Panama.

World War II brought many European refugees and there is now a Babelic quality in the languages one hears in Panama.

Even my limited Persian turned out to be very useful. The best shops in town were owned by Hindus. True to the bazaar tradition of the East they had a madly fluctuating scale of prices. The difference between the asking price and the final price was enormous if one would engage in the arts and skills of haggling, which is fun, but too time-consuming. So I told the proprietor of one of the best shops that I would give him all my patronage but only on condition that he would give me the right prices without bargaining. He agreed happily and I naïvely thought I had brilliantly solved the problem of my shopping.

The next time I visited the store I selected an article, reminded the proprietor of our pact and optimistically inquired the price, with he promptly quoted. On examining the object I noticed a tag. It was a tag written in Arabic script. It gave the authentic sales price for the guidance of the Hindu sales force, and of course, very much lower than what was quoted. It never occurred to any of them that a customer in Panama would be able to decipher the secret.

Having learned Arabic numerals in Iran I read the price aloud. The proprietor was amazed but somehow it struck him as very funny. He was hugely amused and said, "You win." From that time on he never quoted a price but always showed me the tag.

Architects who build embassies are often so impressed by the official significance of the building that they forget they are not constructing a post office or a sarcophagus. They overlook the fact that the Ambassador who has to live there is not an official zombie but a human being, with the human desire for a little privacy.

The architects have also a strange disregard for the exigencies of climate. This stereotyped approach to embassy building is not indigenous to the United States alone. I have seen its manifestations in many parts of the world. A prize example illustrating this disdain for climate, this lack of sympathy for the environment has to do with France. In the Foreign Office in Paris, through some bureaucratic failure, the architectural plans for two embassies got mixed up. Tokyo got the plans designed for Vienna and Vienna received the Tokyo plans. The design was so similar that the mistake was only discovered after the buildings were completed. Not that it mattered. Neither building corresponded to the landscape nor to the needs of the post. The French Embassy in Vienna has one remarkable feature—the handles on the doors and French windows: handles of gilded bronze of the female form without an underdeveloped area. I do not know what propaganda effect this aesthetic manifestation was supposed to have on the Japanese, but the Viennese found it most *gemütlich*.

One delightful exception is our embassy in Panama. It stands on a hill, where I think every house should be, even with the penalty of distorting the shape of the hill. The embassy is right for the size of the post and right for the necessary amount of entertainment. Even the reception rooms were planned with kindness to the guests. The doors were so conveniently placed that the subpoenaed guests at official parties could, after greeting their hosts in the receiving line, saunter out unnoticed through another door and escape undetected into freedom. This is a most humane floor plan, especially in posts where the parties are many, overcrowded, noisy, and unbearably hot.

For once, in Panama, the architects took into consideration the well-being of the Ambassador. By separating the official part from the living quarters, some semblance of private life was made possible. The architect also took the trouble to investigate the climate and instead of an igloo he built a house ideal for the tropics. Large, high-ceilinged rooms that open on screened porches give a sensation of living outdoors.

It is the only safe way to enjoy the unfriendly nature of the tropics. When unprotected by screens, everything stings, bites or poisons. After a few years in the tropics I used to dream of friendly green grass on which I could lie without being chewed up by chiggers, getting tropical fever from some insects or something worse from other creeping things. Panama is blessed by a Sanitary Control Commission that completely eradicated yellow fever and malaria in the cities, but there is still enough insect life—not to mention snakes, and frogs that spit poison— to kill any desire for al fresco picnics.

This inhospitable ground perhaps inspired the Indians to invent one of the great pleasures of life—the hammock. Once you learn that you have to lie in it diagonally so as not to be decanted onto the floor by a careless move, it is the most pleasant way of relaxing and sleeping. My hammock was on the porch of our bedroom. Every moment I could steal from my "meet and mingle" life I would spend rocking, surrounded by trees and singing birds. Science has not sufficiently investigated the therapeutic values of rocking. It works so much better than a tranquilizer.

A hammock is much more comfortable and cooler than a bed and is used by many people in South America. Even the great *libertador* Simón Bolívar always slept in one. Only in order to die in greater dignity did he ask to be transferred to a bed.

In spite of termites, poisonous snakes, and the permanent humid heat, everyday life in Panama was easy and pleasant. At first I was quite startled when I encountered a fer de lance poisonously curled under our bridge table and when I nearly stepped on another snake taking a siesta on the front steps of the embassy. But soon I acquired a philosophical resignation, especially after being told by Panama's greatest herpetologist, Dr. Zetek, that more people are hit by lightning than bitten by snakes. I do not know why the idea of being struck by lightning seemed such a consoling choice, but it worked. I never worried about snakes any more.

An experience that changed completely my relation to all creeping things was our visit to Barro Colorado. There we met not only coral snakes and boa constrictors but also scorpions, tarantulas, alligators, crocodiles, and pumas.

When the canal was built, the Chagres River spread over the valley and only the tops of the hills were above water, forming islands. All the jungle animals took rufuge there. Those islands, like Noah's Ark, contain all samples of jungle life. The largest of them on Gatun Lake, Barro Colorado, became a living museum, a kind of national park, and was made available to the Institute for Research for the study of tropical fauna and flora.

In this "vest-pocket jungle," where all animals roam freely, Dr. Zetek was the curator and the king. He could not understand why many people did not share his passionate admiration for all forms of life and with a kingly hospitality, but with granite firmness, he made us visit every rock and turn of his kingdom. Like a terrified, sweating, exhausted Dante I trailed behind Zetek through all the circles of tropical hell. Our amiable but too thorough Vergil showed us, under the surface of the earth, the marvels of architecture, the tunnels, the long corridors, the underground storerooms and homes of moles, mice, scorpions, ants, and tarantulas. On the next level we were introduced to opossums, tapirs, ocelots, pumas, raccoons, snakes, armadillos and, tortoises. In the next circle of this Dantesque zoo were found the monkeys—howler, capucin, white-faced—and the bats. In the last circle were the birds, more than three hundred species—the pelicans, the eagles, the toucans, the humming-birds, to mention just a few. The background music of those dramatic walks was supplied by mosquitoes, wasps and bees, and the scenery was a rain forest of giant trees festooned with orchids and curtained by lianas.

I would return from those strange and fascinating walks in the uncatalogued jungle of the island, having shed on the way my ready-made attitude toward creation.

A stay in Barro Colorado should be required for anyone assigned to a tropical post. A few days in this wild confusion of jungle life creates a reconcilation with the most bizarre caprice of nature. One is apt to lose, if not all fear, some of the repulsion and squeamishness, when seeing all forms of animal life in their natural habitat.

As for me, I can't say that now, I greet with a welcoming Franciscan smile a scorpion in by bedroom slippers or a black, huge, hairy spider under the mosquito net. But I have lost the sickening repugnance that often clouds one's existence in the tropics. Also in the light of the work of scientists on Barro Colorado, who with patience and affection established quite an understanding with some of the wildlife, the story of St. Rose of Lima does not even seem miraculous. The story is that the saint made a friendly agreement with mosquitoes, that she would not drive them away and they would not bite and annoy her. It is also recorded that at her command the mosquitoes would gently buzz to praise God.

Not only does the jungle present a bewildering variety, but humanity in the Republic of Panama provided a confusing array of different cultures and ethnic groups.

Within a biscuit throw of the Americanized Panama City there is a small island inhabited by Indians which is, I think, the only nudist colony in that part of the world. The people on the island never wear any clothes except when marketing in the city. Then they wrap themselves in a large square of cotton material, but discard it immediately they get into their canoes to go home.

I once saw such a family, father, mother and children, stark-naked, paddling peacefully in their canoe, surrounded by packages of Lux, Wonder bread, canned goods, and Coca-Cola. As a concession to modesty the mother had wrapped a string of sausages around her neck. Their bodies of polished copper had great beauty and there was an atmosphere of serenity about them. It is a great mystery why people leading out of choice a neolithic life would accept grocery store products and nothing else from our civilization.

Another ancient Indian tribe occupies the small group of Panamanian islands of San Blas. Their women are carefully shielded from any contact with men of other races, and the tribe has retained complete racial purity, and (alas) dismal ugliness.

They have a great spirit of independence and refuse to pay taxes or acknowledge any dependence on the Republic of Panama. They live in great isolation, away from material progress but peacefully, simply, and I think happily. Their chieftains—caciques—are often educated men. One of them gave a résumé of their philosophy to an American writer.

"Competition for worldly goods brings progress—as you call it—but it also brings a war every generation," said an island patriarch who had attended Yale. "Peoples everywhere are slaves to the amassing and the protection of that very wealth which they somehow think means independence rather than slavery. The safest course, particularly during this transitional period of history when the nations are struggling against the inevitable world state, is to live so simply that no other people can envy you. For the complexities we avoid, the struggles we evade, and the freedom we enjoy, the price we pay is small."

It is from those islands that comes the strangest propaganda story. In various places we have run into, I suppose, every known form of propaganda, both foreign and domestic. We have encountered countless "ambassadors of good will," many self-appointed. Only one of these enjoyed an unqualified success and left behind him an imperishable memory.

We were very intrigued as we noticed that one could not meet a cacique from San Blas Islands without an anxious query on their part of "When is the yachtsman coming back?" After a lot of scouting around, the mystery was cleared up. We had been in Panama only a short time when the islands were visited by a very distinguished playboy-yachtsman-movie star. To enliven the voyage he had invited as guests a group of young ladies not particularly noted for the inflexible rigidity of their virtue. At each island the local cacique was invited aboard and much was made of him. As each chief disembarked the yachtsman would inform him that as a sign of special friendship his "wife" would accompany the cacique for the night. Then one of the young ladies would duly go ashore with the cacique.

No "ambassador of good will" ever made such a deep impression. It worked better than lend-lease. And to this day the question "When is the yachtsman coming back?" is hopefully asked on the islands.

There was a magical quality in the embassy. Its walls, as if made of rubber, would shrink to create an informal atmosphere when we had small parties and expand to the size of a three-ring circus tent for large, formal receptions. The largest reception was on the occasion of the fiftieth anniversary of the founding of the Republic of Panama.

Delegations came from many countries, including a large one from the United States. There was a period of great festivity. All delegations and their embassies celebrated the great event with appropriate and costly entertainment.

228

John was left holding the bag without one cent for expenses, although the United States was intimately connected with the founding of the republic.

We had to give a dinner for more than nine hundred guests, which included three presidents of republics of Central America.

Even with the accordion quality of our embassy, nine hundred people could not have been invited without the garden. After winning a bitter battle, John had been given enough money to put flagstones on the terrace. In that way we could receive in the garden. Otherwise in the rainy season the terrace was like a marsh.

As our party was given during the rainy season those heavy tropical rains were still a problem. Sheets of water would fall in cascades. These rains rarely lasted more than an hour but that was long enough to ruin a party. Everyone advised me to have a smaller party, even with the penalty of offending or hurting the feelings of many people, and have it indoors. I stubbornly refused. Years ago in Colombia I had learned that when arranging an outdoor party it was customary to light a candle to St. Cecilia, with a prayer for good weather. One would light a candle early in the morning, in the garden, and the saint would take care of the rest. And so I did, and kept the candle burning until the last guest left. And not a drop of rain fell to spoil our big event. Even in trivial things "the saints will aid if men will call."

Another problem was the dinner. I have a deep antipathy for caterers' food, for the monotony of assembly line hams and turkeys, for the glazed, overdecorated, tasteless fish, and for those superbaroque architectural desserts that look and taste like cardboard theater props.

And sometimes they are props. Some years ago there was a French ambassador who was so thrifty that he used the same large lobster for every one of his buffets. He would have the shell stuffed with river fish, and pretended that he was serving lobster. Everybody knew about it, as the lobster, having lost an eye in his numerous apparitions, was easily recognizable. He was named Oscar by the Diplomatic Corps. When, after a year of intense service, Oscar was retired he was missed by all.

Homemade cooking is our motto, even when faced by a crowd of nine hundred people. Thanks to the genius, the patience, the pride in her craft of our cook Aminta, all the food was prepared in the embassy. Curiously enough, among all the *haute cuisine* dishes inspired by John's knowledge of food, the Boston baked beans, also John's idea, were the most popular item. Oceans of baked beans were consumed with such rapidity that the supply was exhausted. I was embarrassed when, late at night, Chichi Remón, the President of Panama, demanded a refill. There was not a bean left.

It turned out to be a magnificent party, due mostly to the armed forces of the Canal Zone. There were 120 men outside the embassy to control traffic and park cars. But, more important, there were the massed bands of the army, navy, and air force, all excellent. Inside the house we had Panamanian music, a band that could take the United States by storm it was so good. It was so good that it melted the diplomatic starch of high officials, and after dinner they never stopped dancing.

It even had too great an effect on one of the presidents. As the evening progressed he became gayer and gayer, which was very gratifying to me as hostess until he started a Nijinski solo in the middle of the ballroom.

I knew that something had to be done to keep him from making a spectacle of himself. There is that delicate line between gaiety and buffoonery which a president of any country cannot cross with impunity. I quickly looked for John, and told him we should get the President to leave the party before something embarrassing happened. But how to ask such an eminent guest to leave without hurting his feelings? I knew
230

nothing in the protocol that covered such an emergency. But, of course, John's Irish imagination always finds the answer. He said, "Let's tell the orchestra to play his national anthem." I must explain that it was arranged for the three presidents to arrive at the party at intervals of fifteen minutes and as each entered the embassy his national anthem was played by the massed bands. This process was to be repeated on their departure.

Our problem child president was dancing a spirited rumba to the music of the Panamanian orchestra when suddenly his national anthem thundered out. He immediately, of course, with the rest of us, stood to attention, and as the playing of his anthem was a signal of departure, he left. He thought that one of his aides had mistakenly conveyed to us his decision to leave and never guessed that he had been eased out. He was, incidentally, a most charming man and a very welcome guest, up to a point.

At another time in Panama protocol was reduced to the simple question of meeting with serenity an entirely unforeseen situation. The Ambassador of a Caribbean country was seated at my left at a formal dinner in our embassy. It was a fairly large dinner. Finally, as usual, finger bowls, each on a dessert plate, were placed before the guests. Following an idiotic tradition, I have a habit of putting flowers and small shells into the water of the finger bowls.

The dessert was served. It consisted of tiny hot cream puffs with a hot chocolate sauce. All the guests meticulously removed the finger bowls from their plates and helped themselves in the usual manner. To my amazed horror, the Caribbean Ambassador dumped his cream puffs into the water of the finger bowl. I gently suggested that he remove his finger bowl from the plate and start all over again with some fresh cream puffs. Vehemently, he replied, "No, no, no! This is the way I like it." Then came the chocolate sauce. That too went into the finger bowl and the Ambassador consumed his dessert, cream puffs, flowers, water, sauce, and, I fear, the shells too, with great gusto. No drugstore ever produced a stranger mixture. Yet he survived and flourished. Perhaps what he consumed came under the heading of roughage.

Panama is a very difficult and exacting social post for an American ambassadress. In other posts one has to be concerned with the government, the people and the Diplomatic Corps. But in Panama there is the great hierarchy of the Canal Zone, including civilians, the army, the navy, and air force. And then very frequently the Panama Line, a beautiful government steamship line, brings a group of congressmen and senators from home.

We were very much in favor of such visits even if they frequently disrupted our routine of work and life. The more senators and congressmen travel the more vividly they see the shape of the world. They recognize problems not unlike those of their own particular backgrounds. Members of Congress are usually intelligent, eager to learn, and very considerate.

One of these visiting congressmen raised our standard of living. He was staying at the embassy and did not like bathing or shaving with cold water. There was no hot water in the embassy, except on the kitchen stove, since the hot-water heater had long before collapsed. John had repeatedly asked the department for a new heater, but to no avail. An ambassador can easily be ignored by the department. It was not a great hardship to take cold showers in the tropics, though the water runs fairly cold, but when one was tired and grimy after a trip into the interior a hot bath could be very welcome.

On returning to Washington the congressman went instantly to see the director of the Foreign Buildings Office of the Department of State, who at that time was a gentleman with a worthy desire to save the taxpayers' money, even if such laudable efforts deprived the Foreign Service of essential facilities.

232

The congressman told him that there was no hot water in the embassy in Panama. Not aware of the congressman's stay at the embassy, the director replied, "Wiley exaggerates!" The congressman then explained that he had lived in the embassy for a week, that not only was there no hot water but that the plaster was falling from the ceiling and that our furniture was full of termites. A month later we got a large hot-water heater, and the ceilings were replastered. We were grateful to the thoughtful and nice Member of Congress.

Through the help of this same nice congressman we also got metal furniture for our porch to replace the cheap rattan pieces. In Panama wood furniture is a menace to life and limb, the termites, with their ferocious appetites and secretive ways, devour the stoutest wooden pieces from within. One does not realize the danger till the furniture crumbles to dust. One day while receiving an official visitor I saw my guest, an elderly, prim ambassadress, with her cup of tea and plate of cake still in her hands, descend in slow motion to the floor, where she sat, dignified but with a startled expression until I picked her up. The legs of her chair had literally melted away.

At one formal embassy dinner, an eminent American doctor, rotund and full of years, ceased to be visible at the festive board. The State Department's dining-room furniture was late Duncan Phyfe, once relabeled by a vague friend of mine as Duncan the Fifth. The doctor's chair must have had succulent glue. The termites had concentrated on the glue! The doctor's chair became unstuck; it disintegrated. Happily, the elderly doctor did not. He was picked up uninjured. John and I had really a moment of panic. For an instant we did not know what had happened to him. His disappearance was so sudden, so silent, it was as though a magician had whisked him away in order to mystify an audience.

Owing to the great variety of people who are of interest to

the Embassy, there was an unending chain of exhausting receptions, masses of people. One could never get past the "how do you do" stage; there were too many people.

Like the star of an old-fashioned opera, I frequently had to disappear and change my clothes, but not merely from a desire for glamour and chic. In the aquarium weather of Panama any dress becomes wilted and soaked in a few minutes. The most carefully dressed woman would quickly acquire that limp, bedraggled look of someone just rescued from a shipwreck.

Cocktail parties, the favorite form of entertainment in Panama, were especially trying for me since I do not drink. A Polish friend of mine once said, "Not drinking is difficult because you have to do it all the time, whereas drinking is done occasionally." He was so right. It is a full-time job to be a nondrinker. One has to use so much tact not to seem patronizing; not to have a holier-than-thou attitude; not to be a walking reproof; and sometimes to know when to take a drink so as not to be different and spoil a party.

After many years in the Foreign Service one develops a sixth sense that indicates which social entertainment is necessary and useful. Some entertainments are an end in themselves. In other posts this knowledge permitted me to avoid the unnecessary parties and find time to study, to work, or to do nothing. But, alas, not in Panama, where practically all entertainments were official. Attendance was *de rigueur*.

Trained by John, who has an acute sense of duty, I faithfully attended the "musts" on the diplomatic calendar. Only once during our stay did I really neglect my ambassadorial chores—it was in order to carve a crucifix for a church.

As I have said before, John always tries to see the country he is stationed in, so we traveled over most of Panama. On one trip, to a most isolated community, Changrinola (a United Fruit Company settlement), I met a young American priest, Father Chaliastre.

The father on his arrival at Changrinola found that there was no Catholic church for miles around. The United Fruit Company provided him with tools and wheelbarrows. With the aid of his Indian parishioners and fruit farm laborers, he built a wooden church with a capacity of two hundred people. The church was not only functional but beautiful in proportion. Those who do not believe in miracles should see what a priest without any knowledge of architecture, and helped by completely untrained people of the soil, equipped with some lumber and primitive tools, and armed with faith and determination was able to produce.

When Father Chaliastre showed me the church in its naked bareness, I asked him if I, as a sculptress, might contribute something. He was delighted and asked for a crucifix. Assuming he wanted an altar cross of possibly one or two feet in dimension, I promptly agreed to make one and promised to deliver it in a few weeks. Before leaving I asked how high it should be. "Six or eight feet," calmly replied Father Chaliastre. I managed not to look too startled. I explained that after consideration it would take me longer than I had at first imagined.

On our return to the embassy I sought and found a beautiful ivory-colored piece of cedar wood. I started the carving at once. By working sometimes ten hours a day, and neglecting all my other duties, I had the figure finished in two months. I mounted it on a mahogany cross, stained green at the suggestion of John. "Green is the color of hope," he explained.

The delivery of the cross was an odyssey, as Changrinola was so lost, deep in the jungle. The United Fruit Company offered their plane for the journey, but I found that the outstretched arm of Christ could not pass through the plane's door. So it went by truck to the pier, was hoisted on a freighter, and finally transferred to a flatcar of a banana railroad that runs through the jungle. It arrived safely in the church, and was installed above the altar.

This episode with Father Chaliastre symbolizes in my memory all the good missionaries we met on our travels.

It is impossible to write about diplomatic life without mentioning that other Diplomatic Corps whose only protocol is charity, the only promotion is sanctity, "who own nothing but possess everything," the missionary corps.

There is unfortunately a widespread belief among some people that missionaries are a hybrid army, a mixture of repressed individuals like the protagonist in Somerset Maugham's *Rain,* or stern tight-lipped, narrow-minded, intolerant men, who like a plague of locusts would destroy all the beauty, all the joy of living wherever they appear. Such people are misinformed. They should see, as I have seen, the missionaries, both Catholic and Protestant, at work in the jungles, in the deserts, in cities, in remote villages. Perhaps my experience was not typical, but I never saw a missionary of any Christian denomination, who did not respect the customs and the traditions of the people he had come to convert.

These people were trying to raise the standard of living; to care for the sick; to build hospitals and schools where there had never before been a doctor or a teacher. They never crammed religion down the throats of their people, never blackmailed them into coming to church in exchange for bread or medicine. They would never try to colonize or to dominate, but always to share.

I have seen them in Persia, where missionary work is more meritorious than anywhere else, as it is so seldom rewarded by conversion. As a rule Moslems are unconvertible. A very old missionary in Persia who had spent sixty years in the Middle East once told me that he could die happy because he had just baptized an octogenarian, blind, beggarwoman—his only convert in all his missionary years.

There was one other conversion in Persia that I remember, a conversion inspired by the loveliest concept of true marital love. A Moslem general came to see a Catholic priest, asking for baptism. The priest, very surprised, asked why he suddenly wanted to become a Catholic. "It is because of my love for my wife," replied the general. "You see, the Moslem Paradise is only for men. The women become houris. I cannot stand the idea that my wife, after death, will be pursued in heaven by some bearded mullah. In the Christian Paradise we will be together as man and wife." And the general faithfully attended instruction and did become a Catholic.

We have seen the missionaries in South America where they would bring comfort, help, and hope to the helpless and hopeless, such as the Polish priest in Colombia who for the past ten years has been living in a leper colony. Once, when he had just come, he went with a few of his leper charges on a long walk. It was a hot day, and the lepers had a bottle of coke; they drank from the bottle first, then passed it to the priest, who drank from it without wiping it. He knew that if he showed any sign of fear or repulsion, he might hurt them or perhaps forfeit their trust.

And what a debt of gratitude is owing to those privileged souls—the nuns! Their work is mostly with children, running nurseries, orphanages, and schools. For the children of Foreign Service and other American families far from home, their schools are sanctuaries in a strange world.

The question of the moral code in education varies widely as a problem once we leave countries which observe Christian ethics. Morals change in every latitude and longitude in the world depending on climate, on standard of living, on the historical past, and on religious beliefs. All beliefs of a highly mystical plane meet in their search for truth, but the merger is often puzzling to the uninitiated. How baffling for a child to find in Russia that it is right to denounce one's mother to the authorities if she opposes the regime; how confusing to see a harem; how depressing to be in a place where there are still human slaves! Of course, if the parents are truly religious, the problem is half solved. The question of right and wrong can only be taught if the ultimate authority is God. A child with his unerring sense of truth can easily grasp that, be it Jehovah, Christ or Allah, the Commandments come from God. If to a Christian child one prefaces one's moral teaching with "Jesus said," he is given the cornerstone on which to build his life. When a child has the words of God to guide him, geography ceases to be a barrier. That is why I firmly believe that for American families abroad, putting a child in a religious school is wise. The nuns have "green" fingers with children: There is no contradictory outside influence to bewilder, puzzle, or unsettle them. And the answer to it is in St. Paul's letter to the Corinthians: "If I should speak with the tongues of men and of angels, but do not have charity, I have become as sounding brass or a tinkling cymbal." Lay teachers too often have all the knowledge, but are only "tinkling cymbals" as their creed sometimes is limited to vitamins, morals, physical hygiene, and science. The nuns, on the other hand, have faith, hope and charity. They teach what they love. A child who knows that he has a "Father who is in heaven" has complete security. A child who has been taught obedience, as distinguished from servility, has independence. A child that has been taught through the Lord's Prayer that loving and glorifying God comes before asking for daily bread will never be selfish, but will have a sense of values. All this is the unconscious secret of nuns' education. Of course, lay teachers who love God can have the same influence as nuns. But alas, in my experience they more often are like the little girl who said, "I believe in God, but I am not nuts about him."

XX

After two and a half years in Panama we were recalled to Washington.

Plunged again into the surrealistic nightmare of packing, I would curse that lunatic urge that drives nearly all diplomats to the amassing of useless possessions. Why, for instance, did we acquire a voodoo drum in Haiti? It is cumbersome, ugly, and not connected with any ritual of either of us.

Perhaps the wisdom in acquiring things is that they become keys to locked doors in one's memory where are stored so many experiences and impressions, often forgotten, gathering dust. It was perhaps wise to get a drum in Haiti, as every time we look at it it brings back to us that enchanted place where we vacationed for two weeks while stationed in Panama.

Apropos of drums, John has a theory that there was never a large-scale slave rebellion in the United States because the American slaveowner did not permit the slaves to retain their African drums. Probably the aristocrats of the South did not wish their slumber disturbed. I was sure it was true after we heard in Haiti drums talking to each other in the night from hilltop to hilltop. Perhaps it was because of these same drums that the Haitian Negroes were able to mass their forces against the French. They drove from the island some of Napoleon's best generals.

Haiti is like Paradise, as the Haitians have not yet eaten the apple of knowledge, but just nibbled at it. When not engaged in revolutions, the people are smiling, dancing, enjoying the simple things of life, like "sunsets and tides," and they ignore the complications of refrigerators and television. How proudly the Haitians walk; theirs is the most beautiful walk in the world.

Even the poorest, the most destitute of them know that the ground they step on is their own, and out of this earth that is free has come a most curious, primitive, but alive pictorial art.

In a village of the deepest jungle lived a young and very poor bricklayer who one day in a dream saw the Blessed Virgin appear and shower over him a rain of color falling like petals of roses. In the morning he went to the village priest and said, "I must have paints, Our Lady wants me to be a painter." And he became a painter, one of the best in Haiti. He sold his first picture to a rich tourist for $20. What do you think a man with wife and many children, living in squalor and want, did with his first big money? He bought the largest bottle of Chanel perfume he could find in Port au Prince and poured it all over himself. "I have always wanted to smell good," he explained. For weeks his approach was heralded by a wave of scent.

But let's return to the problem of possessions in diplomatic life. When one has no permanent home, no roots, when through the window the landscape always changes, from minarets to drugstores, from palms to birches, from jungle to asphalt, and when life is a perpetual gigantic cinerama, inanimate objects become tyrannical. It is in the nature of man to take root in one place. We are like Antaeus; we have to touch the earth to regain our strength. But, unlike Antaeus, we have to touch our *own* earth to recharge our batteries.

We, the wives of Foreign Service officers, suffer more from this mode of life, like living perpetually in a trailer, than do our husbands. They have more continuity, since all embassies, legations, and consulates are pretty much the same. The desks, the chairs, the pictures, are all mass produced somewhere in the United States. And the big wings, the welcoming smile of the American eagle, clutching the thunderbolt, is everywhere; on the walls, on the stationery, over the doors, to make you feel at home. In that way the Foreign Service officer during his working hours is still in the United States.

The lack of permanence or conformity tends to magnify our possessions. That is why when on arrival at a new post our chairs, beds, and tables emerge, even battered, broken and bruised, out of their nests of excelsior, it is as if so many friends and neighbors were coming to surround us.

The tyranny of inanimate objects was looming very big in my life when the war came; I was becoming one of those nervous hostesses who watch their guests with anxious eyes to see that no one places a wet glass on a polished table or uses the wrong ash tray. But after the Russians invaded the Baltic States we had to go, leaving all our belongings in vans on the docks of Riga. We were convinced that we would never see them again and suddenly everything came back into focus. I did not care in the slightest. All furniture, all curios became what they were before we had invested them with a pantheistic life, just pieces of wood, glass, silver; as at the end of Hans Andersen's fairy tales, after the talkative and lively china shepherdess reverted to what she was in the beginning, a piece of clay.

But some objects never lose their magic quality, and those are the presents. As in a fairy tale, one look at them and the giver would materialize.

In the Foreign Service we receive a lot of gifts—not expensive ones, as we are not permitted to accept them. That stern principle of the Foreign Service was drilled into me persistently by John from the minute we were married. It was a very necessary precaution, as I come from a family without any money sense, and my approach was that if you had money you gave it away and when you did not have any you asked for it from those who had. That is akin to giving spectacular presents if you can afford it and accepting such presents as a matter of course. It took me some time to realize that in public life presents have strings attached to them, that they are not simply a manifestation of friendship, but perhaps of an ulterior design. In all fairness I must mention that in the Near East and South America the giving of gifts between friends is like Cardinal Newman's definition of a rose garden, an end in itself. The ever-flowing generosity in those countries is such that when visiting anyone's house it is not safe to admire anything except the ceiling, as with exquisite amiability you will be presented with the object of your admiration.

John had me at first so completely terrified on the subject of receiving presents that when we arrived in Bogotá and an immense basket of orchids was sent to me by a Colombian, I immediately telephoned John at the Chancery to ask if I should not return it. I had been in Colombia only a few days and had not realized that orchids there cost no more than daisies and that the fabulous gift of flowers was merely a normal, unpretentious attention.

I wish I could tell how heroically I returned a ruby tiara to a maharajah, a sable coat to Khrushchev, or a white Cadillac to an Arabian king, but, alas, temptations of that sort were never put in my path. The story is a little different with John, to whom a grateful Chinese once presented a big shiny new limousine, which he of course promptly declined.

The gifts we received were mostly from poor people, from servants, from workmen, and from unmoneyed friends. I wish I knew how to describe the generosity of those without worldly goods or self-seeking goals, their warm, unselfish desire to give, and their good taste.

On the subject of gifts I must mention the habit of the Diplomatic Corps in some posts of offering silver objects ranging from trays to cigarette boxes to departing chiefs of mission. It is, of course, a great help in building up one's household equipment, but there is something so automatic and impersonal in that type of present that I have never enjoyed it. As we were leaving Panama I made a most unsuccessful and unpopular move in trying to change this custom. Quite a lot of money was collected among the colleagues to give us a parting memento. They wanted to give us a silver tray and came to ask me to choose the pattern. Having just heard that there were so few beds in the children's hospital that many little patients had to sleep on the floor, I meekly proposed that it would make us much happier if, instead of giving us a silver tray, the money collected was contributed in our name for the beds. This proposal was met with politeness and cold disfavor, and the end result was that we never got the tray and the children never got the beds.

At last the clouds of packing paper and excelsior settled, the *de capo ad infinitum* rounds of *despedidas* came to an end, and we were ready to depart. For John, after Panama where the conduct of diplomacy is often like eating soup with a fork, it was a welcome change. As for me, even though I never felt that all foreign lands were hotels and only one's own country was a home, it was going to be a novel and delightful experience getting under our own roof.

One of the questions so often asked of a Foreign Service wife, "What is the post you liked the best?" always makes me think of an episode in Austria.

On our arrival in Vienna we rented a very attractive apartment as the temporary Legation residence while waiting for our furniture to arrive. It was very baroque and very Viennese. We were particularly impressed by a massive cabinet in the bathroom. It had four vertical panels each with a handle at the top. Each bore a label: the first read Bed Linen, the second, Table Linen, the third, Starched Linen (stiff collars, dress shirts, etc.), and the fourth, Body Linen, all of course in

German. By pulling the handle, each panel became a chute. We viewed this object with deepest respect; housekeeping had at long last reached a superbly scientific and efficient level.

We immediately called in Fu and Han, explained how the cabinet worked, and gave strict orders that the laundry should be carefully sorted out, with each category going into its proper chute. The Chinese, too, were deeply impressed with this wonder of the Western world.

Unfortunately, John got a little curious the next day. We investigated what he called "the terminal reception." Alas, the carefully sorted laundry merely landed in a heap in a common receptacle, once again unsorted. The Chinese were hugely amused.

As in the Viennese cabinet, our posts abroad have labels, such as Moscow, Lisbon, Teheran, et cetera. But in my heart and memory they are all mixed together like our laundry in Vienna. Instead of a feeling for any particular country, I have developed only a consciousness of the affinity that can exist among peoples everywhere.

Index